MORAL DISAGREEMENTS

"Gowans's compendious volume is rich in examples and philosophical strategies. It is bound to be a very useful text. I recommend it."
Michael Krausz, *Milton C. Nahm Professor of Philosophy,*
Bryn Mawr College, USA

"This excellent collection fills a large gap and will provide an outstanding study text."
David Archard, *University of St. Andrews*

Can moral disagreements be rationally resolved? Does the persistence of moral disagreement undermine the idea of moral objectivity? Can universal human rights be defended in the face of moral disagreements?

Moral disagreement is one of the central problems in moral reflection. It also provides a stimulating introduction to some of the perennial problems of philosophy, such as relativism, skepticism, and objectivity. *Moral Disagreements: Classic and Contemporary Readings* is the first anthology to bring together classic and contemporary readings on this key topic. Clearly divided into five parts – The Historical Debate, Some Voices from Anthropology, Challenges to Moral Objectivity, Defenses of Moral Objectivity, and New Directions – the anthology presents readings from the following key thinkers: Sextus Empiricus, Aquinas, Montaigne, Hume, Nietzsche, Chagnon, Shweder, Turner, Mackie, Williams, Wong, Brink, Nussbaum, Gewirth, Berlin, MacIntyre, Rawls, and Narayan.

A distinctive feature of the anthology is that it brings philosophers into dialog with well-known anthropologists. Also included is a comprehensive introduction by Christopher Gowans, explaining the problem of moral disagreement to those coming to the topic for the first time. An ideal text for courses in ethics and moral philosophy, the anthology will also be an invaluable companion to classroom and seminar debate.

Christopher W. Gowans is Professor of Philosophy at Fordham University, NY. He is the editor of *Moral Dilemmas* (1987) and the author of *Innocence Lost: An Examination of Inescapable Moral Wrongdoing* (1994).

MORAL DISAGREEMENTS

Classic and contemporary readings

Edited by
Christopher W. Gowans

London and New York

First published in 2000
by Routledge
11 New Fetter Lane, London EC4P 4EE

Simultaneously published in the USA and Canada
by Routledge
29 West 35th Street, New York, NY 10001

Routledge is an imprint of the Taylor & Francis Group

Typeset in Times by
J&L Composition Ltd, Filey, North Yorkshire
Printed and bound in Great Britain by
MPG Books Ltd, Bodmin

British Library Cataloguing in Publication Data
A catalogue record for this book is available from the British Library

Library of Congress Cataloging in Publication Data
Moral disagreements: classic and contemporary readings/edited
by Christopher W. Gowans. p. cm.
Includes bibliographical references and index.
1. Ethical problems. I. Gowans, Christopher W.
BJ1031. M666 2000
170–dc21   99–046278

ISBN 0-415-21711-3 (hbk)
ISBN 0-415-21712-1 (pbk)

CONTENTS

CONTENTS

CONTENTS

PREFACE

Moral disagreements that appear to resist rational resolution are a pervasive feature of the modern world. We encounter them in our personal lives, in our neighborhoods, in political debates, and in the interactions across national and cultural boundaries that have become so frequent and visible through increased transportation and communication. For philosophers and others, these disagreements raise both theoretical questions about the objectivity of morality and practical questions about how we should think and act with respect to those with whom we disagree. The purpose of this anthology is to bring together a representative collection of clear, cogent, and important discussions of these questions. The readings should be accessible to students with some philosophy background who are not necessarily advanced students of the subject. The book would be suitable in moral philosophy courses and may be used in conjunction with texts that emphasize meta-ethical topics, historical discussions, and even applied ethics.

A distinctive feature of the book is that it brings a diverse array of contemporary Anglo-American philosophers into dialogue with one another as well as with both historical philosophical figures and contemporary anthropologists. Most of the texts of the philosophers from the tradition are not widely read. It is valuable to see that much of the contemporary debate is anticipated in them, though in many respects their concerns are often very different from our own. As for anthropology, there was once a flourishing interaction between philosophers and anthropologists interested in moral disagreement and diversity (roughly speaking, in the 1950s and 1960s). Nowadays there is relatively little interest in anthropology on the part of moral philosophers, and any reference to it is as likely as not to be to anthropologists such as Ruth Benedict who wrote many decades ago. But among at least some anthropologists today there is considerable interest in issues such as moral relativism and human rights. It would be well for moral philosophers to pay more attention to these discussions. I have included here selections from three contemporary anthropologists: a well-known empirical account in the case of Chagnon, and two very different philosophical approaches in the case of Shweder and Turner.

The order and organization of the chapters is for the most part obvious enough. However, it should not be taken as a suggestion for the order in which the chapters should be read by a class. There are many ways in which this might be done. One could begin with Mackie and Brink, or Shweder and Narayan, or Nietzsche and Gewirth. It would also be interesting to read side-by-side Turner and Wong, or Aquinas and MacIntyre, or even Montaigne and Nussbaum or Berlin. The chapters relate to one another in a variety of ways, and individual professors should decide for themselves how they might best be taught to a particular group of students.

Readers should be aware that I have significantly edited and abridged almost all the selections (omissions are generally indicated with ellipses, but larger omissions are indicated by bracketed ellipses unless this is evident from the numbering system in the text). This was necessary in order to include as many different views as possible and, in the case of most of the historical chapters, to focus on relevant material. I take full responsibility for the editorial work: my aim was to render each chapter as a self-contained whole that accurately represents the argument of its author. I am very grateful to the living authors for their cooperation and suggestions in this regard. Readers who seek greater understanding of these chapters and the issues raised by them should turn to the original sources and follow the recommendations for other relevant works in the Introduction.

The aim of the Introduction is fourfold: to provide some useful background for various aspects of debates about moral disagreements; to give a guide to relevant literature by means of endnote references to entries in the Bibliography; to supply a framework for evaluating different contributions to these debates; and to raise some fundamental questions about the main positions taken. On the last point, the criticisms are mostly familiar concerns; they are not intended to constitute decisive objections, but to encourage reflection by suggesting issues that need to be confronted. The organization of the Introduction is not chapter-by-chapter (though it is often obvious where a particular author is discussed), but is designed to bring the reader into and through the debates in a meaningful and fruitful way.

The literature on moral disagreements is immense. The main focus of the Bibliography is works on moral disagreements, and related topics discussed in this book, in Anglo-American philosophy. In addition, there arc a limited number of references to relevant works primarily in four areas: especially anthropology and the human rights literature, and to a lesser extent political science and theology. The Bibliography also contains everything referred to in the Introduction.

Many people have been very helpful to me with various aspects of this project. I would like to thank in particular Jonathan Adler, Jeff Blustein, John Davenport, Brian Davies, Hilde Nelson, Michael Stocker, Margaret Walker, and the anonymous authors of several readers' reports. I am also grateful to my editor at Routledge, Tony Bruce, for his interest and assistance and to my graduate assistant, Silas Langley, for his help on the Bibliography and the proofs. Very special thanks are owed to my wife Coleen for her love, encouragement, and advice, and to our two-year-old daughter Hannah for the daily joy she brings into our lives.

CWG
New York

ACKNOWLEDGMENTS

Permission given by the following copyright holders and authors is gratefully acknowledged.

Isaiah Berlin, "The Pursuit of the Ideal," from *The Proper Study of Mankind* by Isaiah Berlin (London: Pimlico, 1998), reproduced with permission of Curtis Brown Ltd, London on behalf of The Isaiah Berlin Literary Trust. © 1988 Isaiah Berlin.

David O. Brink, "Moral Disagreement," from *Moral Realism and the Foundation of Ethics* by David O. Brink (Cambridge: Cambridge University Press, 1989), reprinted with the permission of Cambridge University Press. © 1989 Cambridge University Press.

Napoleon A. Chagnon, "Yanomamö: The Last Days of Eden," from *Yanomamö: The Last Days of Eden* by Napoleon A. Chagnon (San Diego, CA: Harcourt, Inc., 1992), reprinted by permission of the publisher. © 1992 Harcourt, Inc.

Alan Gewirth, "Is Cultural Pluralism Relevant to Moral Knowledge?," from *Social Philosophy and Policy* 11 (1) (1994), reprinted with the permission of Cambridge University Press. © 1994 Cambridge University Press.

Alasdair MacIntyre, "The Rationality of Traditions," from *Whose Justice? Which Rationality?* by Alasdair MacIntyre (Notre Dame, IN: University of Notre Dame Press, 1988), reprinted by permission of thie publisher and by permission of Gerald Duckworth & Co Ltd. © 1988 Alasdair MacIntyre and University of Notre Dame Press.

J.L. Mackie, "The Argument from Relativity," from *Ethics: Inventing Right and Wrong* by J.L. Mackie (London: Penguin Books, 1977). © 1977 J.L. Mackie.

Michel de Montaigne, "Apology for Raymond Sebond," from *The Complete Essays of Montaigne*, trans. Donald M. Frame (Stanford, CA: Stanford University Press, 1958), excerpted with the permission of the publisher, Stanford University Press. © 1958 by the Board of Trustees of the Leland Stanford Junior University.

Uma Narayan, "Essence of Culture and a Sense of History: A Feminist Critique of Cultural Essentialism," from *Hypatia* 13 (1998), reprinted by permission of the publisher and the author.

Friedrich Nietzsche, "Beyond Good and Evil," from *The Basic Writings of Nietzsche*, trans. Walter Kaufmann (New York: Random House, Inc., 1966), reprinted by permission of Random House, Inc. © 1966 Walter Kaufmann.

Martha Nussbaum, "Non-relative Virtues: An Aristotelian Approach," from *The Quality of Life*, eds. Martha Nussbaum and Amartya Sen (New York: Oxford University Press, 1993) reprinted by permission of Oxford University Press. © 1993 The United Nations University.

John Rawls, "Political Liberalism and the Idea of an Overlapping Consensus," from *Political Liberalism* by John Rawls (New York: Columbia University Press, 1993), reprinted with the permission of the publisher. © 1993 Columbia University Press.

Sextus Empiricus, "Outlines of Scepticism," from *Sextus Empiricus: Outlines of Scepticism*, trans. Jonathan Barnes and ed. Julia Annas (Cambridge: Cambridge University Press, 1994), reprinted with the permission of Cambridge University Press. © 1994 Cambridge University Press.

Richard A. Shweder, "The Astonishment of Anthropology," from *Thinking through Cultures: Expeditions in Cultural Psychology* by Richard Shweder (Cambridge, MA: Harvard University Press, 1991), reprinted by permission of the publisher. © 1991 by the President and Fellows of Harvard College.

Terence Turner, "Human Rights, Human Difference: Anthropology's Contribution to an Emancipatory Cultural Politics," from the *Journal of Anthropological Research* 53 (3) (Fall 1997), by permission of the publisher, University of New Mexico, and the author, Terence Turner. © 1997 University of New Mexico.

Bernard Williams, "Knowledge, Science, Convergence," from *Ethics and the Limits of Philosophy* by Bernard Williams (Cambridge, MA: Harvard University Press, 1985), reprinted by permission of the publisher. © 1985 by the President and Fellows of Harvard College.

David B. Wong, "Moral Relativity and Tolerance," from *Moral Relativity* by David B. Wong (Berkeley: University of California Press, 1984). © 1984 The Regents of the University of California.

INTRODUCTION
Debates about moral disagreements

Christopher W. Gowans

Yet, I must confess, that this enumeration puts the matter in
so strong a light, that I cannot, *at present*, be more assured
of any truth, which I learn from reasoning and argument,
than that personal merit consists entirely in the usefulness
or agreeableness of qualities to the person himself possessed of them, or to others, who have any intercourse with
him. But when I reflect, that, though the bulk and figure of
the earth have been measured and delineated...yet men still
dispute concerning the foundation of their moral duties:
When I reflect on this, I say, I fall back into diffidence and
scepticism, and suspect, that an hypothesis, so obvious, had
it been a true one, would, long ere now, have been received
by the unanimous suffrage and consent of mankind.

(David Hume,
An Enquiry Concerning the Principles of Morals)[1]

1 Some questions about moral disagreements

Are homosexual relations morally wrong? Is the "female circumcision"
practiced in parts of Africa and elsewhere actually a morally abominable
genital mutilation? Are the polygamous or arranged marriages found in
many traditional societies morally acceptable? Is a first-trimester abortion morally permissible? What about suicide in the face of terminal and
painful illness? Could taking one's life be morally expected upon the
death of one's husband, as in Hindu suttee (*sati*), or upon loss of one's
"honor"? Was the Buddha correct in teaching that it is wrong to kill even
animals? In political affairs, is individual freedom morally more important than the common good? Is a society justified in punishing those
whose writing is deemed blasphemous, as some Iranians think in the case
of Salman Rushdie? Is economic equality morally more valu
political liberty? Are undemocratic forms of government eve
justified? Are men and women morally equal? With respect t

life, is a life of contemplation, or of artistic pursuit, better than a life devoted to more commonplace activities of family, work, or civic affairs? Is Christian humility a virtue and Aristotelian magnanimity a vice? Should we seek the harmony with nature often esteemed in traditional Chinese thought or the mastery of nature advocated in so much of the Western tradition? Is there a single correct moral theory, as proponents of theories of virtue, natural law, deontology, utility, the social contract, etc. sometimes maintain? If so, which theory is it?

It is obvious that people disagree about the answers to these questions. By itself this may have little philosophical significance. But some have argued by reference to examples such as these for a stronger and controversial claim: that there are widespread and deep moral disagreements that appear persistently resistant to rational resolution (hereafter, the *Disagreement Thesis*). We need first to ask: is this thesis true, or perhaps better, to what extent is it true? Among those who think it is true to a significant extent, two further questions have often been thought important. One is *theoretical*: would the Disagreement Thesis undermine the idea that morality is objective? The other is *practical*: with respect to persons with whom we disagree about moral issues that appear, at least so far, resistant to rational resolution, what attitudes and actions should we take, and on what basis might we be able to cooperate with one another? A final question concerns the possibility of a connection among these questions: if the Disagreement Thesis were true and did undermine objectivity, would this imply a specific answer to the practical question, such as that in some respect we ought to tolerate, or refrain from interfering with, those with whom we reasonably disagree? These four questions are central topics in the selections in this anthology. The purpose of this introduction is to provide a context for understanding these readings and a critical framework for assessing their claims (citations of relevant literature may be found in the notes; page references are to this volume unless otherwise noted).

2 The disagreement challenge to moral objectivity: a preliminary statement

It will help to begin with a preliminary account of issues raised by the theoretical question. This question commonly arises when two perspectives on morality are brought to bear on each other. On the one hand, as observers of moral practices, we describe the fact that a group of people, possibly including ourselves, makes specific moral judgments, and we may give explanations of this fact such as the phenomenon of enculturation. The *observer perspective* is the province of social sciences such as anthropology, but it also has informal, commonsense counterparts. On the other hand, as participants in moral practices, we make particular moral judgments – that is, we think some action, person, or institution is right or wrong, good or bad, virtuous or vicious, etc. – and typically we suppose these judgments have authority for people. The *participant perspective* is the province of both deliberation about how to live and evaluation of ourselves and others: it is a habitual perspective for human lives.

Some persons maintain that a commitment of the participant perspective is not only that moral judgments have authority, but that this authority involves the idea that morality is objective, that moral judgments sometimes constitute objective moral knowledge of what is right and wrong, etc. This interpretation of our presuppositions in asserting moral judgments might seem belied by the fact that people sometimes say things such as that morality is just a matter of opinion. But the contention is that our moral practices nonetheless reveal a deeper commitment to objectivity: for example, the assertion that a social policy should be changed because it is unfair implicitly appeals to a moral standard all persons involved may be expected to know. At the same time, some persons argue that the observer perspective supports the Disagreement Thesis and that this thesis puts the objectivity of morality in doubt. However, this argument is rejected by many others as unsound. In order to evaluate this controversy, we need a conception of moral objectivity.[2]

Objective knowledge is commonly thought to require belief, truth, and justification. Following this understanding, let us say that *a person knows a moral proposition* (for example, that we ought to change an unfair policy) only if the person believes it, it is true, and the person is justified in believing it.[3] On this account, asserting that the proposition is true should be understood in a straightforward sense at least in many respects similar to the sense of "true" in statements such as "It is true that the wolves have returned." Thus, the truth of a proposition is usually independent of the attitudes people happen to have towards it.[4] Saying that a person is justified in believing a proposition means that the person has sufficient evidence, reasons, grounds, etc. for believing it is true in this sense. Now, let us say that *morality is objective* only if the following three conditions obtain: (a) moral propositions are ordinarily true or false (they have "truth-value"); (b) many moral propositions are true; and (c) persons have the capacity to be, and in fact often are, justified in believing moral propositions (specifically, believing true ones and disbelieving false ones). On this conception, moral objectivists believe that morality is objective, while moral nonobjectivists deny this because they think either that moral propositions are never true or that no one is ever justified in believing moral propositions (or both).

Various arguments against moral objectivism may be given, but a central one is based on the Disagreement Thesis. According to this argument, the Disagreement Thesis gives us reason to doubt that reasonable and well-informed persons would tend to agree about their moral beliefs. But such agreement is a key indicator of objectivity: we expect and find such agreement in precisely those areas where objective knowledge is achieved – in the natural sciences, for example. Hence, it is unlikely that morality is objective. Moreover, the lack of agreement is better explained by some nonobjectivist position (such as skepticism, anti-realism, or relativism) than by an objectivist position. Hence, we should conclude that morality is not objective, whatever the commitments of the participant perspective may be.

Or so many moral nonobjectivists argue. In response, moral objectivists claim either that the Disagreement Thesis is false or that, even if it were true, it would imply nothing that cannot best be explained by an objectivist account. In short, objectivists argue that whatever disagreement there is in morality can be explained in a variety of ways that do not impugn its objectivity. Such, in brief, is the basic shape of much of the debate concerning the theoretical question.[5]

3 A participant perspective: the international human rights movement

Many people find it natural to make moral judgments in terms of human rights. For example, governments that prevent their citizens from speaking freely, that torture prisoners, or that oppress religious minorities are regularly criticized for violating people's human rights. In making these judgments, it is typically assumed that all human beings have these rights whether or not they are actually recognized or enforced in a particular country. Human rights are thought to have universal authority: they are believed to provide a standard of moral conduct that applies to all persons and states in all places, irrespective of cultural differences. Moreover, judgments affirming human rights are expressed by persons the world over – from Western leaders, to women in Islamic countries, to political dissidents in China. Even governments whose actions appear to violate human rights often speak as if they respect them. If any moral judgments are objective, it would seem, those pertaining to fundamental human rights are surely foremost among them.

However, people have not always found it natural to speak of human rights. The prevalence of human rights as a *de facto* international moral standard is a recent phenomenon that is directly related to the birth of the United Nations. Established in the wake of the Second World War and its atrocities, especially the Holocaust, the United Nations declared in its Charter that it aimed to promote and encourage "respect for human rights" (United Nations 1995a: Article One). In 1948, the General Assembly proclaimed without a single negative vote the Universal Declaration of Human Rights, a document that ever since has been at the center of all human rights discussions.[6] The Declaration is philosophically minimal in that it offers no specific justification for human rights, except perhaps in its reference to "the dignity and worth of the human person" (United Nations 1995b: Preamble). But the Declaration is quite expansive in content: its thirty articles detail a long list of civil and political rights as well as economic, social, and cultural rights; and it states that everyone is entitled to these rights irrespective of "race, colour, sex, language, religion, political or other opinion, national or social origin, property, birth or other status" (United Nations 1995b: Article Two). At the outset, there was no provision for the enforcement of these rights (state sovereignty was challenged only recently). The aim was rather to increase respect for human rights through recommendation and education. By the measure of public affirmations of human rights by individuals and governments alike, this aim appears to have been remarkably successful (though perhaps as much because of the media and non-governmental organizations such as Amnesty International as the United Nations itself). A half-century later, it is often said that there is an international consensus on human rights.[7]

But is this really so? It is obvious that there continue to be massive violations of the human rights specified in the Declaration. What is more important philosophically is that there have always been disagreements concerning these rights. From the start there has been a sharp division about the relative importance of political rights and economic rights. Moreover, some intellectuals have questioned whether there are any human rights (Alasdair MacIntyre claimed they are "fictions" on a par with witches and unicorns) or whether they apply to non-Western countries (Adamantia Pollis and Peter Schwab alleged that in most states human rights are "meaningless" because they "do not have a cultural heritage of individualism").[8]

In recent years, as the Cold War declined and the conflicts between "the West and the rest" increased, the question whether human rights have universal validity or merely represent a Western standard that is inappropriately applied elsewhere has come to the center of international relations and debates.[9] For example, the 1993 "Bangkok Declaration" of Asian states maintained that human rights must be considered in terms of "the significance of national and regional particularities and various historical, cultural and religious backgrounds."[10] This challenge to universality was put forward as a legitimate expression of the distinctive features of Asian cultures. But it has been criticized as being little more than a cover for the actions of oppressive governments. In contrast to the Bangkok Declaration, the Korean dissident Kim Dae Jung has argued that "Asia has a rich heritage of democracy-oriented philosophies and traditions" (Jung 1994: 191). Similar disputes have arisen elsewhere, especially with respect to Islamic states.

There is no question that the human rights stated in the Universal Declaration have a Western intellectual heritage. But this heritage is complex: Thomas Jefferson owned slaves as he declared that "all men are created equal." Uma Narayan points out that the West has a long history of oppression at home and abroad, and she suggests that the development of human rights is in part the result of struggles *against* this oppression (chapter 18). In any case, as she notes, the question of origin does not immediately settle the issue whether or not human rights are now an appropriate cross-cultural moral standard. About this issue, there are continuing disagreements within the Western world and beyond it.

In sum: though those who find it natural to speak of human rights are typically confident about the authority or objectivity of their judgments, there have been and still are serious disagreements about these judgments. The international human rights movement is perhaps the practical context that most clearly gives rise to many of the philosophical debates in this volume. Two rather different defenses of human rights are put forward here by Terence Turner (chapter 8) and Alan Gewirth (chapter 14).[11]

4 An observer perspective: the views from anthropology

If participation in the human rights movement is a central source of belief in moral objectivity, then awareness of the observations of anthropologists is an equally strong source of doubt concerning this objectivity. At least among persons in the West, anthropology has had considerable influence in challenging the authority of moral judgments that is often assumed from the participant perspective. It is not uncommonly believed that cultural anthropology has established answers to all the questions posed in section 1, specifically: the Disagreement Thesis is true to a significant extent; therefore morality is not objective but relative; and therefore we ought to tolerate the moral practices of other cultures. Insofar as anthropology is regarded as a science, it is sometimes vaguely supposed that science requires us to accept these claims. However, though such claims have certainly been suggested by some anthropologists,[12] careful attention needs to be given both to what anthropology as a whole says and to the credibility of its contentions.

Anthropologists have traditionally been fascinated with human diversity, especially as manifested in so-called primitive cultures that appear strikingly different from those of the modern, Western world. In this respect, Napoleon A. Chagnon's account of the Yanomamö is representative (chapter 6). The Yanomamö are an indigenous people who live in remote regions of the Amazon basin in Venezuela and Brazil. At least until recently, their contact with the rest of the world has been very limited, and their level of economic and technological development has been extremely low. Chagnon reports that, among the Yanomamö, men pride themselves on being "fierce," and they treat women as virtual property. As a result, the level of violence of men against women and of different tribes against one another appears extremely high.

Do anthropological data such as this provide evidence for the Disagreement Thesis? In answering this question, at least three considerations should be kept in mind. First, how accurate are the data? Chagnon's work is quite controversial in some respects, and other accounts of the Yanomamö portray a rather different though still quite violent people.[13] (On the question of accuracy, compare the accounts of the Hindu practice of suttee in Richard A. Shweder and Narayan in this volume.) Second, do the data show that the Yanomamö are really so different from "us" morally speaking? The level of violence inflicted by Western nations in the twentieth century was immense, and we need not look far in the Western tradition to find women regarded as a kind of property. Of course, on both counts, Chagnon's Yanomamö do violate human rights stated in the Universal Declaration. But in other respects, the Yanomamö do not appear morally alien: they have capacities for trust and reciprocity not unfamiliar to us. Third, do the data indicate "moral disagreements that appear persistently resistant to rational resolution"? The Yanomamö have been isolated from the rest of the world. Might not awareness of alternative ways of life lead to some rational resolution of differences?[14]

The overall anthropological record certainly suggests a good deal of prima facie moral disagreement, but whether this is sufficient to support the Disagreement Thesis in light of the aforementioned questions is a large issue (see section 8). On the further matter of whether this record casts doubt on the objectivity of morality, anthropology has a complex history of interpretations – one in which "relativism" has played a prominent but by no means uncontroversial or unambiguous role.[15] Nineteenth-century anthropologists, often employed by European colonial states, tended to understand cultural diversity by reference to an "objective" standard of culture or civilization which Europeans had most fully achieved and to which other "primitive races" had not yet evolved. This was famously challenged by Franz Boas who, as part of an effort to render anthropology more scientific and professional, emphasized the importance of understanding each culture in terms of its own distinctive values and circumstances.[16] The relativism implied by this approach was developed and popularized by students of Boas – especially Ruth Benedict, Melville J. Herskovits, and Margaret Mead – who shared his commitment to putting anthropological knowledge in the service of social critique.[17] It was mainly through these figures that the identification of anthropology with relativism came into full being – in reputation, if not reality.

But relativism in what sense? There are at least five ideas associated with the term in the anthropological literature: first, that cultures differ from one another in significant ways; second, that anthropologists as scientists should strive to be impartial and hence should not be judgmental about the cultures they study; third, that epistemic standards are valid only relative to a culture and hence lack objective validity; fourth, that moral standards are valid only relative to a culture and hence lack objective validity; and fifth, that we ought to tolerate the moral values of other cultures. The first two of these claims are fairly uncontroversial. The third is quite controversial and implicates a host of issues concerning the extent to which objective knowledge is possible, the respects in which anthropology can be a science, and the degree to which we can understand other cultures.[18]

It is the last two senses of "relativism" that are most relevant here, and with respect to these the classic expression of relativism in anthropology is the Statement on Human Rights submitted to the United Nations by the American Anthropological Association in 1947 during the preparation of the Universal Declaration. The Statement, authored by Herskovits, contains an unsteady *mélange* of assertions ranging from a condemnation of European and American imperialism to the contentions that moral "values are relative to the culture from which they derive" and "respect for differences between cultures is validated by the scientific fact that no technique of qualitatively evaluating cultures has been discovered" (American Anthropological Association Executive Board 1947: 542; the quoted passages are in italics). As will be seen, philosophers have found much to criticize in such contentions (see especially sections 7–11 and 13).[19] But the Statement was controversial even among anthropologists at the time.[20] Moreover, in the postwar period, some anthropologists began to challenge its relativist outlook by emphasizing the cross-cultural similarities in moral values. For example, Ralph Linton maintained that "the resemblances in ethical concepts so far outweigh the differences" that there is a "sound basis for mutual understanding" between different cultures (Linton 1952: 660).[21]

In recent decades, anthropologists have continued to take a variety of positions on these issues. The tradition that emphasizes moral diversity, lack of moral objectivity, and tolerance certainly continues to flourish. For example, Shweder puts forward an "anthropological relativism" according to which it may be that one ethnic group is justified in thinking Rushdie should be free to write while another is justified in thinking he should be punished (chapter 7).[22] On the other hand, there is another tradition that tries to combine appreciation for diversity with some conception of moral objectivity. In fact, some anthropologists have been involved in the international human rights movement.[23] For example, Turner has been active in supporting the Yanomamö against threats to their population, land, and culture by gold miners in the Amazon basin. He argues for a "transcultural principle of justice" that states that people have an individual and collective "right to their differences" so long as they respect the differences of others (chapter 8).

Anthropology does not hand us a set of scientific facts about moral disagreements that directly undermines moral objectivity. Rather, it is an empirically based discipline that offers us various and often conflicting interpretations of human diversity, interpretations that are typically shaped by theoretical considerations and sometimes informed by deep moral convictions. From this there is much to learn, indeed much that should be learned, but this is possible only if we approach anthropology with the same critical spirit that it proclaims for itself.

5 Debates about moral disagreements in the history of Western philosophy

The human rights movement and the interpretations of anthropology are important aspects of the context in which contemporary philosophical debates about moral disagreements arise. An additional aspect is the history of these debates in the Western philosophical tradition. The disagreement challenge to moral objectivity and related issues are not predominant concerns in this tradition. But they surface often enough to make evident that these concerns are not original with us, though perhaps they are now more evident and pressing due to greater ease of communication and transportation. In fact, many of the standard features of contemporary debates are anticipated in these historical discussions. But the accounts in the tradition also have some distinctive features that contrast with current discussions. This should remind us that our own situation and outlook are themselves distinctive and not simply those of human beings in general.

The ancient world and its philosophers were well aware of moral and other disagreements across different societies. The historian Herodotus and the sophist Protagoras, two prominent and widely traveled figures from the fifth century B.C.E., both may be interpreted as putting moral objectivity in doubt: Herodotus endorsed Pindar's dictum that "Custom is king of all," and Protagoras (at least as presented in Plato's *Theaetetus*) said that "whatever practices seem right and laudable to any particular state are so, for that state."[24] In due course, several nonobjectivist philosophical traditions developed. The best-known and most influential of these (largely because its texts are best preserved) is the Pyrrhonian skepticism of Sextus Empiricus, a Greek physician and philosopher probably from the second century C.E., who enunciated in detail the skepticism that began with Pyrrho several centuries earlier (chapter 1).[25]

The Pyrrhonian skeptic is extraordinary in that he or she is skeptical about everything, not just morality, and professes to have not merely no justified beliefs, but no beliefs at all (or at least none about the real nature of things). The state of complete suspension of belief is said to be produced by the realization, achieved through the examination of skeptical arguments, that for every belief there is as much to be said for it as against it. For example, for any contention that something is good, there is an equally convincing argument both that it is and that it is not. It might be objected (and was) that suspension of belief would make a life of action impossible. To this the Pyrrhonian skeptic claimed to live on the basis of appearances – everyday observances such as feelings or customs – and thereby to have achieved a state of tranquility.

Pyrrhonian skepticism was not so much a doctrine as a way of life that, lacking belief, was supposed to ease the anxieties associated with trying to live in accordance with the truth. Concerning this life, questions may be raised as to whether it is humanly possible (can we really live without beliefs?), whether it is logically coherent (is not the Pyrrhonian skeptic committed to some beliefs, for example, that tranquility is the result of suspension of belief?), and whether a basis for suspension of belief has been provided (is the recitation of mere disagreements sufficient?). Similar questions have confronted nonobjectivist theories ever since: Is the proposed life feasible? Is the theory coherent? And are there adequate grounds for it?

The ancient skeptical texts were virtually unknown during the medieval period. But the Christian philosopher and theologian Thomas Aquinas (1225–74) was aware of the disagreement challenge to moral objectivity,[26] and it is possible to distill from his writings an objectivist response to it (chapter 2).[27] For Aquinas, moral theory has a foundational structure: the first principle "that good is to be sought and done, evil to be avoided" (p. 58) is self-evident; on this are based all secondary principles and ultimately conclusions about what to do in particular circumstances. His basic response to the disagreement challenge is that there is increased disagreement or diversity as we move from the general toward the particular, but this can be accounted for in a variety of ways consistent with his objectivist account. With respect to general principles, Aquinas says, what is "right is the same for all and is equally recognized" (p. 59). But with respect to less general principles as well as conclusions about particular cases, errors may arise on account of sin, passions, wrong persuasions, corrupt habits or customs, and the like. Moreover, in some cases an apparent disagreement may not be real because general rules must be qualified by exceptions (for example, something held in trust should usually but not always be returned). Furthermore, human laws are sometimes rightly changed because of increased understanding (in which case a disagreement may be rationally resolved) or on account of different conditions (in which case there may be no real disagreement).

In many respects, Aquinas's account anticipates contemporary responses to the disagreement challenge. However, like them, it is more the suggestion of an explanation than the development of one. There may be little cause for disagreement about Aquinas's first principle because it is a formal principle that explicates the meaning of "good" and "evil" (though even here Nietzsche would object, as will be seen). But disagreements are likely to arise in the specification of the goods to be sought and evils to be avoided. Are general principles concerning these equally recognized? And are the disagreements we actually find in the world best explained overall along the lines suggested? No doubt they could be, but *are they*? Similar questions confront more recent objectivist responses.

In the sixteenth century, a revival of ancient skepticism came about as a result of translations of Sextus into Latin and the subsequent adaptation of his outlook by Michel de Montaigne (1533–92), a lawyer, politician, and philosopher writing in France during the religious wars between Catholics and Protestants. In his *Essays*, Montaigne undertook an unprecedentedly intimate examination of his self in which he seems to profess both Catholicism and skepticism (his motto was "What do I know?"). As a result, he has been variously interpreted, usually as either a fideist or an outright skeptic in disguise. In his critique of moral objectivism (chapter 3), Montaigne borrows heavily from Sextus. But his assessment of the extent of moral disagreements also owes much to his vast reading of classical literature, the recent discovery of the "new world," and his own travels in Europe. Moreover, his account of our inability rationally to resolve these disagreements depends partly on typical Pyrrhonian themes (for example, the unreliability of the senses, the regress of reasons, and the problem of the criterion) and partly on Montaigne's own distinctive perspective on the human situation: he thinks both we and the world are so contingent and unstable – "flowing and rolling unceasingly" (p. 71) – that we cannot hope truly to understand anything (his unsystematic style is an expression of this instability). Finding no ground for justified belief, Montaigne nonetheless says he chooses to remain in the Catholic faith into which he was born.[28]

Many of the difficulties the Pyrrhonian skeptic faces also confront Montaigne. The complication is that his apparent acceptance of both Catholicism and skepticism presents problems of both interpretation and understanding. Taken at face value, this conjunction may appear inconsistent (as Aquinas presumably would have judged it) or arbitrary (though on Montaigne's view probably no more so than anything else). But perhaps his Catholicism is simply an application of Sextus's advice to suspend all belief and live in accordance with local custom. If so, the questions of the feasibility and coherence of such a life are especially pressing.

Montaigne was known by virtually all philosophers in the seventeenth and eighteenth centuries. His legacy was the preoccupation with skepticism that is the hallmark of the modern period. In moral philosophy, many complained with Rousseau of "his strained efforts to unearth in some corner of the world" a practice that contradicts the plain truths of morality (1975: 262).[29] But others put forward moral philosophies that were, in various ways, skeptical. A complex figure in this regard is the Scottish philosopher and historian David Hume (1711–76).[30] Hume is generally regarded as a moral skeptic because he says the foundation of morality is sentiment rather than reason. But in *An Enquiry Concerning the Principles of Morals*, Hume argues that human beings share "a feeling for the happiness of mankind, and a resentment of their misery" (1998: 158). In virtue of this common sentiment, he says, people accept, as the basic moral principle for evaluating the character traits of a person, their usefulness or agreeableness to the person or others. Though a skeptic in denying a rational foundation to morality, Hume nonetheless believes that experience teaches us that human sentiment is such that there is a moral principle that is universal in the sense of both being accepted by and applied to all persons.[31]

The apparent fact of moral disagreements was the source of an obvious objection to Hume's theory, and he responded to it in "A Dialogue" he attached to the *Enquiry* (chapter 4).[32] In many respects, Hume's argument (in the voice of the narrator) is similar in form to that of Aquinas: there is more agreement than the objection supposes, and apparent disagreements can be explained in a manner that is consistent with universal acceptance of the basic principle.[33] Of course, Hume was also a critic of Christianity whose moral outlook owed much to pagan authors such as Cicero. Hence, he differs from Aquinas both in giving contrary assessments of some character traits (most notably, pride and humility) and in offering partially different diagnoses of moral error: a principal cause for Aquinas is the passions, whereas for Hume religious superstition is stressed. Nonetheless, the basic question in evaluating Hume is the same as for objectivist responses: do his accounts actually explain the disagreements we find in the world?

A new form of skepticism enters the world in the provocative and prophetic voice of the German philosopher Friedrich Nietzsche (1844–1900). In *Beyond Good and Evil* (chapter 5), he chastises philosophers who have sought to justify morality rationally: they were merely expressing "the common *faith* in the prevalent morality" of their time and place (p. 82).[34] Instead, Nietzsche urges the importance of comparing "*many* moralities," and of determining the origin and value of each type. For the most part, however, he speaks mainly of two types. Master morality is the morality of the strong, of those who rule: it declares as "good" or "noble" the values of pride, self-glorification, and even exploitation that typify the strong, and it calls the contrary features of the weak "bad" or "contemptible." Slave (or herd) morality is the morality of the weak, of those who are ruled: in reaction against the strong, it characterizes as "good" values such as humility, obedience, and pity, and it regards the opposite values as "evil." Hence, what is good for master morality is evil for slave morality, and what is good for slave morality is bad for master morality. Nietzsche thinks the values of Christianity, democracy, and human rights are all versions of slave morality.

In accounting for the origin of these values, Nietzsche thinks master and slave moralities are the ways in which the strong consciously and the weak unconsciously expressed their "will to power," his basic explanatory principle of all living things. One question for Nietzsche is whether this is an adequate explanation of moral disagreements. In evaluating these values, Nietzsche professes being concerned, not with their truth, but with the extent to which they are "life-promoting" (1966: 11). He leaves no doubt that he himself has contempt for the values of slave morality, and that the values of the "new philosophers" he heralds have an affinity with those of master morality. Other questions for Nietzsche are whether truth can be so easily set aside, what the criterion of the affirmation of life means, and why it should be accepted.

6 Disagreement arguments against moral objectivity: preliminary clarifications

Let us now turn to recent philosophical debates about moral disagreements. In these debates, arguments against moral objectivity have been widely discussed. Before considering these arguments, several preliminary matters should be addressed. It is important first of all to distinguish disagreement arguments from other arguments against moral objectivity. Three forms of the latter have been especially influential. First, some nonobjectivists maintain that the *practical aspects* of our moral values – that they typically involve feelings and motivate us to act – are difficult to reconcile with an objectivist account.[35] Second, nonobjectivists sometimes argue that objective moral values should be questioned because they have no cogent or essential place in the world as understood by the natural sciences – for example, because they involve peculiar metaphysical properties or play no crucial role in causal explanations of observations.[36] Third, some nonobjectivists reject moral objectivity because they reject objectivity in general, whether in morality, science, or elsewhere. Various reasons may be given for the general rejection of objectivity: classical skeptical considerations such as the contention that the regress argument shows justification to be impossible,

13

claims that no sense can be made of the idea that the mind represents reality, assertions that all beliefs depend on the contingencies of history and culture, contentions that purported objective beliefs are nothing but expressions of the will to power, and so on.[37]

In none of the aforementioned arguments are moral disagreements per se a prominent feature (though there may be indirect connections; see sections 10 and 11). In recent formulations of disagreement arguments, it is usually supposed that objective knowledge is possible and paradigmatically found in the natural sciences. Though morality is often said to compare unfavorably with scientific knowledge, the specific basis of the comparison is our understanding of disagreements and agreements in the two cases (a comparison stressed by Bernard Williams in chapter 10). In these arguments, it is the purported pervasiveness and depth of moral disagreements, and not the practical aspects of moral convictions, that are said to threaten moral objectivity.

It is also important to clarify the meaning of moral disagreements in these arguments. The subject of the disagreements concerns morality; hence, some understanding of morality must be at least tacitly assumed. Usually it is uncontroversial that a disagreement is a moral disagreement (for example, the controversies regarding abortion), but sometimes this is controversial (is the dispute about tattoos cited by Sextus a moral dispute?). It is obvious that disagreements that are not really moral in nature are not directly relevant to a critique of moral objectivity.

Discussions of moral disagreements usually focus on mid-level judgments about what is morally right or wrong, good or bad, virtuous or vicious, etc. – for example, that assisted suicide is wrong or that temperance is a virtue. Of course, these judgments have implications for particular cases and they typically involve more fundamental considerations. There might also be disagreements about the relative importance of general moral values, about the validity of moral theories, and about metaphysical or religious understandings of human nature and the world that figure in moral outlooks. Different accounts of moral disagreements might be given in these different cases; hence, it is important to keep them in mind.

There is also need to consider what it means to disagree. The most obvious and typical case is a situation in which one person affirms a moral proposition and another denies it. But not all disagreements are so explicit. Suppose a group of people regard as objective moral knowledge their belief that killing animals renders a person morally impure. Another group may neither affirm nor deny this explicitly (perhaps because they lack the relevant concepts or because in their moral framework no such statement would make sense), but they regularly kill animals without any expression of disapproval, compunction, remorse, shame, and the like. It seems clear that these two groups have a moral disagreement even though there is no proposition directly affirmed by one and denied by the other: the disagreement is implicit rather than explicit.

Note also that the terminology of the last two paragraphs – judgments, beliefs, propositions – suggests an objectivist understanding of morality. Some nonobjectivists would contest this: properly understood, moral disagreements are disagreements in attitude or feeling rather than in judgment or belief, and so the distinctions in these paragraphs require reformulation in at least some cases. In this respect, it is difficult to describe moral disagreements in language that is neutral vis-à-vis different meta-ethical interpretations of their proper understanding.

Finally, moral disagreements should be distinguished from moral dilemmas as philosophers have employed this term in recent years. Moral dilemmas are standardly defined as situations in which someone morally ought to (and can) do one thing and morally ought to (and can) do another, but cannot do both. The assumption is that the same person (or group) affirms both moral judgments. Hence, a moral dilemma is not a disagreement between persons, but a conflict within a person.[38]

7 A disagreement argument against objective moral knowledge

Disagreement arguments against moral objectivity take a variety of forms that cannot be fully summarized in brief space (for examples in this volume, see J.L. Mackie, Williams, and David B. Wong).[39] The purpose of this section is to describe one version of this kind of argument that suggests both why some have thought such arguments are plausible and what is required to properly evaluate them (for convenience, I will refer to this as "the disagreement argument"). As already noted, the first premise is the Disagreement Thesis:

1   There are widespread and deep moral disagreements that appear persistently resistant to rational resolution.

Recall that a condition of morality's being objective was said to be that persons have the capacity to be, and in fact often are, justified in believing moral propositions. The next premise contends that there is an important, general relationship between this condition and agreement among reasonable and well-informed persons. While it is doubtful that the relationship can be defended in terms of a strict, logical condition, it may be said, more plausibly, that agreement among reasonable and well-informed persons is a key indicator of the justification condition. To say that X is a *key indicator* of Y is to say that (a) X is non-accidentally related to Y in an important respect (causally or logically) such that (b) the absence of X provides strong presumptive but defeasible evidence for the absence of Y. For example, a pattern on an X-ray might be a key indicator of a certain disease; or a configuration of certain kinds of beliefs and practices might be a key indicator of something's being a religion. In these cases, there is no necessary connection; but we may have good reason to suppose there is a significant, non-accidental connection that would properly underwrite compelling albeit fallible inferences. For example, the absence of a specific X-ray pattern might warrant a doctor in thinking it very unlikely that a specific disease is present. Now, the second premise states that:

2   A key indicator of our having the capacity to be, and often being, justified in believing propositions of a particular kind is that, insofar as persons were reasonable and well informed, they would tend to agree in their beliefs about propositions of that kind.

(Henceforth the *Agreement Indicator of Objectivity* refers to the tendency of reasonable and well-informed persons to agree in their beliefs about propositions of a kind.) One rationale for this premise is as follows: to say that a person is justified in believing a proposition is to say that the person has good evidence for it; but if this is so, then we would ordinarily expect that other reasonable and well-informed persons would also possess that evidence and believe the proposition; hence, if our beliefs concerning a class of propositions are often justified, we naturally suppose that, insofar as persons were reasonable and well-informed, they would tend to agree in their beliefs about propositions of that class. Further support for the second premise is found in the fact that those areas where we feel most confident about objectivity are areas where we see much agreement (mathematics and natural sciences, for example), whereas the absence of agreement in an area is likely to make us question objectivity (for example, conceptions of beauty or preferences for foods).

The argument then states that premise (1) gives us grounds for denying that, insofar as persons were reasonable and well informed, they would tend to agree in their beliefs about moral propositions: if such persons would tend to agree, it is unlikely we would find so many deep disagreements that appear persistently resistant to rational resolution. Hence, we have grounds for thinking that:

3   The Agreement Indicator of Objectivity is absent in the class of moral propositions.

But if this is so, then given the meaning of a key indicator:

4   We have strong presumptive but defeasible evidence that it is false that we have the capacity to be, and often are, justified in believing moral propositions.

Of course, since this presumption might be overridden, more needs to be said to conclude that morality is not objective. Specifically, it must be established that:

5   The best overall explanation of the fact that the Agreement Indicator of Objectivity is absent in the class of moral propositions is a nonobjective account of morality.

If this is correct, then we ought to conclude that:

6   It is false that we have the capacity to be, and often are, justified in believing moral propositions.

Since this is one of the necessary conditions of the objectivity of morality, it follows that:

7   Morality is not objective.

A proponent of this argument faces three challenges. First, the Disagreement Thesis (premise 1) must be established. Second, it must be shown that this thesis gives us adequate grounds for thinking the Agreement Indicator of Objectivity is absent in the class of moral propositions (premise 3). Finally, it must be established that some nonobjective account of morality is a better explanation than any objective account of the fact that the Agreement Indicator is absent (premise 5). As stated, the argument does not specify which nonobjective account of morality is the best explanation: the main contenders are anti-realism, skepticism, and relativism (these are defined in section 10). Disagreement arguments are usually put forward in defense of one of these views in particular. To achieve that end, it would also have to be shown that that particular view provides a better overall explanation of the absence of the Agreement Indicator than all objectivist accounts and all other nonobjectivist accounts.

These three challenges will be considered in the next four sections. As a preliminary, it should be observed that premise (2) may also be questioned. Though it is very common to relate objectivity to some form of agreement, sometimes objectivity is understood in more metaphysical terms as requiring reference to a mind-independent world. For example, Williams construes objectivity in terms of agreement that would be explained by "how things actually are" (p. 131). There is clearly something intuitively correct in this formulation, and it appears to contrast with the epistemological formulation favored here. But it is doubtful that the two formulations are completely independent: surely our best indication of the actual nature of things is agreement by reasonable and well-informed persons, especially on the assumption that these persons are independent of one another and in other respects diverse (as is typically taken to be the case in these discussions).

However, there is a serious issue concerning our understanding of the phrase "reasonable and well-informed persons." Many discussions of disagreement arguments tacitly or expressly presuppose that this should be understood in terms of a conception of rationality that is universally valid (for all people at all times and places) and can be specified without reference to morality. But such a conception is quite controversial. It is not uncommon to suppose that good moral reasoning requires having some moral characteristics. Moreover, MacIntyre argues that different conceptions of rationality are connected with different conceptions of justice. If such claims were correct, then the second premise could not be fully understood in the absence of some particular understanding of morality, and any evaluation of the disagreement argument, pro or con, might beg the question. However, it may be that there are some norms shared by any conception of rationality – for example, an openness to evidence, respect for consistency, etc. – even though in other respects conceptions of rationality differ. Insofar as this were the case, discussion of the disagreement argument would obviously be complicated. But it need not be impossible: some beliefs may be unreasonable on any conception of rationality and, as MacIntyre suggests, it may be possible to adjudicate between different conceptions.[40]

8 The Disagreement Thesis

The Disagreement Thesis may be evaluated from two points of view. The first, favored by several of those who reject it, says that the falsehood of this thesis may be established on the basis of a priori considerations, that is, considerations that do not depend on empirical investigation of the extent to which people morally agree or disagree. The second approach says that such investigation is crucial.

The a priori approach takes different forms. One argument was implied by Philippa Foot in opposition to Charles Stevenson and other noncognitivists.[41] Stevenson claimed that moral language can be used only to express or evoke attitudes or emotions. It cannot be used cognitively to express propositions that are true or false. Hence, there is no guarantee of agreement even among reasonable and informed persons. In response, Foot argued that moral concepts are logically connected to human harms and benefits via rules of evidence. As a result, there are limitations on what can properly be said to be morally good or right, and this places a substantial conceptual constraint on how much moral disagreement there could be.

Foot's argument is more convincing with respect to "thick" moral concepts such as courage or charity than "thin" moral concepts such as goodness or rightness (as her own analogy with rudeness implies). It does seem plausible to say that not just anything could be called courageous: it must have something to do with confronting a danger or difficulty in order to achieve some good end. But how much agreement does this establish? Aristotle thought courage was best shown in confronting death while fighting in war.[42] Pacifists would surely disagree; they might claim that courage is best shown in nonviolent resistance to oppression. This is clearly a substantial moral disagreement that is not precluded by conceptual limitations of the concept of courage. If we define courage broadly, it may be said (albeit on empirical grounds) that every society is likely to have a concept of courage; but in that sense very different understandings of courage are possible. If we define courage narrowly, as Aristotle did, it turns out that not all societies have such a concept (for example, Christian or Buddhist pacifist communities); but this is still a serious even if implicit moral disagreement. In his discussion of thick moral concepts, Bernard Williams argues that though a society might know that a person is courageous, given its understanding of the concept, it cannot know that the way of life embodying that understanding is better than others (chapter 10).[43]

A related but broader a priori argument has been advanced by reference to our ability to understand the moral values of another culture.[44] Usually the argument is presented as an application of Donald Davidson's general contention that a disagreement presupposes significant agreement on account of the constraints on translation.[45] To see this, suppose I were to say that another culture seriously disagrees with us about the nature of trees because they think *erbras* – the term I translate as "trees" – are not alive or are only found in caves. The proper response would be, not that I have identified a striking disagreement about trees, but that I have incorrectly translated "*erbras*" by our term "trees." Only insofar as what we believed about trees and what they believed about *erbras* were mostly in agreement could we say there is a common entity about which we are disagreeing in some particular (for example, if they think *erbras* have souls, but otherwise say the same things about *erbras* as we do about trees). To generalize, insofar as translation is successful, there must be a broad measure of cross-cultural agreement: radical disagreement is impossible.

The application of this argument to morality has led some to conclude that any moral disagreement presupposes substantial common moral ground and hence that there cannot be widespread and deep moral disagreements. However, even if we grant Davidson's own controversial argument,[46] there are several difficulties with extending it so as to reach this conclusion. First, the impossibility of radical disagreement in general appears compatible with significant disagreement in a particular area of discourse; specifically, identification of moral disagreements might presuppose considerable agreement, but this agreement need not be primarily moral agreement. Second, even if, for any two societies, moral disagreement requires moral beliefs common to those two societies, it does not follow that there is a set of moral beliefs common to all societies: in a simple case, any two pairs of three societies may have something in common without there being anything that all three have in common. Hence, serious differences that might challenge moral objectivity could remain. Finally, the conclusion that there is common moral ground depends on successful translation. But it is quite possible to acknowledge failure of translation in significant respects and still have good reason to attribute substantial moral disagreements: in the example of an implicit disagreement in section 6, the society that thought killing animals makes a person morally impure could recognize a serious moral disagreement with a society that routinely killed animals, even if it could not adequately understand its moral language (though morality cannot be reduced to behavior, in some cases behavior may be sufficient to show considerable disagreement).

A third a priori argument focuses on the last clause of the Disagreement Thesis: that many disagreements *appear persistently resistant to rational resolution*. According to this argument, whether a disagreement can be rationally resolved is simply the question whether there is a compelling epistemological consideration for a resolution – a good argument, say – and this has nothing to do with what people actually think. Hence, the proper evaluation of the Disagreement Thesis depends, not on inquiry into the extent of moral disagreements in the world, but on whether there are good arguments for resolutions of disagreements: if we discover such arguments, it will no longer appear that disagreements resist rational resolution even if people continue to disagree.

This argument is obviously partly correct: a rational resolution requires something such as a good argument, and whether an argument is good is not simply a function of what people happen to think. However, as the epigram from Hume suggests, it would also be a mistake radically to divorce these two. I might suppose I have a good argument for something even though I recognize that other reasonable and well-informed persons reject it. But if this situation persists, I have to admit that something is amiss. For a good argument ought to convince such persons, and if it never does, then I would have grounds for questioning whether it really is a good argument (though this may not show exactly what is wrong with it).[47] In short, we cannot completely separate the question whether something is a good argument from its ability to persuade reasonable and well-informed persons.

If a priori considerations are insufficient to assess the Disagreement Thesis, then we need to evaluate empirical investigations of people's actual values – something in which philosophers traditionally have shown little interest. As I have already urged, great caution needs to be taken in evaluating the empirical claims of anthropologists and others concerning moral disagreements (see section 4). It also should be stressed that in assessing empirical grounds for the Disagreement Thesis, agreements as well as disagreements are relevant. If there were widespread moral agreements, this might suggest at a minimum that the Disagreement Thesis is true to a lesser extent than is often claimed. However, since what is at issue is a claim concerning disagreements that appear to resist rational resolution, reference to the mere existence of either disagreements or agreements by itself is not enough for proper assessment of the Disagreement Thesis. To this extent the third a priori argument is instructive. Proponents of the thesis need to point to disagreements that prima facie are unlikely to be rationally resolved. Opponents need to point to agreements that prima facie reflect some rational concord and not merely the uniform effects of oppression or irrational passions.

Enough has already been said to indicate the kind of evidence for moral disagreements proponents have in mind. Opponents have not only contested this evidence, they have also argued on a variety of fronts that there are significant cross-cultural moral agreements. Some have observed that ancient ethical codes of different spiritual traditions contain common prohibitions; for example, killing human beings, stealing, lying, and adultery are proscribed in both Christian and Buddhist codes. Others have followed Voltaire in being impressed with the fact that a form of the Biblical Golden Rule may also be found in Confucius. In view of such considerations, some have proposed that there is at least a "minimalist morality" across all cultures. For example, Sissela Bok takes the minimal shared morality to include three kinds of values: duties of mutual support and reciprocity, prohibitions on violence and deception, and a basic understanding of procedural justice.[48] In another example, the 1993 Parliament of the World's Religions, under the leadership of Hans Küng, declared a "global ethic" with four basic principles: "nonviolence and respect for life," "solidarity and a just economic order," "tolerance and a life of truthfulness," and "equal rights and partnership between men and women" (Küng and Kuschel 1995: 24–34).[49] The declaration purported to represent a consensus that already exists; it was signed by representatives of Buddhism, Christianity, Hinduism, Judaism, Islam, and many other traditions. As already seen, other persons have suggested that, whatever may have been true in the past, the international human rights movement of the last half-century is evidence of an emerging consensus on fundamental rights (see section 3).

As with claims about moral disagreements, these contentions need to be subjected to critical scrutiny: in what respects and to what extent do people really have common moral values? It is also important to ask how much establishing rather general, common values really shows. Suppose every society had some concept of property and a prohibition on stealing. Many questions would remain: What are the rules of acquisition and transfer of property? Is this determined by kinship relations or contractual agreements? What rights are involved in ownership? Who may own property, and what – *or who* – may be owned? In what does stealing consist? Is stealing always prohibited or only sometimes, and if the latter, what determines the qualifications? What is the relative importance of the prohibition on stealing in comparison with other values accepted in the society? What justification is given for the prohibition? Since very different answers to these questions may be given, agreement on the prohibition on stealing would be consistent with a great deal of moral disagreement.[50]

It should be clear that evaluating evidence for and against the Disagreement Thesis is a complex task that requires being empirically informed, methodologically sophisticated, philosophically careful, and morally sensitive with respect to a massive body of potentially relevant information.

9 Does morality lack the Agreement Indicator of Objectivity?

Let us suppose it were established that there are widespread and deep moral disagreements that appear to resist rational resolution. The disagreement argument claims that this would give us reason to deny that, insofar as persons were reasonable and well-informed, they would tend to agree in their beliefs about moral propositions. If the Agreement Indicator of Objectivity were present in morality, it is said, it is unlikely we would find the phenomena identified by the Disagreement Thesis. In response, objectivists have argued that even if the Disagreement Thesis were true, this fact could be explained in a variety of ways that are compatible with the objectivity of morality (many of these are defended by David O. Brink in chapter 12). These explanations usually come under one of three categories: the claim that sometimes (a) there is no real disagreement, (b) the disagreement is rationally resolvable, and (c) it is not rationally resolvable but does not threaten moral objectivity. Discussion of the plausibility of these explanations lies at the heart of much of the debate about disagreement arguments against moral objectivity.

(a) No real disagreement. Two common objectivist responses take the form of saying that in some cases, despite the appearance, there is no real disagreement. First, a single principle applied in different circumstances may give different results, but each application may be correct. For example, a principle of distributive justice might justify certain inequalities in some economic circumstances, but not in others. This might look like a disagreement, but in fact it is not. Second, a single principle might be fulfilled in a variety of ways, each of which is morally permissible. For

example, Kant's imperfect duty of benevolence requires us to promote the happiness of others, but (within limits) it leaves it to our discretion how to go about this. Persons promoting happiness in different ways might appear to disagree with one another about benevolence, but in fact they may not be in disagreement.

(b) *Rational resolution.* Perhaps the most common objectivist responses claim that moral disagreements often rest on some kind of error: if two parties morally disagree, then it may be that at least one of them is either mistaken about some nonmoral fact or has made a mistake in reasoning. For example, two persons who disagree about the morality of capital punishment may agree that deterrence is the primary moral consideration; but one thinks capital punishment significantly deters while the other thinks it does not. There is a genuine disagreement here, but it is a disagreement about a matter of fact and not about a moral principle. As such, it may be expected that insofar as these persons agreed on the psychological facts concerning deterrence, they would agree about capital punishment. Objectivists may go on to offer an account of why people tend to make such mistakes. As seen in section 5, Aquinas points to our sinful state, corrupt habits, and unruly passions as sources of defective moral reasoning. Contemporary secular accounts are more likely to explain this by reference to self-interest, ideology, prejudice, or religious superstition. In any case, the conclusion is that, despite appearances, at least many moral disagreements are resolvable in principle: insofar as persons were reasonable and well informed, they would tend to agree. Moreover, it may be added optimistically, in time these disagreements are likely to dissipate as resolutions are achieved.

With respect to both (a) and (b), it is obvious that such explanations are correct accounts of some moral disagreements. A proponent of the disagreement argument cannot plausibly deny this. What is at issue, however, is whether these explanations are sufficiently broad in their application so as to undermine the claim that the Disagreement Thesis makes it unlikely that the Agreement Indicator of Objectivity is present in morality. For example, disagreements about capital punishment sometimes reflect a disagreement about whether the justification of punishment is deterrence or retribution: a retributivist might say it is justified even in the absence of significant deterrent effect. Is one of the parties in this dispute making a mistake? If so, what is it and why is it being made? What the objectivist requires here (and what Williams thinks has not been provided) is a convincing theory of error. In general, adjudication of the issues raised by (a) and (b) would require examination not simply of a few examples, but of the broad range of phenomena identified by the Disagreement Thesis. Such an inquiry has not been undertaken by persons on either side of the debate.

(c) *Irresolvable but unproblematic.* Finally, the objectivist might allow that there are some moral disagreements that cannot be rationally resolved, but argue that these cases are so special and infrequent that they do not threaten the overall objectivity of morality. First, some disagreements may be due to vagueness. It is usually clear whether or not something is blue; but in some close cases people disagree, and no rational resolution may be possible. The same may be true of moral concepts such as generosity. But such cases would not show that either blue or generosity lacks objectivity in general. Second, disagreements may sometimes be due to incommensurability. For example, it might be said that the demands of justice typically take priority over the requirements of friendship, but in some cases it may be true neither that justice has greater value, nor that friendship does, nor that they are equal in value. In these unusual cases, there could be no rational resolution of a disagreement, even though in the vast majority of cases such a resolution would be possible. Similarly, it might be said that one athlete is obviously better than another (say, Michael Jordan and the average playground player), but it might be allowed that in some cases there is no truth about whether one athlete is better than, worse than, or equal to another (say, Michael Jordan and Jack Nicklaus). As before, the absence of objectivity in such limited situations should not be taken to imply a general lack of objectivity.[51]

Since the claim is that these explanations only apply to a few disagreements, it cannot be maintained that by themselves they offer a full response to this step of the disagreement argument. However, it might be and often is contended that some combination of explanations (a), (b), and (c) do constitute a full response. Or, more broadly still, it might be and frequently is argued that such a combination, together with doubts raised in the last section about the extent to which the Disagreement Thesis is true, provide an adequate response to the disagreement argument as a whole. Determining whether or not this is so would require bringing all these considerations to bear on the full range of purported disagreements advanced by proponents of this argument.

10 The plausibility of nonobjectivist accounts

Let us now suppose it were established that we have strong presumptive but defeasible evidence that it is false that we have the capacity to be, and often are, justified in believing moral propositions. To reach the conclusion that morality is not objective, the disagreement argument must show that the best overall explanation of the fact that morality lacks the Agreement Indicator of Objectivity is some nonobjectivist account of morality. To show this would require a comparison of objectivist and nonobjectivist accounts for their general credibility. If it turned out that all nonobjectivist accounts were utterly implausible, and that at least one objectivist account was quite plausible, then it would seem that the best explanation is not a nonobjectivist account. Hence, even if the proponent of the disagreement argument were to succeed in establishing premises (1) through (4), it would still be necessary to compare the over-all plausibility of objectivist and nonobjectivist accounts. This is obviously a very large agenda. All that is possible here is to point to some of the main issues, concentrating on nonobjectivist accounts in this section and objectivist accounts in the next.

Three basic nonobjectivist theories are customarily and naturally distinguished. *Moral skepticism* is the view that, though moral convictions have truth-value and are sometimes true, they are never justified; hence, our moral convictions never constitute knowledge. *Moral anti-realism* is the position that moral convictions are never true, either because they are always false or, more commonly, because they lack truth-value altogether. Finally, *moral relativism* is the view that, though moral convictions are never true in a straightforward sense, they do have relative truth-value, and in this sense, sometimes they are true and some people are justified in believing they are true.

Moral skepticism as just defined is a logically possible position, but it is rarely defended in contemporary discussions (though Sextus and Montaigne often seem to be skeptics in this sense).[52] Skepticism appears to have problems comparable to other nonobjectivist accounts and no offsetting advantages. Moreover, it seems odd to say there are moral truths we can never know: if we can never know them, why suppose they exist? Sextus did hold out the prospect that we might eventually come to know them; but this too seems a peculiar claim if, as he thought, we have had no success so far. By contrast, both anti-realism and relativism have prominent contemporary defenders. Hence, it is best to focus on them.

Moral anti-realism says our moral convictions are never true. This might be because they are always false (as in the "error theory" propounded by Mackie [1977: ch. 1]). But the more typical view is that they are neither true nor false: moral convictions are not beliefs about the world that are true or false, but expressions of attitudes, preferences, feelings, desires, etc. ("noncognitivism"). Sometimes anti-realists say that morality involves the projection of our attitudes onto the world. Moral anti-realism is frequently invoked to explain the fact that morality lacks the Agreement Indicator of Objectivity: such disagreement is just what we would expect if moral convictions were a matter of feeling rather than apprehension of facts in the world.[53] But there are other arguments for anti-realism as well. It is often thought that it better explains the practical aspects of moral convictions (in particular, that they motivate us to act) and that it is the position most compatible with the world understood by the natural sciences (see section 6).

The main objection to anti-realism, especially in its noncognitivist form, is that it cannot account for a variety of *cognitive aspects* of moral judgments that appear implicit in our moral practices: for example, that we speak of moral convictions as being true or false; that we think there are sometimes reasons for these convictions; that we assume logical relations of consistency and inference apply to them, etc. This objection has led to attempts to show how these cognitive aspects – or at least some semblance of them – may make sense on an anti-realist view.[54] Another way of putting the cognitivist objection is to say that the moral anti-realist cannot account for the authority of morality presupposed in the participant perspective. If that authority requires objective moral knowledge, then the anti-realist denies that our moral convictions have such authority. In this case, it would seem that some reform of our moral practices is required, and the anti-realist would have to explain what this involves. However, the anti-realist might challenge the objectivist interpretation of our moral practices: it might be said that the relevant sense of authority does not require objective moral knowledge, and that the anti-realist can make sense of whatever conception of authority we do presuppose. In this case, the anti-realist would need to explain the relevant sense of authority. Such in brief are some of the main issues confronting moral anti-realism.

Moral relativism is the view that moral judgments lack truth-value in any straightforward sense – often called "absolute" in this context – but do have "relative" truth-value and in that sense are sometimes true.[55] Relative truth-value is usually taken to indicate that the truth-value of moral judgments is a function of the convictions and practices of some group of persons such as a society or culture (and so is not independent of people's attitudes). On this view, the judgment that polygamy is morally wrong is neither true nor false in an absolute sense, but it may consistently be true for one society and false for another. Moreover, relativism typically supposes that persons are sometimes justified in their moral judgments understood in this relative way. For example, I may be justified in believing that polygamy is wrong in my society, and you may be justified in believing polygamy is obligatory in your society.

Among persons generally, moral relativism appears to be the most popular nonobjectivist response to moral disagreements; and among philosophers, it is sometimes defended as the best explanation of the fact that morality lacks the Agreement Indicator of Objectivity (a form of this argument is defended by Wong in chapter 11).[56] Other defenses of relativism are possible; but for most, disagreements are the central rationale. Relativism might be thought to have an advantage over anti-realism in that it retains a sense in which moral judgments have truth-value, and so it can account for some of the cognitive aspects of moral judgments – at least understood in terms of relative truth. Since the cognitivist objection is the main problem with anti-realism, this advantage would seem significant. But relativism has several problems of its own.

The central problem for relativism is to explain why moral judgments have relative truth-value (as opposed to absolute truth-value or none at all). Why should the general disapproval of polygamy in my society make it true that polygamy is wrong in my society? In general, why should the fact that there is a common practice in a society render its judgments authoritative for all its members? What if someone disagrees? Is a critic of the common moral values of a society necessarily mistaken? Plausible answers to these questions might be developed from the contention that relative truth resides in the fact that reasonable and informed persons within a society would tend to agree in approving and disapproving various practices. This would be a qualification of typical formulations of relativism, and it would have to be shown both that such persons do tend to agree and that such agreement is adequate to account for the authority of moral judgments. The problem of authority is implicit in many of the difficulties commonly raised against relativism.

Among these are several complications concerning the proper formulation of relativism. First, is the truth of a moral judgment relative to the group of the person who makes the judgment or to the group of the person being judged? This makes a difference when judgments are made about persons in other groups (for example, if someone in England morally judges someone in China). Second, how are we to define the groups that determine the truth of moral judgments? Many criteria appear possible – culture, ethnicity, political territory, religion, race, gender, etc. – and these may be given broader or narrower descriptions. Third, the moral values of a given group are often not homogeneous and may involve serious disagreements: how is the truth of moral judgments to be determined in these cases? Finally, it may be that many persons are members of more than one group: how is the truth of moral judgments to be determined with respect to such persons when the groups have conflicting moral values? These questions suggest that relativism requires a more complete and precise formulation than is often supposed. Moreover, the last three might be taken to point in the direction of subjectivism, the view that the truth-value of moral judgments is a function not of groups but of individuals. This is a very different position: whereas relativism purports to retain a limited sense of intersubjective authority for moral norms, subjectivism allows for no such authority.

The relativist also needs to take into consideration a set of facts concerning similarities and interactions between groups of persons. First, people often make moral judgments about persons in other groups on the basis of values they take to have authority for all (as in international discussions of human rights). Second, moral conflicts between groups sometimes get resolved on the basis of a change in understanding on the part of one or both parties (as perhaps was the case in the change of view concerning slavery in the United States in the last two centuries). Third, it seems that people can learn from other groups (as Gandhi did) or can even find reason to embrace wholly the values of other groups (as in the case of persons in France who have become Buddhists). The traditional relativist image of the world as divided up into different societies, each with its own moral values, leaves it unclear how these facts are to be understood or explained. In any case, the relativist needs to provide some account of them. One approach would be to maintain that some moral judgments have absolute truth-value while others have only relative truth-value. This might be thought the most direct way to account for both the similarities and differences we find in people's moral values. Such a picture of morality would lack unity, but perhaps there is little reason to expect much unity in an account of a phenomenon as complex as morality. Of course, such an approach would need to explain why a given judgment has absolute or relative truth-value as the case may be.

11 The plausibility of objectivist accounts

Moral objectivism is sometimes assessed in general terms. At this level, the question is whether any objectivist account could adequately respond, not only to disagreement arguments, but to other arguments against moral objectivism such as those mentioned at the beginning of section 6. If one of these other arguments established that no form of objectivism could be tenable, then objectivism could not provide an adequate explanation of the fact that morality lacks the Agreement Indicator of Objectivity. However, there is no consensus among philosophers concerning the soundness of these arguments. It is sufficient to note here that a plausible moral objectivism would have to account for the practical aspects of moral convictions, to show that these convictions are not precluded by the understanding of the world provided by the natural sciences, and to overcome the skeptical arguments against objectivity in general.

Moral objectivism may also be evaluated by reference to specific objectivist theories that aim to detail the nature of moral knowledge understood in a particular way. These theories cannot ignore the aforementioned anti-objectivist arguments: they would have to respond to them in the course of developing their positive account of the authority they take moral judgments to have. In this regard, it may be said that objectivists have an embarrassment of riches: there are numerous objectivist theories, and there is about as much disagreement among objectivists as there is between objectivists and nonobjectivists. Two objectivist traditions that are especially influential are represented in this volume by Martha Nussbaum (chapter 13) and Alan Gewirth (chapter 14): the first takes moral knowledge to be based on a detailed empirical understanding of human nature, while the second believes that this knowledge follows from the presuppositions of our nature as rational agents. A brief look at their accounts will suggest some of the kinds of problems moral objectivists face.

Nussbaum presents her theory as a defense of Aristotle. On this view, there is "a single objective account of the human good" that is based on features of human nature and may be used for "the criticism of existing moral traditions" (pp. 168–69). The account focuses on several spheres of human experience such as fear, bodily appetite, management of personal property, social association, etc. These "grounding experiences" are said to be universal in that each person must choose and act in some way with respect to each of them. A virtue in the "thin" sense is defined formally as having a stable disposition to act appropriately in a given sphere. A description of a virtue in the "thick" sense is a specification of what appropriate action would actually be. The aim of ethical theory is to provide objective knowledge of virtues in the thick sense.

Let us suppose Nussbaum is correct in her claim that the grounding experiences are universal and that any adequate account of a good human life will have to specify what appropriate action would be with respect to each. What lends credibility to her theory is the plausibility of this claim. However, Nussbaum acknowledges that people disagree about what precisely would be appropriate action in each case. Moreover, she herself raises an obvious objection: it is one thing to say that any adequate account must specify what actions are appropriate, and it is another thing actually to specify what these actions are. In response, Nussbaum makes four points: that a "plurality of acceptable accounts" may objectively be established (p. 173); that sometimes an adequate account will be quite general, leaving further specification to our choice; that it is essential to pay close attention to particular contexts; and that revision in the face of new circumstances and evidence is always possible. She regards it as an advantage of her theory that in these respects it combines genuine objectivity with a significant measure of flexibility.

But does this establish an objective account of human goods? Consider bodily appetites. Beliefs about proper responses to these range from the severely ascetic to the freely hedonistic: they vary significantly in their view of the respects in which and extent to which bodily pleasures fit into a good human life. By reference to what criteria are these beliefs to be assessed? The difficulty, of course, is that there appear to be serious disagreements about which criteria are relevant. It is at this level that the proponent of the disagreement argument may assert that there is insufficient agreement among reasonable and well-informed persons to render plausible any notion of truly substantial and objective criteria. Perhaps, it may be conceded, some very limited objective constraints are possible. But these would be so minimal as to provide no basis for resolving the main disagreements concerning bodily appetites, and they would hardly suffice to give us "a single objective account of the human good" in this respect. This is one central difficulty Nussbaum's account needs to confront.[57]

Gewirth's approach is quite different. He argues that every actual or prospective agent is logically committed to accepting as a universally valid and supreme moral principle that "all prospective purposive agents have rights to freedom and well-being" (the Principle of Generic Consistency or PGC).[58] The basic argument for the PGC is as follows: every such agent logically must accept (a) "I must have freedom and well-being"; this logically commits every agent to accepting (b) "I have rights to freedom and well-being"; and this in turn commits every agent to accepting (c) all other agents have rights to freedom and well-being. Gewirth says this argument is an application of the principle of non-contradiction: any agent who rejects it is inconsistent. Hence, the PGC is logically binding on any rational agent.

Gewirth's argument is widely questioned by philosophers who do not question the principle of noncontradiction. This suggests at a minimum that the argument involves more than a straightforward application of this principle. Let us suppose that every agent desires freedom and well-being. Why should we believe, more strongly, that every agent, simply in virtue of being an agent, is logically committed to thinking he or she *must* have these things [that is, (a)], where this is understood to imply in turn a *right* to them that others are required to respect [that is, (b)]? The answer, according to Gewirth, is that freedom and well-being are "necessary goods for each agent" in the sense that they are "needed for whatever purpose-fulfillment he may seek to attain by acting." Here a critic of this argument may raise several questions. Are freedom and well-being really necessary in this sense (after all, slaves have performed many successful actions)? Moreover, even if they were necessary, why must each agent infer from this that others must respect a right to them? Does logic compel us to think other people must meet our most fundamental needs? In addition, a critic may wonder whether the inference from (b) to (c) is really just a matter of consistency: someone who accepted (b) and rejected (c) might be selfish, but would the person be irrational? Such are some of the questions Gewirth's theory needs to answer.[59]

12 Could a mixed account be correct?

In view of the complexities and difficulties outlined in the last five sections, it would be hazardous in an introductory essay to offer a definitive conclusion to the debate about disagreement arguments. But there is a preliminary conclusion that should be drawn. Philosophers and others often *come to* this debate with sharply opposed sensibilities: some are confident that we have objective moral knowledge and see little threat from moral disagreements, while others are quite impressed by these disagreements and suspect they undermine moral objectivity. Those with objectivist inclinations can argue with some plausibility that the disagreement argument does not refute their position because there are significant agreements in people's moral values, there are objectivist explanations of why rational and well-informed persons would mostly agree, and all the nonobjectivist theories have difficulties. But those with nonobjectivist proclivities can likewise argue with some plausibility that the disagreement argument supports their position because there are significant disagreements in people's moral values, objectivist attempts to show that rational and well-informed persons would mostly agree are not conclusive, and all the objectivist theories have difficulties. In view of this, it would be arbitrary to say that one side or the other bears the burden of proof in this debate. Hence, it appears that each side has reason to feel some confidence in its own position, but neither side can give those who begin with the opposed sensibility a compelling reason to change their position.

Some might go beyond this conclusion and argue either that no rational resolution of this debate is possible or that none is possible without much more understanding than we now possess. But others might claim that what this apparent impasse suggests is that the correct position is a mixed one: objectivist in some respects and nonobjectivist in others (one version of this was suggested in connection with relativism at the end of section 10). Since many kinds of mixed positions are conceivable, no simple evaluative framework is possible for them. But two of the philosophers in this volume might be interpreted as providing grounds for mixed positions: Isaiah Berlin (chapter 15) and MacIntyre (chapter 16). Both strive to defend moral objectivity, at least to a significant extent, while taking quite seriously the disagreements that have impressed nonobjectivists. A brief look at their views will suggest some characteristic prospects and problems mixed views face.[60]

Berlin acknowledges that there are some common moral values; indeed, he insists that both mutual understanding and the survival of societies require this. But this admission is made by way of qualification of the view that there is a plurality of "objective values" that may conflict and are in some sense incommensurable with one another. This pluralism is Berlin's signature theme; it is rooted less in abstract philosophical analysis than in a lifelong reflection on the history of Western ideas and a counter-Enlightenment ear for cultural diversity.[61] Pluralism has gained a considerable following in recent years, and some believe a version of it offers the best interpretation of the moral agreements and disagreements we find in the world.[62]

Berlin explicitly rejects the relativist label. But where he stands in relation to moral objectivism depends on how incommensurability is understood.[63] It is clear that Berlin thinks no single, rational principle or method may be employed in making the inevitable choices between conflicting values. He might be interpreted as believing that there is no correct answer in these choices or at least that no answer could be known. This would be a mixed position, but it raises the question why we should embrace a measure of nonobjectivism if we already take the conflicting values to be objective (if we have reason to think each is actually good, we might have reason to think one is better than the other). However, Berlin might also be read as thinking that there is a correct and rational choice when values conflict (at least ordinarily), but what makes this so is a full appreciation of the particulars of the context and not the application of an "overarching criterion." This would be an objectivist position, albeit one that is distinctive in its emphasis on the diversity of correct choices that may be made depending on circumstances. The implication might be that there is less disagreement than the Disagreement Thesis supposes (if I correctly choose A in my circumstances and you correctly reject A in yours, our choices reflect no disagreement).

Writing in the tradition of Aquinas, MacIntyre insists that there are moral truths understood in a straightforward, nonrelative sense of the term. But he also thinks we can have justified beliefs concerning these truths only insofar as we belong to a tradition of rational inquiry that is socially embodied in a particular historical-cultural context. As seen at the end of section 7, MacIntyre rejects any conception of rationality as historically and culturally neutral. Moreover, he says that traditions of rationality are often both incompatible and incommensurable in important respects. Despite this, he argues, it can be and has been the case that in times of "epistemological crisis" members of two such "alien" traditions might come to understand one another and even to judge, by reference to their own respective standards, that one of the traditions is rationally superior to the other. Hence, the fact that rationality depends on contingent traditions does not necessitate a nonobjectivist account.

MacIntyre thus intends to defend an objectivist account of both truth and justification. But his argument might be interpreted as successfully establishing only that objective justification of one tradition vis-à-vis another is possible or at best only occasionally actual. It is one thing to say that persons in one tradition *sometimes* have reason to believe an alien tradition is rationally superior to their own (this would imply a limited form of objective justification); it is another to say that this happens *typically* or, stronger yet, that one tradition will emerge in the end as better than all the others (what the objectivist presumably would expect). MacIntyre himself admits that conflicting traditions have coexisted "for very long periods" without rational resolution (p. 215). But if, as might be argued, conflicting and incommensurable traditions continue to persist with no resolution in sight, then that might seem reason to think full justification of no tradition has yet been – or perhaps will be – achieved. To admit this would be to move towards a less objectivist account of justification.

MacIntyre thinks the nonobjectivist has no cogent place to stand: such an account can only be defended from some tradition, and any such tradition will have objectivist commitments. However, even if the latter were true, surely there could be many such places to stand – for example, by immigration, marriage, or upbringing a person might partially occupy two conflicting traditions and conclude that a nonobjectivist account is the best explanation of his or her experience. To defend moral objectivity, it would have to be established that there is some likelihood for the eventual resolution of conflicting and incommensurable moral traditions. The central obstacle to establishing this is MacIntyre's own insistence on the contingency and particularity of the traditions we find in the world.[64]

13 Implications for tolerance

In addition to the theoretical question whether moral disagreements threaten objectivity, there is the practical question how we should act with respect to those with whom we disagree. It has sometimes been supposed, notably by some anthropologists (see section 4), that because disagreements undermine objectivity we ought to tolerate those with whom we disagree. Philosophers are nearly unanimous in rejecting this inference as invalid, but there is controversy about whether a more complex connection between some form of disagreement argument and some form of tolerance may be established.

In the West, the historical origin of an appreciation for tolerance is the emergence of the liberal tradition out of the wars of religion in Europe in the sixteenth and seventeenth centuries: from John Locke's limited defense of religious tolerance in *A Letter Concerning Toleration*, the idea grew into a broader principle that came to be regarded as a cornerstone of liberal society – such as, for example, the principle of liberty famously defended by John Stuart Mill in *On Liberty*.[65] In common usage nowadays, a tolerant person is sometimes thought of as someone who is unconcerned about the affairs of others, has a rather expansive notion of what is morally permissible (for example, with respect to sexual activities), or is not prejudiced against people on account of characteristics such as ethnicity. But indifference and the absence of disapproval need to be distinguished from what philosophers often regard as tolerance. In this view, to say that a person tolerates a class of actions of other persons is to say that the person believes the actions are morally wrong but does not seek to use available means of interference or coercion to prevent persons from performing them. For example, someone who thinks gambling is wrong but should not be illegal may be said to tolerate it. Since it is ordinarily thought implausible to tolerate wrong actions such as rape or murder, the challenge for a proponent of tolerance is to explain why we should tolerate some actions we think are wrong but not others.[66]

Defenses of tolerance range from pragmatic considerations concerning the costs or dangers of interference to principled moral considerations concerning the nature of a good society or the value of autonomy. The main question here is whether a disagreement argument for moral nonobjectivism could have implications for some form of tolerance. It is obvious that nonobjectivists cannot consistently put forward as an objective moral judgment that persons ought to tolerate those with whom they reasonably disagree. Only an objectivist could defend an objective judgment concerning tolerance – as, for example, Gewirth does in his claim that tolerance of the morally permissible is an important implication of his PGC (see pp. 188–89). However, relativists – the most common kind of nonobjectivist in these discussions – could consistently put forward as a judgment that is true and justified for persons in their society that they should tolerate the actions of persons in other societies with whom they reasonably disagree (that is, actions that are regarded as wrong in the relativist's society but are not so regarded in the other society). For example, relativists in a monogamist society might say that their society should tolerate the polygamous practices of another society. However, according to relativism (as usually interpreted), whether or not this or any moral judgment is true and justified depends on what values happen to have authority in the society of the people who make the judgment. Hence, the epistemic status of the judgment prescribing tolerance cannot be a consequence of relativism per se nor of a disagreement argument for relativism. If a fundamental value of their society is that polygamy should be aggressively opposed wherever it is found, then relativists would have to concede that this policy and not tolerance is what is true and justified in their society. Such are the kinds of objections philosophers have typically raised against what Williams once called "the anthropologists' heresy."[67]

In response, Wong argues that these objections leave untouched another relativist argument for tolerance that anthropologists and others may have had in mind. According to this argument, a person who accepted relativism *in conjunction with* an ethical principle could have a reason for tolerance that he or she would not have on the basis of the ethical principle alone (chapter 11).[68] Consider the following "justification principle" (adapted from Kant's idea of respecting persons as ends):

"one should not interfere with the ends of others unless one can justify the interference to be acceptable to them were they fully rational and informed of all the relevant circumstances" (pp. 148–49). Suppose that this principle and the requirement of monogamy were true and justified in our society, and that we also recognized the truth of relativism. If another society required polygamy, we might not be justified in interfering with that practice: since in their society (though not ours) the requirement of polygamy is true and justified, our justification for interference might not be acceptable to them even if they were fully rational and informed. If so, by the justification principle, we should not interfere with their practice of polygamy.

Wong's argument does not purport to establish a general relationship between relativism and tolerance, but it would be significant if it established a relationship for those who accept the justification principle. Of course, to be of interest, Wong would also have to be successful in his attempt to show that, once we accepted relativism, we would continue to have reason to accept a moral principle so closely associated with Kant's universal conception of reason and morality.

14 Liberal political philosophy

The practical import of moral disagreements has been the subject of much recent debate in political philosophy, especially in the liberal tradition. The issues here also pertain to tolerance, but they go beyond it to basic questions concerning the nature and justification of the liberal state. At the center of most of these discussions has been the philosophy articulated by John Rawls in *Political Liberalism* (chapter 17).[69] With respect to moral disagreements, the main problem for Rawls may be seen as arising from two claims: "the liberal principle of legitimacy" and "the fact of reasonable pluralism." According to the first:

> Our exercise of political power is fully proper only when it is exercised in accordance with a constitution the essentials of which all citizens as free and equal may reasonably be expected to endorse in the light of principles and ideals acceptable to their common human reason.[70]
>
> (Rawls 1996: 137)

This principle is fundamental to the social contract tradition of political philosophy, particularly in its Kantian form (it is not unrelated to Wong's principle of justification just discussed). The fact of reasonable pluralism is the fact that in a free society persons affirm, and will continue to affirm, a plurality of reasonable comprehensive doctrines that conflict with one another in many respects. A comprehensive doctrine is a religious, philosophical, or moral understanding of the world and our place in it: it involves both theoretical and practical reason, and is ordinarily rooted in some tradition (the world's major religions are examples, but a comprehensive doctrine may take secular form). It is obvious that such doctrines conflict with one another. Rawls also thinks reasonable persons often disagree about these doctrines. They do so because of what he calls "the burdens of judgment": for example, evidence concerning comprehensive doctrines sometimes conflicts, and conflicting aspects of evidence are weighed differently depending on our overall life experience.

The result of these two claims is that political power cannot be justified on the basis of one particular comprehensive doctrine: for any such doctrine, some reasonable persons may reject it, and so the justification would be illegitimate by the liberal principle. But, then, how can political power be justified? Rawls poses this question with respect to the principles pertaining to liberty and equality in his own theory of "justice as fairness" developed earlier in *A Theory of Justice*.[71] His answer is that reasonable persons who are divided by their comprehensive doctrines may nonetheless have an "overlapping consensus" that the principles of justice as fairness are reasonable (what he calls a "political conception of justice"). Reasonable persons are construed as accepting the burdens of judgment and being willing to adhere to fair terms of cooperation so long as others do likewise. In the overlapping consensus, everyone has moral grounds for accepting the principles of justice; but since these grounds are rooted in each person's respective comprehensive doctrine, not everyone has the same grounds. The central thought is that agreement about the fundamentals of justice may be possible among reasonable persons despite the fact that agreement on other serious issues pertaining to comprehensive doctrines is not possible. Hence, a constitution consonant with these fundamentals may be justified consistent with the liberal principle and the fact of reasonable pluralism.

Among the issues about which comprehensive doctrines differ is the question of moral objectivism: some affirm a form of this and others dissent. For this reason, the object of the overlapping consensus is neutral with respect to this question. All persons in the consensus affirm the principles of justice as reasonable; depending on their comprehensive doctrine, some persons may also affirm them as true, while others may deny this or take no position. Since the object of the consensus as such includes no affirmation of the truth of the principles, it might seem that the shared, political conception of justice involves a form of moral nonobjectivism. Rawls denies that this is the case, at least with respect to what he calls "skepticism." If it were the case, then the political conception would be incompatible with the many nonskeptical comprehensive doctrines, and the overlapping consensus would collapse.

But is not a form of skepticism implied by the view that, on account of the burdens of judgment, reasonable persons disagree about conflicting comprehensive doctrines? Rawls says this view is not the skeptical position that "the necessary conditions of knowledge can never be satisfied." Rather, it is the recognition of "the practical impossibility of reaching reasonable and workable political agreement in judgment on the truth of comprehensive doctrines" (1996: 63). Much depends on the interpretation of this "practical impossibility." Since the recognition of it is said to be permanent and inevitable, it might be thought to involve a form of skepticism that many comprehensive doctrines would deny. If so, then it seems unlikely that there is or will be an overlapping consensus in Western countries, such as the United States, that Rawls has in mind. This is one aspect of a broader question that confronts Rawls: is there any real prospect that all persons ordinarily thought of as reasonable – including, as Rawls hopes, those who have conservative, religious comprehensive doctrines – would join in a consensus affirming his liberal principles of justice?

15 Feminist approaches to moral disagreements

Feminist ethics has brought a distinctive array of perspectives to understanding the nature of moral disagreements, the relation of these to moral objectivity, and the implications of such considerations for moral practice.[72] These perspectives are united in their opposition to the oppression of women, in their critiques of patriarchy in moral and political theory, and in their emphasis on the theoretical and practical importance of the moral experiences and outlooks of women. Beyond this, feminist ethics is itself the scene of much moral and philosophical disagreement. For example, feminist critics have pointed out that philosophers in the Western tradition have typically regarded women as morally inferior to men, and that these philosophers have tended to feature circumstances, experiences, traits, and modes of thinking that are customarily associated with men rather than women. As a result of these critiques, some feminists have largely rejected this tradition while others have critically appropriated aspects of it they continue to regard as worthwhile. In a similar vein, the observation that in both theory and practice the liberal political tradition has discriminated against women has resulted in the complete repudiation of this tradition by some feminists and the attempt by others to reform it on the basis of a consistent application of the principle of gender equality.

An important area of disagreement among feminist philosophers is the issue of moral objectivity. Many feminist condemnations of the oppression of women appear to presuppose an objective understanding of morality. In fact, many who express these condemnations intend them to be so understood. But some feminist philosophers are deeply suspicious of the whole idea of moral objectivity. They point out that this idea has been closely connected, historically and philosophically, to moral outlooks that have oppressed women. In addition, they sometimes stress the importance of recognizing relevant differences between men and women instead of falsely presenting as "objective" or "universal" what is true only of men or of some men. Finally, some feminist critiques of moral objectivity draw on broader contextualist or postmodern misgivings about objectivity in general. In opposition to these critiques, other feminist philosophers argue that they threaten to undermine feminism itself: in the absence of some objective standard – universal human rights, for example – there is no basis for criticizing many practices such as "genital mutilation" that are deeply harmful to women, but are common in societies where sexism has a long and deep hold.[73]

An important aspect of this objectivity debate concerns the proper representation of the values, outlooks, experiences, and situations of women vis-à-vis both men and one another. In an influential contribution to this discussion, the developmental psychologist Carol Gilligan suggested that male and female moral thinking may be incommensurably different, with men favoring a "justice" perspective that stresses equality and the protection of rights, and women preferring a "care" perspective that emphasizes compassion and the preservation of relationships.[74] This contention raises numerous theoretical and practical questions, and it was greeted with an enormous critical response, both favorable and unfavorable, among feminist moral philosophers and others.[75] Another dimension of this discussion is the claim that many feminist representations of women (including Gilligan's) are true only of some women, usually white, heterosexual, rather well-off women in Western countries. The result has been an increased emphasis on the importance of differences among women throughout the world.

In response, Uma Narayan argues that this emphasis may be as problematic as the false generalizations it seeks to replace because it sometimes uncritically identifies the values of particular women with the values of a local culture that has frequently been constructed and defined by social and political interests harmful to women (chapter 18). Moreover, Narayan maintains, an adequate sense of history shows that cultures are heterogeneous and complex, undergo processes of change, and often have unclear borders. There are real cultural differences, but they do not correspond in any simple fashion to the customary ways in which cultures are individuated. Hence, we should be careful in presuming to know the values of persons in a particular context as well as in drawing comparisons between, for example, the respective values of "Western" and "non-Western" cultures. These are important cautions that have relevance for discussions throughout this volume.

Apropos the objectivity debate, Narayan tries to weaken the feminist "temptation to relativism" by pointing out that the oppression of women has sometimes been associated historically with both relativism and the emphasis on difference. While remaining "agnostic" about the existence of "one neat and complete universal set of values," she contends that many feminist values may be "meaningful and efficacious in a variety of global contexts" (p. 239). One question is whether this is sufficient for the concerns about objectivity of some feminist moral philosophers. In any case, given Narayan's emphasis on the complexities of cultures, she sets a difficult task – empirically, philosophically, and morally – for an international feminist program. But it may be that no moral philosophy that truly aspires to speak to and for human beings across cultures can escape this burden.

Notes

1 Hume (1998: 152).
2 The terminology I employ here and in what follows is mostly common among philosophers; but since they do not always use terms in the same way, my terminology is in part stipulative.
3 The claim is only that these conditions are necessary, not sufficient. Cf. Williams, pp. 132–33 in this volume.
4 The "mind-independence" of truth requires careful formulation with respect to moral truth, since morality is about people and their attitudes. Theories that make the truth of a basic moral principle depend on the nature of rational agency are naturally thought of as objective because this truth does not depend on the attitudes that anyone in particular has (see Gewirth, ch. 14). In section 10, this conception of truth as mind-independent is contrasted with a relativist conception.
5 This debate is discussed in some detail in sections 7–11.
6 The vote was forty-eight in favor and none against, but there were eight abstentions.
7 For example, see Henkin (1990: 26) and Perry (1998: 88).
8 See MacIntyre (1984: 70) and Pollis and Schwab (1980: 13).
9 The quoted phrase is from Huntington (1996); he argues that Western values such as human rights are alien to other civilizations, especially in Asia and the Islamic world.
10 Quoted in Cerna (1994: 743).
11 For general discussions of human rights and moral diversity, see An-Na' im (1990b), Cerna (1994), Donnelly (1984) and (1989), Donoho (1991), Drydyk (1997), Little (1999), Milne (1986), Perry (1997) and (1998), Pollis (1996), Pollis and Schwab (1980), Renteln (1985), (1988), and (1990), Shute and Hurley (1993), and Twiss (1998). For accounts of human rights vis-à-vis a variety of different cultures and religions, see Afshari (1994), An-Na'im (1987) and (1990a), An-Na'im and Deng (1990), Bauer and Bell (1999), Bloom *et al.* (1996), Breslauer (1993), De Bary (1998), Donnelly (1990), Dwyer (1991), Gustafson and Juviler (1999), Howard (1986) and (1990), Ilesanmi (1995), Inada (1990), Little (1990), Little *et al.* (1988), Marfording (1997), Monshipouri (1998), Rouner (1988), Swidler (1982), Thurman (1988) and (1996), Tibi (1990), and Welch and Leary (1990).
12 Most famously by Benedict (1934a: 278) and most recently by Hatch (1997: 374).

13 For example, see Ferguson (1995), Lizot (1985), and Ramos (1987). In a well-known controversy, Margaret Mead's data concerning the Samoan people was later challenged (see Mead [1928] and D. Freeman [1983]; for a discussion of the controversy, see Scheper-Hughes [1984]).

14 Chagnon himself says the Yanomamö are both "exotic" and "fundamentally like all the rest of us in universally human ways" (Chagnon 1992: xvi). But some philosophers have drawn on his work in challenges to moral objectivism (see Bennigson [1996] and [1998], and Miller [1985] and [1992]). Another empirical study that has attracted the attention of philosophers is Turnbull (1973). For some recent empirical studies of morality by anthropologists, see Howell (1997).

15 I have benefited from the interpretation in Hatch (1983).

16 For representative work, see Boas (1974).

17 For example, see Benedict (1934a) and (1934b), Herskovits (1948: ch. 5) and (1972), and Mead (1928) and (1935). See also Sumner (1906) and Westermarck (1932). Though Boas is commonly referred to as a relativist, he denied that he was a moral relativist (Boas [1938: 202]; cf. Cook [1999: 74] and Stocking [1992: 110–11]).

18 In these connections, see the following anthologies: Borofsky (1994); Haan *et al.* (1983), Hollis and Lukes (1982); Krausz (1989); Krausz and Meiland (1982); Shweder and Levine (1984); and Wilson (1970). See also D'Andrade (1995), Fay (1996), Geertz (1973), Hanson (1975), Scheper-Hughes (1984), Spiro (1986), (1992a), and (1992b), and Wainwright (1986).

19 During the 1950s there was considerable interest and engagement in anthropology by moral philosophers, usually with respect to moral relativism. In particular, see Brandt (1954), Edel and Edel (1959), Ladd (1957), and MacBeath (1952). Other philosophical discussions of anthropology in the postwar period include Beis (1964), Brandt (1959: chs 5 and 11), Edel (1955), Edel and Edel (1963), Ladd (1963), Lazari-Pawlowska (1970), Louch (1963), McClintock (1963), Nielsen (1966), (1971), and (1974), Schmidt (1955), P. W. Taylor (1958) and (1963), Tennekes (1971), and Wellman (1963). In recent years, there has been renewed interest in anthropology by moral philosophers; see especially Cook (1999) and Moody-Adams (1997).

20 For example, see the critiques of H.G. Barnett (1948), Bennett (1949), and Steward (1948); there is a response in Herskovits (1972: 44 ff.). For an early critique of relativism by a psychologist, see Duncker (1939).

21 For other discussions of relativism by anthropologists during this period, see Bidney (1953) and (1959), Ginsberg (1953), Kluckhohn (1955) and (1962), Redfield (1953) and (1957), and E. Williams (1947).

22 For other relevant works, see Shweder (1989), (1991), and (1996), as well as Shweder *et al.* (1997). Another prominent recent figure in this tradition is Clifford Geertz; see especially (1986) and (1989).

23 See American Anthropological Association Commission for Human Rights (1993), C.R. Barnett (1988), Downing and Kushner (1988), Messer (1993) and (1997), Nagengast (1997), Salmon (1997), Scheper-Hughes (1995), Schirmer (1988), Washburn (1987), R.A. Wilson (1997), and Zechenter (1997).

24 See Herodotus (1987: 3.38) and Plato (1961: 167c). A rather different Protagoras appears in Plato's *Protagoras.*

25 For the main works, see Sextus Empiricus (1994) and (1997). For useful commentary, see Annas (1986), Annas and Barnes (1985), Barnes (1988–90) and (1990), Hankinson (1995), McPherran (1990), and Nussbaum (1994: ch. 8).

26 See Aquinas (1964: 18).

27 The central text is the Second Part of Aquinas (1964–75). For general discussions of Aquinas's moral philosophy, see Davies (1992: chs. 12–13), Finnis (1998), and McInerny (1993); on his response to the disagreement challenge, see Doolan (1999), Finnis (1980: ch. 2), and Wiles (1989). In editing ch. 2 I have benefited from references in Finnis (1980).

28 Montaigne (1965) is the main work; with respect to moral disagreements and skepticism, see especially: bk. I, chs. 23, 27, 31, 37, and 53; bk. II, chs. 3 and 12; and bk. III, chs. 1 and 13. Two important studies pertaining to Montaigne are Friedrich (1991) and Popkin (1979). On Montaigne and moral philosophy, see Schneewind (1998: ch. 3) and C. Taylor (1989: ch. 10).

29 In his *Essay Concerning Human Understanding*, John Locke describes moral disagreements at great length (though not with reference to Montaigne) in order to show that moral principles are not innate in the mind (1959: bk. 1, ch. II). But Locke did not think these disagreements challenged the truth and certainty of these principles.

30 Hume's moral philosophy is contained primarily in Hume (1967: bk. III) and (1998). For accounts of Hume's moral philosophy, see Beauchamp's Introduction in Hume (1998), J. Harrison (1976), Mackie (1980), and D.F. Norton (1982) and (1993).

31 On the two senses of moral universality, see Hume (1998: 147–48).

32 For commentary specifically on "A Dialogue," see Abramson (1999) and Beauchamp's annotations in Hume (1998: 250–57).

33 Parts of Hume's argument may also be compared with an argument of Dugald Stewart, a follower of Thomas Reid, the commonsense philosopher and critic of Hume. Reid and Stewart supposed all human beings possess a rational moral faculty that reveals some moral principles as self-evident. Stewart argued that this is consistent with "the diversity of opinions" in morality (1859: 233–51). For a brief critique of Stewart, see MacIntyre (1988: 329–32).

34 Nietzsche speaks of morality throughout his works, but the two most important for moral philosophy are Nietzsche (1966) and (1994). For discussions of Nietzsche's moral philosophy, see Schacht (1983: ch. 7) and the essays collected in Schacht (1994).

35 For examples of accounts that emphasize these aspects, see Blackburn (1993: chs. 5 and 6) and Gibbard (1990).

36 For example, see Harmon (1977: chs. 1 and 2) and Mackie (1977: ch. 1).

37 For a prominent example of a general critique of objectivity, see R. Rorty (1979). The citations in note 18 are relevant to these issues.

38 The classic papers in the moral dilemmas literature are contained in Gowans (1987). There is controversy about the proper interpretation of the standard definition of moral dilemmas; I discuss this in Gowans (1994: 4–5 and 59–62). In my view, the key idea is inescapable moral wrongdoing.

39 These arguments are usually considered in connection with either anti-realism or relativism. Those that focus on anti-realism include Bennigson (1996) and (1998), Blackburn (1985), Boyd (1988), Brink (1984) and (1989: ch. 7), Goldman (1987), Loeb (1998), Nagel (1986: 147–9), Railton (1993) and (1996), Schiffer (1990), Shafer-Landau (1994), Snare (1984), Sosa (1998), Tersman (1998), Tolhurst (1987), and Wellman (1975). For mostly recent discussions of disagreements that concern relativism, see Arrington (1983) and (1989), Brandt (1984), Bunting (1996), Cook (1999), Cooper (1978), Darwall (1998), DeCew (1990), Dustin (1995), Fleischacker (1992), Foot (1982), French (1992), Garcia (1988), Garmon (1995), Harman (1991), (1996), (1998a) and (1998b), Lukes (1974), Lyons (1976), McClintock (1969),

41

MacIntyre (1989) and (1994), Matilal (1989), Postow (1979), Rotenstreich (1977), Scanlon (1998: ch. 8), Stewart and Thomas (1991), Sturgeon (1994), and B. Williams (1981). For anthologies on relativism, see Brown (1984), Krausz (1989), Krausz and Meiland (1982), Ladd (1985), Odegard and Stewart (1991), and Paul *et al.* (1994). For earlier discussions of relativism by philosophers, see note 19. Other accounts of disagreements include Bambrough (1979), Beardsmore (1969: chs. 4, 9, and 10), Dworkin (1996), Ewing (1953: 111–18), Hampshire (1983) and (1989), Hurley (1985) and (1989), Kolnai (1978), Kukathas (1994), Lean (1970), McNaughton (1988: ch. 10), Miller (1985) and (1992), Milo (1986), Modood (1982–83), Moody-Adams (1990) and (1997), Nielsen (1974), Phillips and Mounce (1970: ch. 9), Ross (1930: 12–15), Russell (1984), Scanlon (1995), Seabright (1988), Silver (1994), Snare (1980), Stout (1988), and Walzer (1987) and (1994).

40 On this issue, see the citations in note 18; cf. Gewirth, p. 185, this volume.

41 See Stevenson (1944) and (1963), and Foot (1978a) and (1978b).

42 See Aristotle (1985: 1115a30).

43 See also B. Williams (1995). For critical discussion of Williams, see McDowell (1986), Quinn (1993), and Tasioulas (1998), as well as the essays and response by Williams in Altham and Harrison (1995).

44 For example, see Cooper (1978), French (1992: ch. 10), Garcia (1988), Hurley (1985) and (1989: ch. 2), McNaughton (1988: ch. 10), Moody-Adams (1997: 55–56), and Stout (1988: ch. 1).

45 See especially Davidson (1982).

46 For a recent critique, see Forster (1998).

47 If good arguments could exist but never persuade reasonable and well-informed persons, then the existence of such arguments would be compatible with such persons having no awareness of their existence; it would then be odd to equate a rational resolution of a disagreement with the existence of a good argument. A rational resolution is presumably an epistemic state reasonable and well-informed persons consciously achieve.

48 See Bok (1993) and (1995: ch. 1); see also Harbour (1995), Walzer (1994) and J.Q. Wilson (1993), as well as the papers in Outka and Reeder (1993).

49 For diverse reactions, see Küng (1996). Cf. Donovan (1986).

50 Cf. Snare (1980).

51 On incommensurability, see the papers in Chang (1997).

52 For a qualified defense of skepticism, see Sinnott-Armstrong (1996).

53 However, recall that Hume, often claimed by anti-realists, saw things rather differently.

54 For example, see Blackburn (1993: chs. 5 and 6) and Gibbard (1990).

55 The term "moral relativism" is understood in a wide variety of ways, many but not all of which are captured by this definition.

56 See also Wong (1986a) and (1995). For discussions of Wong's book, see Devine (1987), Kupperman (1986), and Narveson (1987); Wong responds to Kupperman in (1986b). Another prominent defender of this argument is Harman (1991), (1996), and (1998a).

57 For a response to Nussbaum, see Hurley (1993) and Moody-Adams (1998). Nussbaum answers the latter in (1998) and develops her position in (1995b) and (forthcoming).

58 All references to Gewirth are to pp. 183–84.

59 For Gewirth's full defense of the argument, see Gewirth (1978); also relevant is Gewirth (1982). For criticism of the argument and a response by Gewirth, see the papers in Regis (1984). A detailed defense of Gewirth's argument is given in Beyleveld (1991).

60 Other authors in this book might also be interpreted as providing grounds for a mixed account, but I take these two to be the most obvious.

61 Connected with his pluralism are two themes: tragedy (choices between goods may involve an "irreparable loss") and liberalism (political society should minimize interference in people's lives).

62 For recent pluralist accounts, see Gaut (1993), Kekes (1993) and (1994), McKnight (1996), Rescher (1993), Skorupski (1996), Stocker (1990), and Wolf (1992).

63 For other relevant work, see Berlin (1969) and (1998), and Berlin and Williams (1994). For interpretations of Berlin, see Crowder (1994), Frisch (1998), Galipeau (1994), Gray (1996), and Lukes (1994). On incommensurability, see the essays in Chang (1997).

64 For other relevant work by MacIntyre, see all the entries in the Bibliography. Pertinent critiques of MacIntyre include Annas (1989), Dahl (1991), and Schneewind (1991); MacIntyre responds to the last two in (1991). See also the papers and response by MacIntyre in Horton and Mendus (1994). Also of interest are Fowl (1991), Sreenivasan (1998), and C. Taylor (1993).

65 See Locke (1991) and Mill (1956).

66 For discussions of tolerance, see the papers in Heyd (1996) and Mendus (1988).

67 See Williams (1972: 20–26) and G. Harrison (1976).

68 For a related discussion, see Wong (1992).

69 Rawls (1996); for earlier presentations of the relevant ideas, see Rawls (1987) and (1989); for a more recent account, see (1997). The critical literature is already very large. For discussion of political liberalism and moral disagreements, mostly apropos Rawls, see Adams (1993), K. Baier (1989), Bohman (1995), Cohen (1993) and (1994), Freeman (1994), Greenawalt (1995: ch. 10), Gutmann (1993), Gutmann and Thompson (1990) and (1996), Hampton (1993) and (1994), Larmore (1994), Lukes (1991), Moon (1993), Nagel (1987), Raz (1994a) and (1994b), Richardson (1990), Solum (1994), Waldron (1994), Weinstock (1994), and Weithman (1994). Some of these accounts overlap with the philosophy of law; in that connection, see especially Sunstein (1996) and Waldron (1999).

70 Rawls originally said he was especially concerned with stability. But his Introduction to the 1996 paperback edition (the book was first published in 1993) makes clear that what is crucial is stability and consensus "for the right reasons," and I take this to indicate the importance of the liberal principle. See pp. 220 and 224–25 in this volume.

71 Rawls (1971).

72 For example, see Baylis and Downie (1997), Benhabib (1992), Brems (1997), Bunch (1992), Code (1995) and (1998), Farley (1993), Li (1995), Morgan (1991), Nagengast (1997), Narayan (1997) and (1998), Nussbaum (1995a), (1999a) and (1999b), Okin (1994), (1995), and (1998), Sherwin (1991), Shrage (1994: ch. 7), and Walker (1998).

73 On this topic, see James (1994) and Nussbaum (1999c).

74 See Gilligan (1982) and (1987).

75 For some philosophical responses, see the essays in Kittay and Meyers (1987). An influential development of an ethics of care is Noddings (1984).

Part I

THE HISTORICAL DEBATE

1

OUTLINES OF SCEPTICISM

Sextus Empiricus

Book I

(i) The most fundamental difference among philosophies

... [3] Those who are called Dogmatists in the proper sense of the word
think that they have discovered the truth – for example, the schools of
Aristotle and Epicurus and the Stoics, and some others. The schools of
Clitomachus and Carneades, and other Academics, have asserted that
things cannot be apprehended. And the Sceptics are still investigating. [4]
Hence the most fundamental kinds of philosophy are reasonably
thought to be three: the Dogmatic, the Academic, and the Sceptical. The
former two it will be appropriate for others to describe: in the present
work we shall discuss in outline the Sceptical persuasion. By way of pref-
ace let us say that on none of the matters to be discussed do we affirm
that things certainly are just as we say they are: rather, we report descriptively on each item according to how it appears to us at the time. ...

(iv) What is Scepticism?

[8] Scepticism is an ability to set out oppositions among things which
appear and are thought of in any way at all, an ability by which, because
of the equipollence in the opposed objects and accounts, we come first to
suspension of judgement and afterwards to tranquillity. ...

[10] By "opposed accounts" we do not necessarily have in mind affirmation and negation, but take the phrase simply in the sense of "con-

From *Sextus Empiricus: Outlines of Scepticism*, translated and edited by Julia Annas and
Jonathan Barnes, Cambridge: Cambridge University Press, 1994, pp. 3–11, 188, 194–200,
and 204. Notes of the translators are not included.

Sextus Empiricus was a Greek physician and philosopher who probably lived in the second
century C.E.

flicting accounts." By "equipollence" we mean equality with regard to being convincing or unconvincing: none of the conflicting accounts takes precedence over any other as being more convincing. Suspension of judgement is a standstill of the intellect, owing to which we neither reject nor posit anything. Tranquillity is freedom from disturbance or calmness of soul. . . .

(vii) Do Sceptics hold beliefs?

[13] When we say that Sceptics do not hold beliefs, we do not take "belief" in the sense in which some say, quite generally, that belief is acquiescing in something; for Sceptics assent to the feelings forced upon them by appearances – for example, they would not say, when heated or chilled, "I think I am not heated (or: chilled)." Rather, we say that they do not hold beliefs in the sense in which some say that belief is assent to some unclear object of investigation in the sciences; for Pyrrhonists do not assent to anything unclear.

[14] Not even in uttering the Sceptical phrases about unclear matters – for example, "In no way more," or "I determine nothing" . . . – do they hold beliefs. For if you hold beliefs, then you posit as real the things you are said to hold beliefs about; but Sceptics posit these phrases not as necessarily being real. . . .

[15] . . . [I]n uttering these phrases, they say what is apparent to themselves and report their own feelings without holding opinions, affirming nothing about external objects.

(viii) Do Sceptics belong to a school?

[17] . . . [I]f you count as a school a persuasion which, to all appearances, coheres with some account, the account showing how it is possible to live correctly (where "correctly" is taken not only with reference to virtue, but more loosely, and extends to the ability to suspend judgement) – in that case we say that Sceptics do belong to a school. For we coherently follow, to all appearances, an account which shows us a life in conformity with traditional customs and the law and persuasions and our own feelings. . . .

(x) Do Sceptics reject what is apparent?

[19] Those who say that the Sceptics reject what is apparent have not, I think, listened to what we say. As we said before, we do not overturn anything which leads us, without our willing it, to assent in accordance with a passive appearance – and these things are precisely what is apparent. When we investigate whether existing things are such as they appear, we

grant that they appear, and what we investigate is not what is apparent but what is said about what is apparent – and this is different from investigating what is apparent itself. [20] For example, it appears to us that honey sweetens (we concede this inasmuch as we are sweetened in a perceptual way); but whether (as far as the argument goes) it is actually sweet is something we investigate – and this is not what is apparent but something said about what is apparent. . . .

(xi) The standard of Scepticism

[21] That we attend to what is apparent is clear from what we say about the standard of the Sceptical persuasion. "Standard" has two senses: there are standards adopted to provide conviction about the reality or unreality of something (we shall talk about these standards when we turn to attack them); and there are standards of action, attending to which in everyday life we perform some actions and not others – and it is these standards which are our present subject.

[22] We say, then, that the standard of the Sceptical persuasion is what is apparent, implicitly meaning by this the appearances; for they depend on passive and unwilled feelings and are not objects of investigation. . . .

[23] Thus, attending to what is apparent, we live in accordance with everyday observances, without holding opinions – for we are not able to be utterly inactive. These everyday observances seem to be fourfold, and to consist in guidance by nature, necessitation by feelings, handing down of laws and customs, and teaching of kinds of expertise. [24] By nature's guidance we are naturally capable of perceiving and thinking. By the necessitation of feelings, hunger conducts us to food and thirst to drink. By the handing down of customs and laws, we accept, from an everyday point of view, that piety is good and impiety bad. By teaching of kinds of expertise, we are not inactive in those which we accept.

And we say all this without holding any opinions.

(xii) What is the aim of Scepticism?

[25] It will be apposite to consider next the aim of the Sceptical persuasion. Now an aim is that for the sake of which everything is done or considered, while it is not itself done or considered for the sake of anything else. Or: an aim is the final object of desire. Up to now we say the aim of the Sceptic is tranquillity in matters of opinion and moderation of feeling in matters forced upon us. [26] For Sceptics began to do philosophy in order to decide among appearances and to apprehend which are true and which false, so as to become tranquil; but they came upon equipollent dispute, and being unable to decide this they suspended judgement. And

when they suspended judgement, tranquillity in matters of opinion followed fortuitously.

[27] For those who hold the opinion that things are good or bad by nature are perpetually troubled. When they lack what they believe to be good, they take themselves to be persecuted by natural evils and they pursue what (so they think) is good. And when they have acquired these things, they experience more troubles; for they are elated beyond reason and measure, and in fear of change they do anything so as not to lose what they believe to be good. [28] But those who make no determination about what is good and bad by nature neither avoid nor pursue anything with intensity; and hence they are tranquil.

A story told of the painter Apelles applies to the Sceptics. They say that he was painting a horse and wanted to represent in his picture the lather on the horse's mouth; but he was so unsuccessful that he gave up, took the sponge on which he had been wiping off the colours from his brush, and flung it at the picture. And when it hit the picture, it produced a representation of the horse's lather. [29] Now the Sceptics were hoping to acquire tranquillity by deciding the anomalies in what appears and is thought of, and being unable to do this they suspended judgement. But when they suspended judgement, tranquillity followed as it were fortuitously, as a shadow follows a body.

We do not, however, take Sceptics to be undisturbed in every way – we say that they are disturbed by things which are forced upon them; for we agree that at times they shiver and are thirsty and have other feelings of this kind. [30] But in these cases ordinary people are afflicted by two sets of circumstances: by the feelings themselves, and no less by believing that these circumstances are bad by nature. Sceptics, who shed the additional opinion that each of these things is bad in its nature, come off more moderately even in these cases. . . .

Book III

(xxi) The ethical part of philosophy

[168] There remains the ethical part of philosophy, which is thought to deal with the distinction among fine, bad and indifferent things. In order to give a summary account of this part too, let us investigate the reality of good, bad and indifferent things. . . .

(xxiii) Is anything by nature good, bad or indifferent?

[179] Fire, which heats by nature, appears heating to everyone; and snow, which chills by nature, appears chilling to everyone: indeed, everything which affects us by nature affects in the same way everyone who is in

what they call a natural state. But none of the so-called good things affects everyone as good, as we shall suggest. Nothing, therefore, is by nature good.

That none of the things said to be good affects everybody in the same way is, they say, clear. [180] Let us pass over ordinary people – of whom some deem bodily well-being good, others sex, others overeating, others drunkenness, others gambling, others still worse things. Among the philosophers themselves some say (e.g. the Peripatetics) that there are three kinds of goods – some concern the soul (e.g. the virtues), some the body (e.g. health and the like), and others are external (e.g. friends, wealth and the like). [181] The Stoics also say that there is a triple division of goods – some concern the soul (e.g. the virtues), some are external (e.g. virtuous people and friends), and others neither concern the soul nor are external (e.g. the virtuous in relation to themselves). The things concerning the body, however, which the Peripatetics say are good they say are not good.

Some have embraced pleasure as a good, while others say that it is downright bad – so that one philosopher exclaimed: "I would rather go mad than feel pleasure."

[182] If, then, things which affect us by nature affect everyone in the same way, while we are not all affected in the same way in the case of so-called goods, then nothing is by nature good. It is impossible to be convinced either by all the positions set out above (because of the conflict) or by any one of them. For anyone who says that we should find this position convincing but not that one has opposing him the arguments of those who take different views and becomes a part of the dispute. And so he will himself need to be judged along with the rest rather than being a judge of others. Since, then, there is no agreed standard or proof (because of the undecidable dispute about them), he will end up in suspension of judgement and hence be able to make no affirmation as to what is by nature good. . . .

[190] . . . For these reasons nothing is by nature bad either. Things which some think bad others pursue as goods – for example, indulgence, injustice, avarice, lack of self-control and the like. Hence, if things which are so and so by nature naturally affect everyone in the same way, while so-called bad things do not affect everyone in the same way, nothing is by nature bad.

[191] Similarly, nothing is by nature indifferent, because of the dispute over indifferent things. The Stoics, for example, say that among indifferents some are preferred, others dispreferred, others neither preferred nor dispreferred. Preferred are things which have an adequate value, such as health and wealth. Dispreferred are things which have an inadequate value, such as poverty and disease. Neither preferred nor dispreferred are such things as stretching out or crooking your finger. [192] But some say

that nothing indifferent is by nature either preferred or dispreferred: each indifferent thing appears sometimes preferred, sometimes dispreferred, depending on the circumstances. For instance, they say, if a tyrant were to plot against the rich while the poor were left in peace, everyone would choose to be poor rather than rich, so that wealth would become dispreferred. [193] Hence, since each so-called indifferent is said by some to be good and by others to be bad, while if it were by nature indifferent everyone would deem it indifferent in the same way, nothing is by nature indifferent. . . .

[197] Those who say that the life of virtue is by nature good are turned about in the same way – by the fact that some sages choose a life including pleasure, so that the dispute among them overthrows the claim that anything is thus-and-so by nature. [198] In addition, it is no doubt not out of place to dwell briefly in a more specific way on the suppositions made about what is shameful and not shameful, unlawful and not so, about laws and customs . . . and the like. In this way we shall discover much anomaly in what ought to be done and not done.

[199] Among us, for instance, homosexual sex is shameful – or rather, has actually been deemed illegal – but among the Germani, they say, it is not shameful and is quite normal. It is said that among the Thebans in the old days it was not thought shameful, and that Meriones the Cretan was so called to hint at this Cretan custom. And some refer to this the ardent friendship of Achilles for Patroclus. [200] What wonder, when Cynic philosophers and the followers of Zeno of Citium and Cleanthes and Chrysippus say that it is indifferent?

Having sex with a woman in public, though shameful among us, is deemed not shameful among some Indians – at any rate, they have sex indifferently in public – and we hear the same about the philosopher Crates. [201] Among us it is shameful and a matter of reproach for women to prostitute themselves; but with many Egyptians it is glorious – at any rate, they say that the women who have been with the most men wear amulets or ornaments, tokens of the esteem they enjoy; and among some of them the girls collect their dowry before marriage from prostitution and then marry. We see the Stoics too saying that there is nothing out of place in cohabiting with a prostitute or living off a prostitute's earnings.

[202] Further, among us tattooing is thought to be shameful and a dishonour, but many Egyptians and Sarmatians tattoo their babies. [203] Among us it is shameful for men to wear earrings, but among some foreigners, such as the Syrians, this is a token of noble birth – and some of them extend this token of noble birth by piercing their children's nostrils and hanging silver or gold rings from them, something no-one among us would do. [204] In the same way no male here would wear a brightly-coloured full-length dress, although among the Persians this, which among us is shameful, is thought highly becoming. . . .

[205] Among us it is unlawful to marry your own mother or sister; but the Persians – especially those of them thought to practise wisdom, the Magi – marry their mothers, Egyptians take their sisters in marriage . . . Again, Zeno of Citium says that there is nothing out of place in rubbing your mother's private parts with your own – just as nobody would say that it was bad to rub any other part of her body with your hand; and Chrysippus in his *Republic* expresses the belief that fathers should have children by their daughters, mothers by their sons, and brothers by their sisters. Plato asserted even more generally that women should be held in common.

[206] Zeno does not rule out masturbation, which among us is condemned; and we hear of others, too, who engage in this bad practice as though it were something good.

[207] Again, tasting human flesh is among us unlawful; but it is indifferent among entire foreign nations. And why speak of foreigners when even Tydeus is said to have eaten his enemy's brains, and when the Stoics say that there is nothing out of place in eating human flesh, others' or your own? [208] Among most of us it is unlawful to defile the altar of a god with human blood; but Spartans are flogged mercilessly at the altar of Artemis Orthosia so that the blood may flow freely on the altar of the goddess. Further, some make human sacrifice to Cronus, just as the Scythians sacrifice strangers to Artemis; but we think that holy places are polluted by the killing of a human being.

[209] Adulterers are, among us, punished by law; but among some people it is indifferent whether you have sex with other men's wives; and some philosophers say that it is indifferent whether you have sex with another's wife.

[210] Among us the law orders that fathers should get proper care from their sons; but the Scythians cut the throats of everyone over sixty. . . . Again, Cronus decided to destroy his own children, [211] and Solon laid down for the Athenians the law of immunity, according to which he permitted every man to kill his own child. But among us the laws forbid killing children. The Roman lawgivers order sons to be their fathers' subjects and slaves, and the fathers – not the sons – to control the sons' property until the sons obtain their freedom, just like bought slaves. But among others this has been rejected as tyrannical.

[212] There is a law punishing manslaughter; but gladiators who kill often obtain honour. Again, the laws forbid the striking of free men; but athletes who strike free men, often actually killing them, are thought worthy of honours and prizes. [213] The law among us orders each man to have only one wife; but among the Thracians and the Gaetuli (a nation in Libya) each man has several. [214] Among us piracy is illegal and unjust; but among many foreigners it is not out of place. They say that the Cilicians deemed it actually to be glorious, so that they thought people killed during pirate raids worthy of honour. . . .

[215] Again, among us stealing is unjust and illegal; but people who call Hermes a most thieving god bring it about that this is not considered unjust – for how could a god be bad? And some say that the Spartans used to punish people who had stolen not for having stolen but for having been caught.

[216] Again, cowards and men who throw away their shields are in many places punished by law; which is why the Spartan woman, when she gave her son his shield as he left for war, said: "Either with it, or on it." But Archilochus, as though boasting to us about having thrown away his shield and fled, says about himself in his poems:

> Some Saian gloats over the shield which by a bush
> I left behind unwillingly, unblemished armour:
> myself, I escaped death's end.

[217] The Amazons used to lame the male children they bore, to make them unable to do anything manly, and they looked after warfare themselves; but among us the opposite has been deemed fine. The Mother of the Gods accepts effeminate men; and the goddess would not have made this judgement if being unmanly were by nature bad. [218] Thus there is much anomaly about just and unjust things, and about how fine it is to be manly. . . .

[235] The Sceptics, then, seeing such anomaly in objects, suspend judgement as to whether anything is by nature good or bad, or generally to be done, here too refraining from dogmatic rashness; and they follow the observance of everyday life without holding opinions. They therefore remain without feeling in matters of opinions and with moderation of feeling in matters forced upon them: [236] being human, they are affected by way of their senses; but, not having the additional opinion that the way they are affected is by nature bad, their feelings are moderate. For having such an additional opinion about something is worse than actually feeling it.

2

NATURAL LAW AND MORAL DISAGREEMENTS

Thomas Aquinas

58, 5 Can there be intellectual virtue without moral virtue?

Other intellectual virtues, but not prudence, can exist without moral virtue. The reason for this is that prudence is right judgment about things to be done, and this not merely in general, but also in the particular instance, wherein action takes place. Prerequisite for right judgment are principles from which reason proceeds. Yet when reason is concerned with the particular, it needs not only universal principles, but also particular ones. So far as the general principles of practice are concerned, a man is rightly disposed by a natural understanding, by which he knows that he should do no evil, and by some normative science. Yet this is not enough in order that a man may reason rightly about particular cases. In fact, it happens sometimes that general principles and conclusions of understanding and science are swept away in the particular case by a passion. Thus to one who is overcome by lust, the object of his desire then seems good, although it is against his general convictions. Consequently, as by the habits of natural understanding and science, a man is rightly disposed with regard to general truths, so, in order that he be rightly disposed with regard to the particular principles of action, namely, their ends, he needs to be perfected by certain habits, whereby it becomes, as it

From Thomas Aquinas, *Summa Theologiae*, translated by T. Gilby, *et al.*, New York: McGraw-Hill, 1964–75, vol. 23, pp. 77 and 79, vol. 25, pp. 163, 165, and 167, vol. 28, pp. 57, 79, 81, 83, 87, 89, 91, 93, 97, 143, and 145, vol. 29, pp. 35, 37, 59, 61, and 105. The title is supplied by CWG. The numbers at the head of each section refer to the question and article in the *Summa I–II*. For each article, all of the "Reply" and nothing else is included, with three exceptions: 97, 1 and 99, 2 also include a portion of the responses to the views of others, and 100, 11 includes only a portion of the "Reply." Notes of the translators and the Latin text are not included.

Thomas Aquinas was a thirteenth-century Dominican philosopher and theologian at the University of Paris.

were, connatural to him to judge rightly about an end. This is done by moral virtue, for the virtuous man judges rightly of the end of virtue, because, as Aristotle says, "such as a man is, such does the end seem to him." Consequently right judgment about things to be done, namely prudence, requires that a man has moral virtue. . . .

77, 2 Can emotion overcome the better judgment of reason?

Aristotle says that Socrates was of the opinion that knowledge could never be overcome by emotion. Hence he held that virtue consisted in knowledge and sin in ignorance.

There is something to be said for this opinion. Since the object of the will is the good, or at least the apparent good, the will is never attracted by evil unless it appears to have an aspect of good about it, so that the will never chooses evil except by reason of ignorance or error. Thus it says in *Proverbs*, "Do not those who plot evil go astray?"

However, since experience shows that many do act against their better judgment and Scripture confirms this; e.g. "The servant who knew his master's will and did not make ready for him will be beaten with many stripes," and "He who knows how to do good, and does not do it, commits a sin," Socrates could be misleading, as Aristotle in fact points out.

Right behavior presupposes knowledge of both the particular and the general, so that the absence of either precludes both right choice and action.

It can happen that one who knows that it is true that all fornication is wrong is unaware that a given act is fornication and therefore to be avoided. And thus the will fails to follow the general rule.

Moreover, it must be observed that a man can know a thing as a matter of course but not think about it when he is acting. Thus a man can have habitual knowledge of both the general rule and the particular case, but fail to think about it at the moment. And thus it is not difficult to see that a man could act contrary to his habitual knowledge.

That a man should not consciously avert to something he knows habitually sometimes happens because he simply does not think, e.g. the geometrician who at the moment is not thinking of geometry. Sometimes this happens because his mind is distracted by other things, e.g. an external diversion or bodily pain.

This is another way in which a man who is emotionally aroused fails to consider in particular what he knows in general, for the emotion hinders such consideration.

This happens in three ways. The first way is by a kind of dispersion of energy.

The second way is by a kind of opposition, since emotion frequently pulls one in a direction contrary to better judgment.

The third way is by way of a physical condition which somehow hampers reason so that one is unable to act freely, e.g. the way sleep or drunkenness physically disables one for rational accomplishments.

This last can also occur by reason of emotional pressure which can be so intense that a man is completely deprived of the use of reason, for many men are completely carried out of their minds by excessive wrath or love. This is yet another way in which a man who is emotionally aroused might be moved to make a particular judgment contrary to his general convictions. . . .

93, 2 Is the Eternal Law recognized by all?

A thing may be known in two ways, the first, in itself, the other, in its effects, in which some likeness to it is discovered, as when not seeing the sun itself we nevertheless see daylight. So then it should be said that no one, except God himself and the blessed who see him in his essence, can know the Eternal Law as it is in itself, but that every rational creature can know about it according to some dawning, greater or lesser, of its light.

For every knowing of truth catches some radiance from the Eternal Law, which is the unchangeable truth, as Augustine says, and everybody in some manner knows truth, at least as regards the general principles of natural law. As for its other commands, people share in the truth in varying degrees, and accordingly know the Eternal Law, some more, some less. . . .

94, 2 Does natural law contain many precepts or only one?

We have drawn a parallel between the precepts of natural law for the practical reason and the axioms of science for the theoretical reason: both are kinds of self-evident beginnings.

Now a truth is self-evident at two stages, one, in itself, two, in our minds. A proposition is self-evident in itself when the Predicate is of the essence of the Subject. At the same time the proposition may not be self-evident to a man who does not know the definition of the Subject. For instance, "Man is a rational animal," is a self-evident proposition of its nature, since to say "man" is to say "rational." Yet to somebody who does not grasp what man really is, the proposition is not self-evident. That is why Boëthius says, "There are some axioms or self-evident propositions generally known to all", such are the terms of which everybody recognizes, such as, "The whole is greater than the part," or, "Things equal to a third thing are equal to one another."

Sometimes, however, propositions are self-evident only to the well informed, who know what the terms of the proposition mean. Thus to one who appreciates that an angel is not a bodily substance it is self-evident that an angel is not circumscribed in place. This, however, is not manifest to those who are uninstructed and do not grasp what is meant.

Now we discover that the things which enter into our apprehension are ranged in a certain order. That which first appears is *the real*, and some insight into this is included in whatsoever is apprehended. This first indemonstrable principle, "There is no affirming and denying the same simultaneously," is based on the very nature of the real and the non-real: on this principle, as Aristotle notes, all other propositions are based.

To apply the analogy: as to be *real* first enters into human apprehending as such, so to be *good* first enters the practical reason's apprehending when it is bent on doing something. For every agent acts on account of an end, and to be an end carries the meaning of to be good. Consequently the first principle for the practical reason is based on the meaning of good, namely that it is what all things seek after. And so this is the first command of law, "That good is to be sought and done, evil to be avoided"; all other commands of natural law are based on this. Accordingly, then, natural-law commands extend to all doing or avoiding of things recognized by the practical reason of itself as being human goods.

Now since being good has the meaning of being an end, while being an evil has the contrary meaning, it follows that reason of its nature apprehends the things toward which man has a natural tendency as good objectives, and therefore to be actively pursued, whereas it apprehends their contraries as bad, and therefore to be shunned.

Let us continue. The order in which commands of the law of nature are ranged corresponds to that of our natural tendencies. Here there are three stages. There is in man, first, a tendency toward the good of the nature he has in common with all substances; each has an appetite to preserve its own natural being. Natural law here plays a corresponding part, and is engaged at this stage to maintain and defend the elementary requirements of human life.

Secondly, there is in man a bent toward things which accord with his nature considered more specifically, that is in terms of what he has in common with other animals; correspondingly those matters are said to be of natural law which nature teaches all animals, for instance the coupling of male and female, the bringing up of the young, and so forth.

Thirdly, there is in man an appetite for the good of his nature as rational, and this is proper to him, for instance, that he should know truths about God and about living in society. Correspondingly whatever this involves is a matter of natural law, for instance that a man should shun ignorance, not offend others with whom he ought to live in civility, and other such related requirements. . . .

94, 4 Is natural law the same for all?

As we have shown, the objects to which men have a natural tendency are the concern of natural law, and among such tendencies it is proper to man to act according to reason. Now a characteristic of reason is to proceed from common principles to particular conclusions: this is remarked in the *Physics*. However, the theoretic reason and the practical reason set about this somewhat differently. The business of the theoretic reason is with natural truths that cannot be otherwise, and so without mistake it finds truth in the particular conclusions it draws as in the premises it starts from. Whereas the business of the practical reason is with contingent matters which are the domain of human acts, and although there is some necessity in general principles, the more we get down to particular cases the more we can be mistaken.

So then in questions of theory, truth is the same for everybody, both as to principles and to conclusions, though admittedly all do not recognize truth in the conclusions, but only in those principles which are called "common conceptions." In questions of action, however, practical truth and goodwill are not the same for everybody with respect to particular decisions, but only with respect to common principles; and even those who are equally in the right on some particular course of action are not equally aware of how right they are.

So then it is evident that with respect to general principles of both theory and practice what is true or right is the same for all and is equally recognized. With respect to specific conclusions of theory, the truth is the same for all, though all do not equally recognize it, for instance some are not aware that the angles of a triangle together equal two right angles. With respect to particular conclusions come to by the practical reason, there is no general unanimity about what is true or right, and even when there is agreement there is not the same degree of recognition.

All hold that it is true and right that we should act intelligently. From this starting point it is possible to advance the specific conclusion, that goods held in trust are to be restored to their owners. This is true in the majority of cases, yet a case can crop up when to return the deposit would be injurious, and consequently unreasonable, as for instance were it to be required in order to attack one's country. The more you descend into the detail the more it appears how the general rule admits of exceptions, so that you have to hedge it with cautions and qualifications. The greater the number of conditions accumulated, the greater the number of ways in which the principle is seen to fall short, so that all by itself it cannot tell you whether it be right to return a deposit or not.

To sum up: as for its first common principles, here natural law is the same for all in requiring a right attitude toward it as well as recognition. As for particular specific points, which are like conclusions drawn from common principles, here also natural law is the same for most people in their feeling for and awareness of what is right. Nevertheless, in fewer cases either the desire or the information may be wanting. The desire to do right may be blocked by particular factors – so also with physical things that come to be and die away there are occasional anomalies and failures due to some obstruction – and the knowledge also of what is right may be distorted by passion or bad custom or even by racial proclivity; for instance, as Julius Caesar narrates, the Germans did not consider robbery wicked, though it is expressly against natural law.

94, 5 Can natural law be changed?

A change can be understood to mean either addition or subtraction. As for the first, there is nothing against natural law being changed, for many things over and above natural law have been added, by divine law as well as by human laws, which are beneficial to social life.

As for change by subtraction, meaning that something that once was of natural law later ceases to be so, here there is room for a distinction. The first principles of natural law are altogether unalterable. But its secondary precepts, which we have described as being like particular conclusions close to first principles, though not alterable in the majority of cases where they are right as they stand, can nevertheless be changed on some particular and rare occasions, as we have mentioned in the preceding article, because of some special cause preventing their unqualified observance.

94, 6 Can natural law be abolished from the human heart?

As we noticed when speaking of what belongs to natural law to begin with there are certain most general precepts known to all; and next, certain secondary and more specific precepts which are like conclusions lying close to the premises. As for these first common principles in their universal meaning, natural law cannot be cancelled in the human heart, nevertheless it can be missing from a particular course of action when the reason is stopped from applying the general principle there, because of lust or some other passion, as we have pointed out.

As for its other and secondary precepts, natural law can be effaced, either by wrong persuasions – thus also errors occur in theoretical matters concerning demonstrable conclusions – or by perverse customs and corrupt habits; for instance robbery was not reputed to be wrong among some people, nor even, as the Apostle mentions, some unnatural sins. . . .

97, 1 May a human law be altered in some way?

In the statement that human law is a kind of dictate of reason directing human acts, there are two clauses, and under both a cause for just change can arise, namely because of the workings of reason and because of the human lives which are regulated by law.

First, from the side of the reason. To advance step by step from an undeveloped to a developed position seems natural to the human reason. We see this in the theoretic sciences, where the incomplete teachings of early thinkers have been followed by teachings more fully worked out by their successors. So also in practical questions; those who first attempted to draw up useful regulations for the human community were of themselves unable to take everything into consideration; they set up certain institutions which were lacking in many respects, yet which served for their successors to work on and make alterations, so that they might in fewer respects prove defective for the common benefit.

Second, from the side of the human beings whose acts it regulates. Law may be justly altered because of changed conditions of life, which make for differences in what is beneficial. So Augustine puts forward an example:

> If a people have a sense of moderation and responsibility, and are most careful guardians of the commonwealth, then it is a rightly enacted law for them to appoint their own magistrates for their public governance. But if, as time goes on, they become so corrupt as to sell their votes and entrust the government to scoundrels and criminals, then they rightly forfeit their power of electing to office, and this devolves on a few sound men.

. . . [N]atural law is a sharing in the Eternal Law. Hence it endures without change, owing to the perfection and immutability of the divine reason, which institutes nature. Human reason, however, is imperfect and mutable, so as well, therefore, is the law it makes, and therefore its law is the same. Furthermore, natural law comprises universal commands which are everlasting, whereas human positive law comprises particular commands to meet the various situations that arise.

A measure should be as permanent as possible. Yet in a world of change there can be nothing that is altogether and immutably stable. Consequently human law cannot be entirely unalterable. . . .

99, 2 Whether the Old Law contains moral precepts

The Old Law did contain certain moral precepts, as "Thou shalt not kill . . . Thou shalt not steal." And this is reasonable. For just as human law is principally designed to achieve harmonious relationships between men, so divine law is principally designed to establish loving and harmonious relations between man and God. Now love is based on likeness, for "every living thing loves its own sort." On this principle it is impossible for man to love God, who is most of all good, unless men themselves are made good. Hence we read, "You shall be holy because I am holy." Now human goodness consists in virtue, which "renders its possessor good." For this reason it was right for the Old Law to contain special precepts relating to the performance of virtuous acts, and it is these that are the moral precepts of the Law. . . .

It was consistent with the divine law that it should provide for man's needs not only in matters unattainable by reason but in matters in which man's reason may be prevented from its proper function as well. Turning then to the question of the moral precepts, let us consider first those precepts of the natural law which are absolutely universally accepted. Regarding these, man's reason could not be misled in principle, but even so it could be confused by the effect of habitual sin as to what ought to be done in particular cases. A second group of moral precepts consists of those which, so to say, are deduced as conclusions from the general principles of natural law. Regarding these, the minds of many were led astray to the extent that certain actions which are intrinsically evil were adjudged by the minds of many to be lawful. Hence it was right for the authority of divine law to be brought to man's assistance in helping him to overcome both of these deficiencies. . . .

100, 1 Whether all the moral precepts of the Old Law come under the law of nature

The moral precepts, as distinct from the ceremonial and judicial, are concerned with matters which, of their very nature, belong to right conduct. Now since human conduct is such by its relation to reason, whatever conforms with reason is called good, and whatever is in disaccord with reason is called bad. And just as every judgment of reason in the speculative order springs from the natural knowledge of first principles, so does every judgment of reason in the practical order spring from certain naturally known principles, as we said above. From these premises our conclusions will differ according to the different classes of actions. For the moral character of some human actions is so evident that they can be assessed as good or bad in the light of these common first principles straightaway with a minimum of reflection. Others, however, need a great deal of consideration of all the various circumstances, of which not everyone is capable, but only those endowed with wisdom, just as not every man, but only philosophers, can reflect upon the findings of the sciences. And there is another class of actions which require for their assessment the aid of divine instruction, such as those which belong to the province of faith.

It is clear, then, that since the moral precepts are concerned with right conduct, which is what conforms with reason, and, further, every judgment of human reason derives, in some way, from natural reason, all the moral precepts must, of necessity, belong to the law of nature, though not all in the same way. There are some which the natural reason of every man judges straightaway to be done or not to be done, such as "Honour thy father and thy mother," and "Thou shalt not kill. Thou shalt not steal." These belong to the law of nature absolutely. Others there are which are judged by the wise to be done in the light of more careful consideration. These, indeed, belong to the law of nature, but as necessitating instruction on the part of ordinary people by the wise: for instance, "Rise up before the hoary head, and honour the person of the aged man," and the like. Lastly, there are actions to judge of which human reason needs divine instruction, which teaches us about the things of God: for instance, "Thou shalt not make to thyself a graven thing, nor the likeness of anything"; "Thou shalt not take the name of the Lord Thy God in vain." . . .

100, 11 Should the Law contain other moral precepts besides the decalogue?

[T]he judicial and ceremonial precepts derive their force solely from their institution; since, before they were instituted, it seemed a matter of indifference what form they should take. But the moral precepts derive their force from the dictate of natural reason, even if they had not been expressed in the Law. Now they fall into three groups. Some are absolutely certain, and so evident as not to need promulgation, such as the commandments about love of God and one's neighbor, and others of the sort, . . . which constitute, as it were, the end of the precepts; and so no one could be mistaken about them. Others are more determinate in character, yet the reason for them can easily be seen even by the most ordinary intelligence. Yet since, in a few cases, human judgment may be misled about them, they need to be promulgated. These are the precepts of the decalogue. Others, however, there are whose reason is not so evident to all, but only to the wise. These are the moral precepts superadded to the decalogue, given by God through Moses and Aaron.

Since, however, those which are evident are the principles by which we come to know those not so evident, the other moral precepts are reducible to those of the decalogue, by way of addition to them.

3

RENAISSANCE SKEPTICISM

Michel de Montaigne

We have as our share inconstancy, irresolution, uncertainty, grief, superstition, worry over things to come, even after our life, ambition, avarice,
jealousy, envy, unruly, frantic, and untameable appetites, war, falsehood,
disloyalty, detraction, and curiosity. Indeed we have strangely overpaid
for this fine reason that we glory in, and this capacity to judge and know,
if we have bought it at the price of this infinite number of passions to
which we are incessantly a prey. Unless we like to make much, as indeed
Socrates does, of this notable prerogative over the other animals, that
whereas Nature has prescribed to them certain seasons and limits to the
pleasures of Venus, she has given us free rein at all hours and occasions.

> As with wine for sick men, since it is rarely good and often bad,
> it is better not to use it at all, than in the hope of a doubtful ben-
> efit to incur a manifest risk; so I hardly know whether it would
> not have been better for the human race if this swift movement
> of thought, this acumen, this cleverness, which we call reason,
> had not been given to man at all, since it is a plague to many and
> salutary only to a few, rather than given so abundantly and so
> lavishly.
>
> (Cicero)

What good can we suppose it did Varro and Aristotle to know so
many things? Did it exempt them from human discomforts? Were they
freed from the accidents that oppress a porter? Did they derive from
logic some consolation for the gout? For knowing how this humor lodges

From Michel de Montaigne, "Apology for Raymond Sebond," in *The Complete Essays of
Montaigne*, translated by Donald M. Frame, Stanford, CA: Stanford University Press
[1958] 1965, pp. 358–60, 425–27, 435–40, and 454–57. The title is supplied by CWG.
Notes and sub-titles of the translator are not included.

Michel de Montaigne was a sixteenth-century French lawyer, politician, and philosopher.

in the joints, did they feel it less? Were they reconciled to death for knowing that some nations rejoice in it, and with cuckoldry for knowing that wives are held in common in some region? On the contrary, though they held the first rank in knowledge, one among the Romans, the other among the Greeks, and in the period when knowledge flourished most, we have not for all that heard that they had any particular excellence in their lives; in fact the Greek has a hard time to clear himself of some notable spots in his. . . .

[H]umility and submissiveness alone can make a good man. The knowledge of his duty should not be left to each man's judgment; it should be prescribed to him, not left to the choice of his reason. Otherwise, judging by the imbecility and infinite variety of our reasons and opinions, we would finally forge for ourselves duties that would set us to eating one another, as Epicurus says.

The first law that God ever gave to man was a law of pure obedience; it was a naked and simple commandment about which man had nothing to know or discuss; since to obey is the principal function of a reasonable soul, recognizing a heavenly superior and benefactor. From obeying and yielding spring all other virtues, as from presumption all sin. And on the contrary, the first temptation that came to human nature from the devil, its first poison, insinuated itself into us through the promises he made us of knowledge and intelligence: "Ye shall be as gods, knowing good and evil" (*Genesis*). And the Sirens, in Homer, to trick Ulysses and lure him into their dangerous and ruinous snares, offer him the gift of knowledge. The plague of man is the opinion of knowledge. That is why ignorance is so recommended by our religion as a quality suitable to belief and obedience. "Beware lest any man spoil you through philosophy and vain deceit, after the rudiments of the world" (*Colossians*).

[. . .]

I who spy on myself more closely, who have my eyes unceasingly intent on myself, as one who has not much business elsewhere—

> Quite without care
> What king, in frigid lands beneath the Bear,
> Is feared, or what makes Tiridates quake
> (Horace)

— I would hardly dare tell of the vanity and weakness that I find in myself. My footing is so unsteady and so insecure, I find it so vacillating and ready to slip, and my sight is so unreliable, that on an empty stomach I feel myself another man than after a meal. If my health smiles upon me, and the brightness of a beautiful day, I am a fine fellow; if I have a corn bothering my toe, I am surly, unpleasant, and unapproachable. One and the same pace of a horse seems to me now rough, now easy, and the same road at one time shorter, another time longer, and one and the same shape now more, now less agreeable. Now I am ready to do anything, now to do nothing; what is a pleasure to me at this moment will some time be a trouble. A thousand unconsidered and accidental impulses arise in me. Either the melancholic humor grips me, or the choleric; and at this moment sadness predominates in me by its own private authority, at that moment good cheer.

When I pick up books, I will have perceived in such-and-such a passage surpassing charms which will have struck my soul; let me come upon it another time, in vain I turn it over and over, in vain I twist it and manipulate it, to me it is a shapeless and unrecognizable mass.

Even in my own writings I do not always find again the sense of my first thought; I do not know what I meant to say, and often I get burned by correcting and putting in a new meaning, because I have lost the first one, which was better.

I do nothing but come and go. My judgment does not always go forward; it floats, it strays,

Like a tiny boat,
Caught by a raging wind on the vast sea.
(Catullus)

Many times (as I sometimes do deliberately), having undertaken as exercise and sport to maintain an opinion contrary to my own, my mind, applying itself and turning in that direction, attaches me to it so firmly that I can no longer find the reason for my former opinion, and I abandon it. I draw myself along in almost any direction I lean, whatever it may be, and carry myself away by my own weight.

Nearly every man would say as much of himself, if he considered himself as I do. Preachers know that the emotion that comes to them as they talk incites them toward belief; and that in anger we give ourselves up more completely to the defense of our proposition, imprint it on ourselves, and embrace it with more vehemence and approval than we do in our cool and sedate mood.

You recite a case simply to a lawyer, he answers you wavering and doubtful: you feel that it is a matter of indifference to him whether he undertakes to support one party or the other. Have you paid him well to get his teeth into it and get excited about it; is he beginning to be involved in it; has he got his will warmed up about it? His reason and his knowledge are warmed up at the same time. Behold an evident and indubitable truth that appears to his intelligence. He discovers a wholly new light on your case, and believes it in all conscience, and persuades himself that it is so.

Indeed, I do not know if the ardor that is born of spite and obstinacy against the pressure and violence of authority, and of danger, or the concern for reputation, has not sent some men all the way to the stake to maintain an opinion for which, among their friends and at liberty, they would not have been willing to burn the tip of their finger. . . .

What differences in sense and reason, what contradictions of ideas are offered us by the diversity of our passions! What assurance can we then take of a thing so unstable and mobile, subject by its condition to the mastery of disturbance, never going except with a forced and borrowed pace? If our judgment is in the hands even of sickness and perturbation; if it is from folly and heedlessness that it is bound to receive its impression of things, what certainty can we expect of it?

[. . .]

There is no combat so violent among the philosophers, and so bitter, as that which arises over the question of the sovereign good of man, out of which, by Varro's reckoning, 288 sects were born. "But he who disagrees about the supreme good, disagrees about the whole principle of philosophy" (Cicero).

> Three guests of mine differ on what is good;
> Their various palates call for various food.
> What shall I serve? What not? What makes one glad,
> You don't enjoy; what you like, they find bad.
> (Horace)

Nature should reply thus to their arguments and disputes.

Some say that our good lies in virtue, others in sensual pleasure, others in conforming to nature; one man in knowledge, one in having no pain, one in not letting ourselves be carried away by appearances. And this notion seems to resemble this other, of the ancient Pythagoras:

> Wonder at nothing: that is all I know
> To make men happy and to keep them so;
> (Horace)

which is the goal of the Pyrrhonian school.

Aristotle attributes wondering at nothing to greatness of soul. And Arcesilaus used to say that to suspend the judgment and keep it upright and inflexible is a good thing, but to consent and incline it is a vice and a bad thing. It is true that by establishing this by a certain axiom, he was departing from Pyrrhonism. The Pyrrhonians, when they say that the sovereign good is Ataraxy, which is the immobility of the judgment, do not mean to say it in an affirmative way; but the same impulse of their soul that makes them avoid precipices and take cover in the cool of the evening, itself offers them this fancy and makes them refuse any other. . . .

Moreover, if it is from ourselves that we derive the ruling of our conduct, into what confusion do we cast ourselves! For the most plausible advice that our reason gives us in the matter is generally for each man to obey the laws of his country, which is the advice of Socrates, inspired, he says, by divine counsel. And what does reason mean by that, unless that our duty has no rule but an accidental one?

Truth must have one face, the same and universal. If man knew any rectitude and justice that had body and real existence, he would not tie it down to the condition of the customs of this country or that. It would not be from the fancy of the Persians or the Indians that virtue would take its form. . . .

And here at home I have seen things which were capital offenses among us become legitimate; and we who consider other things legitimate are liable, according to the uncertainty of the fortunes of war, to be one day guilty of human and divine high treason, when our justice falls into the mercy of injustice, and, after a few years of captivity, assumes a contrary character.

How could that ancient god more clearly accuse human knowledge of ignorance of the divine being, and teach men that religion was only a creature of their own invention, suitable to bind their society together, than by declaring, as he did, to those who sought instruction therein at his tripod, that the true cult for each man was that which he found observed according to the practice of the place he was in?

O God, what an obligation do we not have to the benignity of our sovereign creator for having freed our belief from the folly of those vagabond and arbitrary devotions, and having based it on the eternal foundation of his holy word?

What then will philosophy tell us in this our need? To follow the laws of our country – that is to say, the undulating sea of the opinions of a people or a prince, which will paint me justice in as many colors, and refashion it into as many faces, as there are changes of passion in those men? I cannot have my judgment so flexible.

What am I to make of a virtue that I saw in credit yesterday, that will be discredited tomorrow, and that becomes a crime on the other side of the river? What of a truth that is bounded by these mountains and is falsehood to the world that lives beyond?

But they are funny when, to give some certainty to the laws, they say that there are some which are firm, perpetual, and immutable, which they call natural, which are imprinted on the human race by the condition of their very being. And of those one man says the number is three, one man four, one more, one less: a sign that the mark of them is as doubtful as the rest. Now they are so unfortunate (for what else can I call it but misfortune, that out of such an infinite number of laws not even one is found that fortune and the heedlessness of chance have allowed to be universally accepted by the consent of all nations?), they are, I say, so wretched that of these three or four selected laws there is not a single one that is not contradicted and disavowed, not by one nation but by many. Now the only likely sign by which they can argue certain laws to be natural is universality of approval. For what nature had truly ordered for us we would without doubt follow by common consent. And not only every nation, but every individual, would resent the force and violence used on him by anyone who tried to impel him to oppose that law. Let them show me just one law of that sort – I'd like to see it.

Protagoras and Aristo assigned no other essence to the justice of the laws than the authority and judgment of the lawgiver; and said that apart from that, the good and the honest lost their qualities and remained empty names of indifferent things. Thrasymachus, in Plato, thinks that there is no other right than the advantage of the superior.

There is nothing in which the world is so varied as in customs and laws. A given thing is abominable here, which brings commendation elsewhere: as in Lacedaemon cleverness in stealing. Marriages between close relatives are capital offenses among us, elsewhere they are in honor:

> There are some nations, it is said,
> Where mothers sons, and fathers daughters wed;
> And thus affection grows, doubled by love.
>
> (Ovid)

The murder of infants, the murder of fathers, sharing of wives, traffic in robberies, license for all sorts of sensual pleasures, nothing in short is so extreme that it is not accepted by the usage of some nation.

It is credible that there are natural laws, as may be seen in other creatures; but in us they are lost; that fine human reason butts in everywhere, domineering and commanding, muddling and confusing the face of things in accordance with its vanity and inconsistency. "Nothing is ours any more; what I call ours is a product of art" (Cicero).

Things may be considered in various lights and from various viewpoints: it is principally from this that diversity of opinions arises. One nation looks at one side of a thing and stops there; another at another.

There is nothing so horrible to imagine as eating one's father. The nations which had this custom in ancient times, however, regarded it as testimony of piety and good affection, trying thereby to give their progenitors the most worthy and honorable sepulture, lodging in themselves and as it were in their marrow the bodies of their fathers and their remains, bringing them to life in a way and regenerating them by transmutation into their living flesh by means of digestion and nourishment. It is easy to imagine what a cruelty and abomination it would have been, to men saturated and imbued with this superstition, to abandon the mortal remains of their parents to the corruption of the earth and to let it become the food of beasts and worms.

Lycurgus considered in theft the quickness, diligence, boldness, and adroitness that there is in taking something from one's neighbor by surprise, and the useful return to the public in that every man looks more carefully to the conservation of what is his; and he thought that from this double training, in attack and defense, there resulted an increase in military efficiency (which was the principal science and virtue in which he wished to train this nation) that more than offset the disorderliness and injustice of helping oneself to other people's property. . . .

I have heard tell of a judge who, when he came across a sharp conflict between Bartolus and Baldus, or some matter debated with many contradictions, used to put in the margin of his book "Question for my friend"; that is to say, that the truth was so embroiled and disputed that in a similar case he could favor whichever of the parties he saw fit. It was only for lack of wit and competence that he could not write everywhere: "Question for my friend."

The lawyers and judges of our time find enough angles for all cases to arrange them any way they please. In a field of knowledge so infinite, depending on the authority of so many opinions, and in so arbitrary a subject, it is impossible that there should not arise an extreme confusion of judgments. And so there is hardly a lawsuit so clear that opinions do not differ on it. The judgment one court has given is reversed by another, which reverses itself another time. Whereof we see common examples in the licentious practice, which is a monstrous stain on the ceremonious authority and luster of our justice, of not letting the decisions decide, and running from one judge to another to settle the same case. . . .

The laws take their authority from possession and usage; it is dangerous to trace them back to their birth. They swell and are ennobled as they roll, like our rivers: follow them uphill to their source, it is just a little trickle of water, barely recognizable, which thus grows proud and strong as it grows old. Look at the ancient considerations that gave the first impetus to this famous torrent full of dignity, awe, and reverence; you will find them so trivial and frail that it is no wonder that these people who weigh everything and refer it to reason, and who accept nothing by authority and on credit, have judgments often far removed from popular judgments. Since they are men who take as their pattern the original image of nature, it is no wonder if in most of their opinions they deviate from the common way.

As, for example: few of them would have approved the conditions and constraints of our marriages, and most of them have wanted wives to be held in common and without obligation.

[. . .]

To judge the appearances that we receive of objects, we would need a judicatory instrument; to verify this instrument, we need a demonstration; to verify the demonstration, an instrument: there we are in a circle.

Since the senses cannot decide our dispute, being themselves full of uncertainty, it must be reason that does so. No reason can be established without another reason: there we go retreating back to infinity.

Our conception is not itself applied to foreign objects, but is conceived through the mediation of the senses; and the senses do not comprehend the foreign object, but only their own impressions. And thus the conception and semblance we form is not of the object, but only of the impression and effect made on the sense; which impression and the object are different things. Wherefore whoever judges by appearances judges by something other than the object.

And as for saying that the impressions of the senses convey to the soul the quality of the foreign objects by resemblance, how can the soul and understanding make sure of this resemblance, having of itself no communication with foreign objects? Just as a man who does not know Socrates, seeing his portrait, cannot say that it resembles him.

Now if anyone should want to judge by appearances anyway, to judge by all appearances is impossible, for they clash with one another by their contradictions and discrepancies, as we see by experience. Shall some selected appearances rule the others? We shall have to verify this selection by another selection, the second by a third; and thus it will never be finished.

Finally, there is no existence that is constant, either of our being or of that of objects. And we, and our judgment, and all mortal things go on flowing and rolling unceasingly. Thus nothing certain can be established about one thing by another, both the judging and the judged being in continual change and motion.

We have no communication with being, because every human nature is always midway between birth and death, offering only a dim semblance and shadow of itself, and an uncertain and feeble opinion. And if by chance you fix your thought on trying to grasp its essence, it will be neither more nor less than if someone tried to grasp water: for the more he squeezes and presses what by its nature flows all over, the more he will lose what he was trying to hold and grasp. Thus, all things being subject to pass from one change to another, reason, seeking a real stability in them, is baffled, being unable to apprehend anything stable and permanent; because everything is either coming into being and not yet fully existent, or beginning to die before it is born. . . .

But then what really is? That which is eternal: that is to say, what never had birth, nor will ever have an end; to which time never brings any change. . . .

Wherefore we must conclude that God alone *is* – not at all according to any measure of time, but according to an eternity immutable and immobile, not measured by time or subject to any decline; before whom there is nothing, nor will there be after, nor is there anything more new or more recent; but one who really is – who by one single *now* fills the *ever*; and there is nothing that really is but he alone – nor can we say "He has been," or "He will be" – without beginning and without end.

To this most religious conclusion of a pagan I want to add only this remark of a witness of the same condition, for an ending to this long and boring discourse, which would give me material without end: "O what a vile and abject thing is man," he says, "if he does not raise himself above humanity!"

That is a good statement and a useful desire, but equally absurd. For to make the handful bigger than the hand, the armful bigger than the arm, and to hope to straddle more than the reach of our legs, is impossible and unnatural. Nor can man raise himself above himself and humanity; for he can see only with his own eyes, and seize only with his own grasp.

He will rise, if God by exception lends him a hand; he will rise by abandoning and renouncing his own means, and letting himself be raised and uplifted by purely celestial means.

It is for our Christian faith, not for his Stoical virtue, to aspire to that divine and miraculous metamorphosis.

4

A DIALOGUE

David Hume

My friend, Palamedes, who is as great a rambler in his principles as in his person, and who has run over, by study and travel, almost every region of the intellectual and material world, surprised me lately with an account of a nation, with whom, he told me, he had passed a considerable part of his life, and whom he found, in the main, a people extremely civilized and intelligent.

There is a country, said he, in the world, called Fourli, no matter for its longitude or latitude, whose inhabitants have ways of thinking, in many things, particularly in morals, diametrically opposite to ours. When I came among them, I found that I must submit to double pains; first, to learn the meaning of the terms in their language, and then to know the import of those terms, and the praise or blame attached to them. After a word had been explained to me, and the character which it expressed had been described, I concluded, that such an epithet must necessarily be the greatest reproach in the world; and was extremely surprised to find one in a public company apply it to a person, with whom he lived in the strictest intimacy and friendship. . . .

[B]eing desired by Alcheic to live with him, I readily accepted of his invitation; as I found him universally esteemed for his personal merit, and indeed regarded by everyone in Fourli as a perfect character.

One evening he invited me, as an amusement, to bear him company in a serenade, which he intended to give to Gulki, with whom, he told me, he was extremely enamoured; and I soon found that his taste was not singular: For we met many of his rivals, who had come on the same errand. I very naturally concluded, that this mistress of his must be one of the finest women in town; and I already felt a secret inclination to see her, and be acquainted with her. But as the moon began to rise, I was much

From David Hume, *Essays and Treatises on Several Subjects*, vol. II, London: J. Jones, 1822, pp. 356–78. Original punctuation and spellings of this essay have been retained.

David Hume was a seventeenth-century Scottish philosopher and historian.

surprised to find, that we were in the midst of the university where Gulki studied: And I was somewhat ashamed for having attended my friend on such an errand.

I was afterwards told, that Alcheic's choice of Gulki was very much approved of by all the good company in town. . . .

It gave me some surprise, that Alcheic's wife (who, by the by, happened also to be his sister) was nowise scandalized at this species of infidelity.

Much about the same time I discovered (for it was not attempted to be kept a secret from me or any body) that Alcheic was a murderer and a parricide, and had put to death an innocent person, the most nearly connected with him, and whom he was bound to protect and defend by all the ties of nature and humanity. When I asked, with all the caution and deference imaginable, what was his motive for this action? he replied coolly, that he was not then so much at ease in his circumstances as he is at present, and that he had acted, in that particular, by the advice of all his friends. . . .

I have lately received a letter from a correspondent in Fourli; by which I learn, that, since my departure, Alcheic, falling into a bad state of health, has fairly hanged himself; and has died universally regretted and applauded in that country. So virtuous and noble a life, says each Fourlian, could not be better crowned than by so noble an end. . . .

Pray, said I, Palamedes, when you were at Fourli, did you also learn the art of turning your friends into ridicule, by telling them strange stories, and then laughing at them, if they believed you [?] . . . But you think, then, [he replied] that my story is improbable; and that I have used, or rather abused, the privilege of a traveller? To be sure, said I, you were but in jest. Such barbarous and savage manners are not only incompatible with a civilized, intelligent people, such as you said these were, but are scarcely compatible with human nature. They exceed all we ever read of among the Mingrelians and Topinambous.

Have a care, cried he, have a care! You are not aware that you are speaking blasphemy, and are abusing your favourites the Greeks, especially the Athenians, whom I have couched all along under these bizarre names I employed. If you consider aright, there is not one stroke of the foregoing character which might not be found in the man of highest merit at Athens, without diminishing in the least from the brightness of his character. The amours of the Greeks, their marriages, and the exposing of their children, cannot but strike you immediately. . . .

I might have been aware, replied I, of your artifice. You seem to take pleasure in this topic: And are indeed the only man I ever knew, who was well acquainted with the ancients, and did not extremely admire them. But instead of attacking their philosophy, their eloquence, or poetry, the usual subjects of controversy between us, you now seem to impeach their morals, and accuse them of ignorance in a science, which is the only one, in my opinion, in which they are not surpassed by the moderns. Geometry, physics, astronomy, anatomy, botany, geography, navigation; in these we justly claim the superiority: But what have we to oppose to their moralists? Your representation of things is fallacious. You have no indulgence for the manners and customs of different ages. Would you try a Greek or Roman by the common law of England? Hear him defend himself by his own maxims; and then pronounce.

There are no manners so innocent or reasonable, but may be rendered odious or ridiculous, if measured by a standard unknown to the persons; especially if you employ a little art or eloquence in aggravating some circumstances and extenuating others, as best suits the purpose of your discourse. All these artifices may easily be retorted on you. Could I inform the Athenians, for instance, that there was a nation in which adultery, both active and passive, so to speak, was in the highest vogue and esteem; in which every man of education chose for his mistress a married woman, the wife, perhaps, of his friend and companion; and valued himself upon these infamous conquests, as much as if he had been several times a conqueror in boxing or wrestling at the Olympic games: In which every man also took a pride in his tameness and facility with regard to his own wife, and was glad to make friends or gain interest by allowing her to prostitute her charms; and even, without any such motive, gave her full liberty and indulgence: I ask what sentiments the Athenians would entertain of such a people; they who never mentioned the crime of adultery but in conjunction with robbery and poisoning? Which would they admire most, the villany or the meanness of such a conduct?

. . . [N]o disgrace, no infamy, no pain, no poverty, will ever engage these people to turn the point of [their sword] against their own breast. A man of rank would row in the gallies, would beg his bread, would languish in prison, would suffer any tortures; and still preserve his wretched life. Rather than escape his enemies by a generous contempt of death, he would infamously receive the same death from his enemies, aggravated by their triumphant insults, and by the most exquisite sufferings.

. . . But this nation gravely exalts those whom nature has subjected to them, and whose inferiority and infirmities are absolutely incurable. The women, though without virtue, are their masters and sovereigns: These they reverence, praise, and magnify: To these they pay the highest deference and respect: And in all places and all times, the superiority of the females is readily acknowledged and submitted to by every one who has the least pretentions to education and politeness. Scarce any crime would be so universally detested as an infraction of this rule.

You need go no farther, replied Palamedes: I can easily conjecture the people whom you aim at. The strokes with which you have painted them are pretty just; and yet you must acknowledge, that scarce any people are to be found, either in ancient or modern times, whose national character is, upon the whole, less liable to exception. But I give you thanks for helping me out with my argument. I had no intention of exalting the moderns at the expence of the ancients. I only meant to represent the uncertainty of all these judgments concerning characters; and to convince you that fashion, vogue, custom, and law, were the chief foundation of all moral determinations. The Athenians surely were a civilized, intelligent people, if ever there were one; and yet their man of merit might, in this age, be held in horror and execration. The French are also, without doubt, a very civilized, intelligent people; and yet their man of merit might, with the Athenians, be an object of the highest contempt and ridicule, and even hatred. And what renders the matter more extraordinary: These two people are supposed to be the most similar in their national character, of any in ancient and modern times; and while the English flatter themselves that they resemble the Romans, their neighbours on the continent draw the parallel between themselves and those polite Greeks. What wide difference, therefore, in the sentiments of morals, must be found between civilized nations and barbarians, or between nations whose characters have little in common? How shall we pretend to fix a standard for judgments of this nature?

By tracing matters, replied I, a little higher, and examining the first principles, which each nation establishes, of blame or censure. The Rhine flows north, the Rhone south; yet both spring from the same mountain, and are also actuated, in their opposite directions, by the same principle of gravity. The different inclinations of the ground, on which they run, cause all the difference of their courses.

In how many circumstances would an Athenian and a French man of merit certainly resemble each other? Good sense, knowledge, wit, eloquence, humanity, fidelity, truth, justice, courage, temperance, constancy, dignity of mind: These you have all omitted; in order to insist only on the points in which they may, by accident, differ. Very well: I am willing to comply with you; and shall endeavour to account for these differences, from the most universal, established principles of morals.

The Greek loves, I care not to examine more particularly. I shall only observe, that, however blameable, they arose from a very innocent cause, the frequency of the gymnastic exercises among that people; and were recommended, though absurdly, as the source of friendship, sympathy, mutual attachment, and fidelity; qualities esteemed in all nations and all ages.

The marriage of half-brothers and sisters seems no great difficulty. Love between the nearer relations is contrary to reason and public utility; but the precise point, where we are to stop, can scarcely be determined by natural reason; and is therefore a very proper subject for municipal law or custom. If the Athenians went a little too far on the one side, the canon law has surely pushed matters a great way into the other extreme.

Had you asked a parent at Athens, why he bereaved his child of that life which he had so lately given it? It is because I love it, he would reply; and regard the poverty which it must inherit from me, as a greater evil than death, which it is not capable of dreading, feeling, or resenting. . . .

Have the gods forbid self-murder? An Athenian allows that it ought to be forborn. Has the Deity permitted it? A Frenchman allows that death is preferable to pain and infamy.

You see then, continued I, that the principles upon which men reason in morals are always the same; though the conclusions which they draw are often very different. That they all reason aright with regard to this subject, more than with regard to any other, it is not incumbent on any moralist to show. It is sufficient, that the original principles of censure or blame are uniform, and that erroneous conclusions can be corrected by sounder reasoning and larger experience. Though many ages have elapsed since the fall of Greece and Rome; though many changes have arrived in religion, language, laws, and customs; none of these revolutions has ever produced any considerable innovation in the primary sentiments of morals, more than in those of external beauty. Some minute differences, perhaps, may be observed in both. . . .

It appears, that there never was any quality recommended by any one, as a virtue or moral excellence, but on account of its being useful or agreeable to a man himself, or to others. For what other reason can ever be assigned for praise or approbation? Or where would be the sense of extolling a good character or action, which, at the same time, is allowed to be good for nothing? All the differences, therefore, in morals, may be reduced to this one general foundation, and may be accounted for by the different views which people take of these circumstances.

Sometimes men differ in their judgment about the usefulness of any habit or action: Sometimes also the peculiar circumstances of things render one moral quality more useful than others, and give it a peculiar preference.

It is not surprising, that, during a period of war and disorder, the military virtues should be more celebrated than the pacific, and attract more the admiration and attention of mankind. . . . So different is even the same virtue of courage among warlike or peaceful nations! And indeed we may observe, that, as the difference between war and peace is the greatest that arises among nations and public societies, it produces also the greatest variations in moral sentiment, and diversifies the most our ideas of virtue and personal merit. . . .

Different customs have also some influence as well as different utilities; and by giving an early bias to the mind, may produce a superior propensity, either to the useful or the agreeable qualities; to those which regard self, or those which extend to society. These four sources of moral sentiment still subsist; but particular accidents may, at one time, make any one of them flow with greater abundance than at another.

The customs of some nations shut up the women from all social commerce: Those of others make them so essential a part of society and conversation, that, except where business is transacted, the male-sex alone are supposed almost wholly incapable of mutual discourse and entertainment. As this difference is the most material that can happen in private life, it must also produce the greatest variation in our moral sentiments.

Of all nations in the world, where polygamy was not allowed, the Greeks seem to have been the most reserved in their commerce with the fair sex, and to have imposed on them the strictest laws of modesty and decency. . . .

We may be assured, that an extreme purity of manners was the consequence of this reserve. Accordingly we find, that, except the fabulous stories of an Helen and a Clytemnestra, there scarcely is an instance of any event in the Greek history which proceeded from the intrigues of women. On the other hand, in modern times, particularly in a neighbouring nation, the females enter into all transactions and all management of church and state: And no man can expect success, who takes not care to obtain their good graces. Harry the third, by incurring the displeasure of the fair, endangered his crown, and lost his life, as much as by his indulgence to heresy.

It is needless to dissemble: The consequence of a very free commerce between the sexes, and of their living much together, will often terminate in intrigues and gallantry. We must sacrifice somewhat of the useful, if we be very anxious to obtain all the agreeable, qualities; and cannot pretend to reach alike every kind of advantage. . . .

Nor will these different customs of nations affect the one sex only: Their idea of personal merit in the males must also be somewhat different with regard, at least, to conversation, address, and humour. The one nation, where the men live much apart, will naturally more approve of prudence; the other of gaiety. With the one, simplicity of manners will be in the highest esteem; with the other, politeness. The one will distinguish themselves by good sense and judgment; the other, by taste and delicacy. The eloquence of the former will shine most in the senate; that of the other, on the theatre.

These, I say, are the natural effects of such customs. For it must be confessed, that chance has a great influence on national manners; and many events happen in society, which are not to be accounted for by general rules. . . .

What you insist on, replied Palamedes, may have some foundation, when you adhere to the maxims of common life and ordinary conduct. Experience and the practice of the world, readily correct any great extravagance on either side. But what say you to artificial lives and manners? How do you reconcile the maxims on which, in different ages and nations, these are founded?

What do you understand by artificial lives and manners? said I. I explain myself, replied he. You know, that religion had, in ancient times, very little influence on common life; and that, after men had performed their duty in sacrifices and prayers at the temple, they thought that the gods left the rest of their conduct to themselves, and were little pleased or offended with those virtues or vices, which only affected the peace and happiness of human society. In those ages, it was the business of philosophy alone to regulate men's ordinary behaviour and deportment. . . . . Its place is now supplied by the modern religion, which inspects our whole conduct, and prescribes an universal rule to our actions, to our words, to our very thoughts and inclinations; a rule so much the more austere, as it is guarded by infinite, though distant rewards and punishments; and no infraction of it can ever be concealed or disguised.

Diogenes is the most celebrated model of extravagant philosophy. Let us seek a parallel to him in modern times. We shall not disgrace any philosophic name by a comparison with the Dominics or Loyolas, or any canonized monk or friar. Let us compare him to Pascal, a man of parts and genius as well as Diogenes himself; and perhaps, too, a man of virtue, had he allowed his virtuous inclinations to have exerted and displayed themselves.

The foundation of Diogenes's conduct was an endeavour to render himself an independent being, as much as possible, and to confine all his wants, and desires, and pleasures, within himself and his own mind: The aim of Pascal was to keep a perpetual sense of his dependence before his eyes, and never to forget his numberless wants and infirmities. The ancient supported himself by magnanimity, ostentation, pride, and the idea of his own superiority above his fellow-creatures. The modern made constant profession of humility and abasement, of the contempt and hatred of himself; and endeavoured to attain these supposed virtues, as far as they are attainable. . . .

In such a remarkable contrast do these two men stand: Yet both of them have met with general admiration in their different ages, and have been proposed as models of imitation. Where then is the universal standard of morals which you talk of? And what rule shall we establish for the many different, nay contrary, sentiments of mankind?

An experiment, said I, which succeeds in the air, will not always succeed in a vacuum. When men depart from the maxim of common reason, and affect these artificial lives, as you call them, no one can answer for what will please or displease them. They are in a different element from the rest of mankind; and the natural principles of their mind play not with the same regularity as if left to themselves, free from the illusions of religious superstition, or philosophical enthusiasm.

5

BEYOND GOOD AND EVIL

Friedrich Nietzsche

186

The moral sentiment in Europe today is as refined, old, diverse, irritable, and subtle, as the "science of morals" that accompanies it is still young, raw, clumsy, and butterfingered – an attractive contrast that occasionally even becomes visible and incarnate in the person of a moralist. Even the term "science of morals" is much too arrogant considering what it designates, and offends *good* taste – which always prefers more modest terms.

One should own up in all strictness to what is still necessary here for a long time to come, to what alone is justified so far: to collect material, to conceptualize and arrange a vast realm of subtle feelings of value and differences of value which are alive, grow, beget, and perish – and perhaps attempt to present vividly some of the more frequent and recurring forms of such living crystallizations – all to prepare a *typology* of morals.

To be sure, so far one has not been so modest. With a stiff seriousness that inspires laughter, all our philosophers demanded something far more exalted, presumptuous, and solemn from themselves as soon as they approached the study of morality: they wanted to supply a *rational foundation* for morality – and every philosopher so far has believed that he has provided such a foundation. Morality itself, however, was accepted as "given." How remote from their clumsy pride was that task which they considered insignificant and left in dust and must – the task of description – although the subtlest fingers and senses can scarcely be subtle enough for it.

Just because our moral philosophers knew the facts of morality only very approximately in arbitrary extracts or in accidental epitomes – for

From Friedrich Nietzsche, "Beyond Good and Evil," translated by Walter Kaufmann in *The Basic Writings of Nietzsche*, New York: Random House, 1966, pp. 287–88, 305–308, and 393–98.

Friedrich Nietzsche was a nineteenth-century German philosopher.

example, as the morality of their environment, their class, their church, the spirit of their time, their climate and part of the world – just because they were poorly informed and not even very curious about different peoples, times, and past ages – they never laid eyes on the real problems of morality; for these emerge only when we compare *many* moralities. In all "science of morals" so far one thing was *lacking*, strange as it may sound: the problem of morality itself; what was lacking was any suspicion that there was something problematic here. What the philosophers called "a rational foundation for morality" and tried to supply, was, seen in the right light, merely a scholarly variation of the common *faith* in the prevalent morality; a new means of *expression* for this faith; and thus just another fact within a particular morality; indeed, in the last analysis a kind of denial that this morality might ever be considered problematic – certainly the very opposite of an examination, analysis, questioning, and vivisection of this very faith. . . .

202

Let us immediately say once more what we have already said a hundred times, for today's ears resist such truths – *our* truths. We know well enough how insulting it sounds when anybody counts man, unadorned and without metaphor, among the animals; but it will be charged against us as almost a *guilt* that precisely for the men of "modern ideas" we constantly employ such expressions as "herd," "herd instincts," and so forth. What can be done about it? We cannot do anything else; for here exactly lies our novel insight. We have found that in all major moral judgments Europe is now of one mind, including even the countries dominated by the influence of Europe: plainly, one now *knows* in Europe what Socrates thought he did not know and what that famous old serpent once promised to teach – today one "knows" what is good and evil.

Now it must sound harsh and cannot be heard easily when we keep insisting: that which here believes it knows, that which here glorifies itself with its praises and reproaches, calling itself good, that is the instinct of the herd animal, man, which has scored a breakthrough and attained prevalence and predominance over other instincts – and this development is continuing in accordance with the growing physiological approximation and assimilation of which it is the symptom. *Morality in Europe today is herd animal morality* – in other words, as we understand it, merely *one* type of human morality beside which, before which, and after which many other types, above all *higher* moralities, are, or ought to be, possible. But this morality resists such a "possibility," such an "ought" with all its power: it says stubbornly and inexorably, "I am morality itself, and nothing besides is morality." Indeed, with the help of a religion which indulged and flattered the most sublime herd-animal desires, we have reached the point where we find even in political and social institutions an ever more visible expression of this morality: the *democratic movement is the heir of the Christian movement.

But there are indications that its tempo is still much too slow and sleepy for the more impatient, for the sick, the sufferers of the instinct mentioned: witness the ever madder howling of the anarchist dogs who are baring their fangs more and more obviously and roam through the alleys of European culture. They seem opposites of the peacefully industrious democrats and ideologists of revolution, and even more so of the doltish philosophasters and brotherhood enthusiasts who call themselves socialists and want a "free society"; but in fact they are at one with the lot in their thorough and instinctive hostility to every other form of society except that of the *autonomous* herd (even to the point of repudiating the very concepts of "master" and "servant" – *ni dieu ni maître* runs a socialist formula). They are at one in their tough resistance to every special claim, every special right and privilege (which means in the last analysis, *every* right: for once all are equal nobody needs "rights" any more). They are at one in their mistrust of punitive justice (as if it were a violation of those who are weaker, a wrong against the *necessary* consequence of all previous society). But they are also at one in the religion of pity, in feeling with all who feel, live, and suffer (down to the animal, up to "God" – the excess of a "pity with God" belongs in a democratic age). They are at one, the lot of them, in the cry and the impatience of pity, in their deadly hatred of suffering generally, in their almost feminine inability to remain spectators, to *let* someone suffer. They are at one in their involuntary plunge into gloom and unmanly tenderness under whose spell Europe seems threatened by a new Buddhism. They are at one in their faith in the morality of *shared* pity, as if that were morality in itself, being the height, the *attained* height of man, the sole hope of the future, the consolation of present man, the great absolution from all former guilt. They are at one, the lot of them, in their faith in the community as the *savior*, in short, in the herd, in "themselves" . . .

203

We have a different faith; to us the democratic movement is not only a form of the decay of political organization but a form of the decay, namely the diminution, of man, making him mediocre and lowering his value. Where, then, must *we* reach with our hopes?

Toward *new philosophers*; there is no choice; toward spirits strong and original enough to provide the stimuli for opposite valuations and to revalue and invert "eternal values"; toward forerunners, toward men of the future who in the present tie the knot and constraint that forces the will of millennia upon *new* tracks. To teach man the future of man as his *will,* as dependent on a human will, and to prepare great ventures and overall attempts of discipline and cultivation by way of putting an end to that gruesome dominion of nonsense and accident that has so far been called "history" – the nonsense of the "greatest number" is merely its ultimate form: at some time new types of philosophers and commanders will be necessary for that, and whatever has existed on earth of concealed, terrible, and benevolent spirits, will look pale and dwarfed by comparison. It is the image of such leaders that *we* envisage: may I say this out loud, you free spirits? The conditions that one would have partly to create and partly to exploit for their genesis; the probable ways and tests that would enable a soul to grow to such a height and force that it would feel the *compulsion* for such tasks; a revaluation of values under whose new pressure and hammer a conscience would be steeled, a heart turned to bronze, in order to endure the weight of such responsibility; on the other hand, the necessity of such leaders, the frightening danger that they might fail to appear or that they might turn out badly or degenerate – these are *our* real worries and gloom – do you know that, you free spirits? – these are the heavy distant thoughts and storms that pass over the sky of *our* life.

There are few pains as sore as once having seen, guessed, felt how an extraordinary human being strayed from his path and degenerated. But anyone who has the rare eye for the overall danger that "man" himself *degenerates*; anyone who, like us, has recognized the monstrous fortuity that has so far had its way and play regarding the future of man – a game in which no hand, and not even a finger, of God took part as a player; anyone who fathoms the calamity that lies concealed in the absurd guilelessness and blind confidence of "modern ideas" and even more in the whole Christian-European morality – suffers from an anxiety that is past all comparisons. With a single glance he sees what, given a favorable accumulation and increase of forces and tasks, might yet *be made of man;* he knows with all the knowledge of his conscience how man is still unexhausted for the greatest possibilities and how often the type "man" has already confronted enigmatic decisions and new paths – he knows still better from his most painful memories what wretched things have so far usually broken a being of the highest rank that was in the process of becoming, so that it broke, sank, and became contemptible.

The *overall degeneration of man* down to what today appears to the socialist dolts and flatheads as their "man of the future" – as their ideal – this degeneration and diminution of man into the perfect herd animal (or, as they say, to the man of the "free society"), this animalization of man into the dwarf animal of equal rights and claims, is *possible*, there is no doubt of it. Anyone who has once thought through this possibility to the end knows one kind of nausea that other men don't know – but perhaps also a new *task! . . .*

259

Refraining mutually from injury, violence, and exploitation and placing one's will on a par with that of someone else – this may become, in a certain rough sense, good manners among individuals if the appropriate conditions are present (namely, if these men are actually similar in strength and value standards and belong together in *one* body). But as soon as this principle is extended, and possibly even accepted as the *fundamental principle of society*, it immediately proves to be what it really is – a will to the *denial* of life, a principle of disintegration and decay.

Here we must beware of superficiality and get to the bottom of the matter, resisting all sentimental weakness: life itself is *essentially* appropriation, injury, overpowering of what is alien and weaker; suppression, hardness, imposition of one's own forms, incorporation and at least, at its mildest, exploitation – but why should one always use those words in which a slanderous intent has been imprinted for ages?

Even the body within which individuals treat each other as equals, as suggested before – and this happens in every healthy aristocracy – if it is a living and not a dying body, has to do to other bodies what the individuals within it refrain from doing to each other: it will have to be an incarnate will to power, it will strive to grow, spread, seize, become predominant – not from any morality or immorality but because it is *living* and because life simply *is* will to power. But there is no point on which the ordinary consciousness of Europeans resists instruction as on this: everywhere people are now raving, even under scientific disguises, about coming conditions of society in which "the exploitative aspect" will be removed – which sounds to me as if they promised to invent a way of life that would dispense with all organic functions. "Exploitation" does not belong to a corrupt or imperfect and primitive society: it belongs to the *essence* of what lives, as a basic organic function; it is a consequence of the will to power, which is after all the will of life.

If this should be an innovation as a theory – as a reality it is the *primordial fact* of all history: people ought to be honest with themselves at least that far.

260

Wandering through the many subtler and coarser moralities which have so far been prevalent on earth, or still are prevalent, I found that certain features recurred regularly together and were closely associated – until I finally discovered two basic types and one basic difference.

There are *master morality* and *slave morality* – I add immediately that in all the higher and more mixed cultures there also appear attempts at mediation between these two moralities, and yet more often the interpenetration and mutual misunderstanding of both, and at times they occur directly alongside each other – even in the same human being, within a *single* soul. The moral discrimination of values has originated either among a ruling group whose consciousness of its difference from the ruled group was accompanied by delight – or among the ruled, the slaves and dependents of every degree.

In the first case, when the ruling group determines what is "good," the exalted, proud states of the soul are experienced as conferring distinction and determining the order of rank. The noble human being separates from himself those in whom the opposite of such exalted, proud states finds expression: he despises them. It should be noted immediately that in this first type of morality the opposition of "good" and "*bad*" means approximately the same as "noble" and "contemptible." (The opposition of "good" and "*evil*" has a different origin.) One feels contempt for the cowardly, the anxious, the petty, those intent on narrow utility; also for the suspicious with their unfree glances, those who humble themselves, the doglike people who allow themselves to be maltreated, the begging flatterers, above all the liars: it is part of the fundamental faith of all aristocrats that the common people lie. "We truthful ones" – thus the nobility of ancient Greece referred to itself.

It is obvious that moral designations were everywhere first applied to *human beings* and only later, derivatively, to actions. Therefore it is a gross mistake when historians of morality start from such questions as: why was the compassionate act praised? The noble type of man experiences *itself* as determining values; it does not need approval; it judges, "what is harmful to me is harmful in itself"; it knows itself to be that which first accords honor to things; it is *value-creating*. Everything it knows as part of itself it honors: such a morality is self-glorification. In the foreground there is the feeling of fullness, of power that seeks to overflow, the happiness of high tension, the consciousness of wealth that would give and bestow: the noble human being, too, helps the unfortunate, but not, or almost not, from pity, but prompted more by an urge begotten by excess of power. The noble human being honors himself as one who is powerful, also as one who has power over himself, who knows how to speak and be silent, who delights in being severe and hard with himself and respects all severity and hardness. "A hard heart Wotan put into my breast," says an old Scandinavian saga: a fitting poetic expression, seeing that it comes from the soul of a proud Viking. Such a type of man is actually proud of the fact that he is *not* made for pity, and the hero of the saga therefore adds as a warning: "If the heart is not hard in youth it will never harden." Noble and courageous human beings who think that way are furthest removed from that morality which finds the distinction of morality precisely in pity, or in acting for others, or in *désintéressement*; faith in oneself, pride in oneself, a fundamental hostility and irony against "selflessness" belong just as definitely to noble morality as does a slight disdain and caution regarding compassionate feelings and a "warm heart."

It is the powerful who *understand* how to honor; this is their art, their realm of invention. The profound reverence for age and tradition – all law rests on this double reverence – the faith and prejudice in favor of ancestors and disfavor of those yet to come are typical of the morality of the powerful; and when the men of "modern ideas," conversely, believe almost instinctively in "progress" and "the future" and more and more lack respect for age, this in itself would sufficiently betray the ignoble origin of these "ideas."

A morality of the ruling group, however, is most alien and embarrassing to the present taste in the severity of its principle that one has duties only to one's peers; that against beings of a lower rank, against everything alien, one may behave as one pleases or "as the heart desires," and in any case "beyond good and evil" – here pity and like feelings may find their place. The capacity for, and the duty of, long gratitude and long revenge – both only among one's peers – refinement in repaying, the sophisticated concept of friendship, a certain necessity for having enemies (as it were, as drainage ditches for the affects of envy, quarrelsomeness, exuberance – at bottom, in order to be capable of being good *friends*): all these are typical characteristics of noble morality which, as suggested, is not the morality of "modern ideas" and therefore is hard to empathize with today, also hard to dig up and uncover.

It is different with the second type of morality, *slave morality*. Suppose the violated, oppressed, suffering, unfree, who are uncertain of themselves and weary, moralize: what will their moral valuations have in common? Probably, a pessimistic suspicion about the whole condition of man will find expression, perhaps a condemnation of man along with his condition. The slave's eye is not favorable to the virtues of the powerful: he is skeptical and suspicious, *subtly* suspicious, of all the "good" that is honored there – he would like to persuade himself that even their happiness is not genuine. Conversely, those qualities are brought out and flooded with light which serve to ease existence for those who suffer: here pity, the complaisant and obliging hand, the warm heart, patience, industry, humility, and friendliness are honored – for here these are the most useful qualities and almost the only means for enduring the pressure of existence. Slave morality is essentially a morality of utility.

Here is the place for the origin of that famous opposition of "good" and "evil": into evil one's feelings project power and dangerousness, a certain terribleness, subtlety, and strength that does not permit contempt to develop. According to slave morality, those who are "evil" thus inspire fear; according to master morality it is precisely those who are "good" that inspire, and wish to inspire, fear, while the "bad" are felt to be contemptible.

The opposition reaches its climax when, as a logical consequence of slave morality, a touch of disdain is associated also with the "good" of this morality – this may be slight and benevolent – because the good human being has to be *undangerous* in the slaves' way of thinking: he is good-natured, easy to deceive, a little stupid perhaps, *un bonhomme*. Wherever slave morality becomes preponderant, language tends to bring the words "good" and "stupid" closer together.

One last fundamental difference: the longing for *freedom*, the instinct for happiness and the subtleties of the feeling of freedom belong just as necessarily to slave morality and morals as artful and enthusiastic reverence and devotion are the regular symptom of an aristocratic way of thinking and evaluating.

This makes plain why love *as passion* – which is our European specialty – simply must be of noble origin: as is well known, its invention must be credited to the Provençal knight-poets, those magnificent and inventive human beings of the *"gai saber"* to whom Europe owes so many things and almost owes itself.

Part II

SOME VOICES FROM ANTHROPOLOGY

6

YANOMAMÖ: THE LAST DAYS OF EDEN

Napoleon A. Chagnon

Daily life among the Yanomamö

Males and females

A number of distinctions based on status and physiology are important in Yanomamö daily life. Perhaps the most conspicuous and most important of these are the distinctions between males and females – what each sex goes through in growing to adulthood and what their roles are after achieving it.

Yanomamö society is decidedly masculine – male chauvinistic, if you will. One hears many statements like "Men are more valuable than women" or "Boys are more valuable than girls." Both men and women say that they want to produce as many children as they can, but they especially want boys. . . .

Female children assume responsibilities in the household long before their brothers are obliged to perform domestic tasks. At an early age, girls are expected to tend their younger brothers and sisters and help their mothers with such chores as cooking, hauling water, and collecting firewood. By the time girls have reached puberty, they have learned that their world is decidedly less attractive than that of their brothers. And most of them have been promised in marriage by then.

Yanomamö girls – and to a lesser extent boys – have almost no voice in the decisions of their older kin as to whom they will marry. They are largely pawns for their kinsmen to dispose of, and their wishes get almost no consideration. A girl is often promised to someone well before she reaches puberty, and sometimes the husband-elect takes over her rearing

From Napoleon A. Chagnon, *Yanomamö: the Last Days of Eden*, San Diego CA: Harcourt, 1992, pp. 144–45, 147, 149–53, and 182–89.

Napoleon A. Chagnon is Professor of Anthropology at the University of California, Santa Barbara.

for part of her childhood. Boys seem better able to initiate the marital process and to have their older kin make the first inquiries. But the males marry later than the females do, so these boys are really young men, and the girls they are interested in are much younger, often just children. Girls do not participate as equals in any of the political affairs of the corporate kinship group, and they seem to inherit most of the duties without enjoying any of the privileges, largely because the husband is older than she is at first marriage and thus has a higher status.

Marriage does not automatically enhance a girl's status or even change her life much. There is no marriage ceremony as such; public awareness of it begins with no more than a comment like "Her father has promised her to so-and-so." The girl usually does not start living with her husband until after she has had her first menstrual period, although she may have been officially married for several years. Her duties as wife require her to continue the laborious tasks she has already been performing, such as the daily collecting of firewood and fetching of water. . . .

Women are expected to respond quickly to the wishes – sometimes the demands – of their husbands and even to anticipate their needs. It is interesting to watch the women's behavior when their husbands return from a hunting trip or a visit to another village. The men march proudly across the village and retire silently to their hammocks, especially when they have brought home some choice item of food. The women, no matter what they have been doing, hurry home and quietly but rapidly prepare a meal. If the wife is slow about it, she may be scolded or even beaten.

Most physical reprimands take the form of kicks or blows with the hand or a piece of firewood, but a particularly nasty husband might hit his wife with the sharp edge of a machete or ax or shoot a barbed arrow into some nonvital area, such as the buttocks or a leg. Another brutal punishment is to hold the glowing end of a piece of firewood against the wife's body, producing painful and serious burns. Normally, however, the husband's reprimands are consistent with the perceived seriousness of the wife's shortcomings, his more drastic measures being reserved for infidelity or suspicion of infidelity. It is not uncommon for a man to seriously injure a sexually errant wife, and some husbands have shot and killed unfaithful wives.

I was told about one young man in Monou-teri who shot and killed his wife in a rage of sexual jealousy, and during one of my stays in the villages a man shot his wife in the stomach with a barbed arrow. She suffered extensive internal injuries, and the missionaries had her flown to the territorial capital for surgery, but by then the wound had become infected and she was near death. Another man chopped his wife on the arm with a machete; some tendons to her fingers were severed, and it was feared that she would lose the use of her hand, but eventually the wound healed.

A club fight involving a case of infidelity took place in one of the villages just before the end of my first field trip. The male paramour was killed, and the enraged husband cut off both of his wife's ears. A number of women have had their ears badly mutilated. The women wear short pieces of arrow cane in their pierced earlobes; these are easily grabbed by an angry husband – and, once in a while, jerked so hard that the earlobes are torn open.

There is one somewhat rare way for a woman to escape the anguish of marriage to an especially unpleasant husband. The Yanomamö even have a word for it, *shuwahimou*, and the word is applied to a woman who, on her own, flees from her village to live in another village and find a new husband there. It is rare to do this because it is dangerous. If the woman's own village is stronger than the one she flees to, the men will pursue her and forcibly take her back – and mete out a very severe punishment to her for having run away. They might even kill her. Most of the women who have fled have done so to escape particularly savage and cruel treatment, and they try to flee to a more powerful village.

But a woman can usually count on her brothers for protection against a cruel husband. If the husband mistreats her too severely, the brothers may take her away from him and give her to another man. Women dread the possibility of being married to men in distant villages, because they know that their brothers will not be able to protect them.

Some women – provided they have not been too severely treated – even seem to measure their husbands' concern for them in terms of the minor physical damage they have sustained. On several occasions, I have overheard young women examining each other's scalp scars and remarking, for instance, that a woman's husband must really care for her, since he hit her on the head so frequently. Both husbands and wives often laugh and joke with each other about past incidents in which the woman received a serious wound.

A woman who has married a male cross-cousin may have the best of it, for she is related to her husband by blood ties of kinship as well as by marriage. Bahimi, for example, is Kaobawä's mother's brother's daughter, and their marital relationship is very tranquil. He reprimands her occasionally, but never cruelly.

I am sometimes asked what the Yanomamö idea of love is. They have a concept, *buhi yabraö*, that at first I thought could be translated into our notion of love. I remember being very excited when I discovered it, and I ran around asking lots of questions like these: "Do you love so-and-so?"– naming a brother or sister. "Yes!" "Do you love so-and-so?" – naming a child. "Yes!" "Do you love so-and-so?" – naming the man's wife. A stunned silence, peals of laughter, and then this: "You don't *love* your wife, you idiot!" One could go so far as to say that, if love in their culture is restricted to the kind of feelings they have toward close blood relatives, then they are more likely to have those feelings toward a spouse if, as in Kaobawä's case, the spouse is a blood relative – a first cousin – as his is.

The women tend to lose their shapes by the time they are thirty, because of the children they have borne and nursed for up to three years each and because of their years of hard work. They seem to be much more subject to bad moods than the men are – moods in which they display a sullen attitude toward life in general and men in particular. To an outsider, the older women appear to speak constantly in what sounds like a whine, punctuated with contemptuous remarks and complaints. When the women are happy or excited, the whining tone disappears, and they laugh gleefully, make wisecracks, and taunt the men, or each other, with biting insults and clever – usually bawdy – jokes.

A woman gains increasing respect as she ages, especially when she becomes old enough to have adult children to look out for her. The oldest women occupy a unique position in intervillage warfare and politics. Immune from the incursions of raiders, they can go from one village to another in complete safety, and they are sometimes employed as messengers and, occasionally, as the retrievers of dead bodies. If a man is killed near the village of an enemy, old women from the slain man's village are permitted to recover his body, or old women from the killers' village may take the body back to his kinsmen.

All women except the very old live in constant fear of being abducted by raiders when their village is at war. Whenever they leave the village, they take their children with them, particularly the younger ones, so that if they are abducted, the child will not be separated from its mother. The fear of abduction gives the women a special concern with the political behavior of their men, and they occasionally try to goad the men into action against an enemy by caustic accusations of cowardice. The men, of course, cannot stand being belittled in this fashion, and they may be badgered into acting.

Children and grown-ups

Although the children of both sexes spend much more time with their mothers, it is the fathers who, largely by example, teach the boys their sex-specific roles and masculine attitudes. The distinction between male and female status develops early in the socialization process. The boys, encouraged to be fierce, are rarely punished for hitting their parents or the hapless girls of the village. Kaobawä, for example, would let his son, Ariwari, beat him on the face and head in a fit of temper, laughing and commenting about the boy's ferocity. Although Ariwari was only about four years old at the time, he had already learned that an acceptable expression of anger was to strike someone with his hand or something else, and it was not uncommon for him to smack his father in the face if something displeased him. He was frequently egged on in this by the teasing and good-natured attitude of his mother and other adults in the household.

When Kaobawä's group was traveling, Ariwari would emulate his father by copying him on a child's scale. For example, he would erect a temporary hut made of small sticks and leaves and would play happily in his own camp, while his sisters were pressed into helping their mother with domestic tasks. Still, young girls are given some freedom to play, and they have their moments of fun with their mothers or other children – such as the merry games of tug-of-war with long vines in the village plaza, especially when it is raining hard.

But a girl's childhood ends sooner than a boy's. Her game of playing house fades imperceptibly into a constant responsibility to help her mother. By the time a girl is about ten years old, she has become an economic asset to her mother and spends much of her time working. Boys, by contrast, spend hours playing together, and many manage to prolong their childhoods into their late teens or early twenties – by which time a girl will have married and may have a child or two. The young men (usually unmarried) called *huyas* are a social problem in almost all Yanomamö villages; their attempts to seduce the young women, almost all of whom are married, are the source of much sexual jealousy. Their equivalent in our culture is teenage boys who are juvenile delinquents or gang members.

A girl's transition to womanhood is obvious because of its physiological manifestations. At first menses (*yöbömou*), Yanomamö girls are confined to their homes and hidden behind a screen of leaves. Their old cotton garments are discarded and replaced by new ones made by their mothers or by older female friends. During this week of confinement, the girl is fed sparingly by her relatives, and the food must be eaten with a stick, as she is not allowed to come into contact with it in any other fashion. She speaks in whispers, and then only to close kin. She must also scratch herself with a second set of sticks. After her puberty confinement, a girl usually takes up residence with her promised husband and begins her life as a married woman.

Women in our culture often ask me, "What do the women do during their menstrual periods? What do they wear for sanitary napkins?" The Yanomamö word for menstruation translates literally as "squatting" (*roo*), and that is a fairly accurate description of what the pubescent females, and the adult women, do. They remain inactive, squatting on their haunches and allowing the menstrual blood to drip on the ground, usually into a shallow hole scraped out for the purpose. The Yanomamö women do not use the equivalent of tampons or sanitary napkins, and herein lies an important difference between our "environment" and theirs. Sanitary napkins are a useful invention for those who need them regularly, but the Yanomamö women menstruate with relative infrequency because for much of their adult lives they are either pregnant or nursing infants. . . .

Finally, Yanomamö children differ from adults in their presumed susceptibility to supernatural hazards. A great deal of Yanomamö sorcery and mythological references to harmful magic focuses on children as the targets of malevolence. Shamans constantly send their *hekura* to enemy villages to secretly attack and devour the vulnerable portions of children's souls, causing much sickness and death, and the shamans spend equal amounts of time warding off enemy malevolent spirits. The children are especially vulnerable because their souls are not firmly established within their physical beings and can wander out of the body almost at will – most commonly escaping through the mouth when the child cries. A mother is quick to hush her bawling baby in order to prevent its soul from escaping, usually by sticking one of her nipples in its mouth. A child's soul can be recovered by sweeping the ground around the place where the soul probably escaped, sweeping with a particular kind of branch while calling for the soul. I helped several times to lure the soul of a sick child back into the child's body by such calling and sweeping. But I also contributed a dose of medicine for the child's diarrhea.

[. . .]

The art, politics, and etiquette of entertaining guests

Yanomamö feasts are political events. They are held whenever one sovereign group entertains the members of an allied group. To be sure, they have significant economic and ceremonial implications, but those are minor when compared to the feast's importance in the forming and maintaining of alliances. The chief purpose of entertaining allies is to reaffirm and cultivate intervillage amity in the intimate, sociable context of having a festive meal together. The allied group then feels obligated to reciprocate in its own village with another feast, and more intervillage amity. The feasts are an important element in reducing the possibility of warfare between groups.

Significant factors in the formation of alliances are trade, economic specialization, historical ties between groups, patterns of warfare, and intervillage marriage exchanges, all of which are intimately connected and interact with each other in the development of alliances. . . .

Yanomamö alliances

One of the benefits that the Yanomamö expect from an alliance is the obligation of the partners to shelter each other whenever one of them is driven from its village and garden by an enemy.

Sometimes the beleaguered partner has to remain in the host village for a year or longer – approximately the length of time required to establish a new garden and a productive base for an independent existence. The members of Kaobawä's group were driven from their gardens twice in their recent history and forced to take refuge in the village of an ally, where they remained for about a year. In both cases, the hosts seized the opportunity to demand a number of women from Kaobawä's homeless group without reciprocating in kind. The longer a group remains under a host's protection, the higher the cost in terms of the loss of women, so visitors always try to establish their new gardens and move as quickly as possible. Without allies, however, the members of a village would have to remain at their old garden, suffering the attacks of their enemies, or else break up into small groups and join other villages permanently, losing many of their women to their protectors. Living in the jungle is not a desirable option; it does not produce enough wild foods to permit a large group to remain in one place, and a small group would soon be overrun by its enemies.

The risk of being driven from one's garden is so pervasive in Kaobawä's area that no village can continue to exist as a sovereign entity unless it has alliances. The Yanomamö take the bellicose position that the stronger villages should always act ready to take advantage of weaker ones and to coerce women from them; to counter this, the members of all villages try to behave as if they are strong. The result of the constant military posturing is to make intervillage alliances desirable, but it also spawns an attitude that inhibits the formation of alliances: allies *need* each other but do not *trust* each other.

Alliances are usually the outcome of a sequence that starts with casual trading, goes on to mutual feasting, and finally leads to an exchange of women between villages to cement the alliance. The most intimate allies are those who, in addition to trading and feasting together, exchange women in marriage. A developing alliance may stabilize at the trading or feasting stage, without proceeding further, but these are weak alliances, serving mainly to limit the degree of fighting if relations turn hostile. The Yanomamö tend not to attack villages with which they trade and feast, unless a specific incident, like the abduction of a woman, provokes them. Allies linked by trade and feasting, for example, will rarely accuse each other of practicing harmful magic, often the trigger for war. Allies bound to each other by affinal kinship ties – relatedness created through intermarriage – are more interdependent, however, because they are

97

under an obligation to each other to continue exchanging women. It is, in fact, through the exchange of women that historically independent villages expand their kinship ties.

Alliances almost always begin with trading between men from different villages, a phase that can last for years. Men go off to another village alone, leaving their women behind – but often making concealed camps in the forest for the women to hide in while the men are away. Indeed, suspicions may be so high that even after the trading phase has moved into feasting the men will continue to leave the women at home, for fear their new allies will appropriate some of them. Not until trust and confidence have developed will they bring their wives and children along.

Members of allied villages are usually reluctant to take the final step in alliance formation of ceding women to their partners, for they always worry that a partner might not reciprocate as promised. This attitude is especially conspicuous in small villages, whose larger alliance partners often try to pressure them into demonstrating their friendship by ceding women. The strong can and do coerce the weak in Yanomamö politics, forcing the weak into a posture of bluff and intimidation to make themselves appear stronger than they really are. Such behavior tells the larger partner that any attempt to coerce women will be met with an appropriate reaction, such as a chest-pounding duel or a club fight. Still, each partner in an alliance expects to gain women by it – indeed, enters it with this in mind – and each hopes to gain more women than it loses. . . .

The women who are exchanged are the ones who like it least of all, for in their new village they will have no brothers or other kinsmen to protect them from a cruel husband. And often their parents share the feeling. . . .

But this is only a thumbnail sketch of the necessary steps in the development of an alliance. Rarely do relations reach the stage at which women are actually exchanged, particularly if the two villages are approximately equal in military strength. Fights and arguments break out over women, food, etiquette, generosity, status, and the like, and the principals may withdraw on semihostile terms, perhaps attempting a rapprochement later on. Or, if the principals are obviously unequal militarily, the stronger of them will try to coerce its weaker partner into ceding women early on, taking advantage of its military strength but impeding the development of the alliance. . . .

Trading and feasting to make friends of enemies

There is little in the way of natural encouragement for two groups to begin visiting each other. One group is always ready to take advantage of the other's weaknesses, especially when the alliance is just developing. Pride and status preclude open attempts to develop stable and predictable alliances. The Yanomamö cannot simply arrive at the village of a potential ally and declare that they are being harassed by a powerful neighbor and need help. To do so would concede their vulnerability and perhaps even invite a raid from the potential ally. Instead, they subsume the true motive for forming an alliance in the vehicles of trading and feasting, developing these institutions over months and sometimes years. In this way they retain their sovereignty and pride while working toward their objective of intervillage solidarity and military interdependence.

Three distinct features of Yanomamö trading practices are important in the context of alliance formation. First, each item traded must be paid for with a different kind of item, in a type of exchange called *no mraiha*. To the inexperienced observer, a person who gives something *no mraiha* appears to be giving it for free, as a gift. But someday the giver remembers it and uses it as a lever to ask for a gift in return. The delayed repayment is a second feature of the *no mraiha*. Taken together, these two features mean that one trade always calls forth another and gives the members of different villages both an excuse and an opportunity for visiting. And the trading tends to continue, for the members of one village always owe the members of the other some trade goods from their last meeting. . . .

The third significant trade feature is a peculiar kind of specialization in the production of items for trade. Each village has one or more products that it provides to its allies. These might include dogs, hallucinogenic drugs (both cultivated and wild), arrow points, arrow shafts, bows, cotton yarn, cotton and vine hammocks, baskets of several varieties, clay pots, and, in the case of villages that have contact with outsiders, steel tools, fishhooks, fish line, and aluminum pots.

The specialization has nothing to do with the availability of natural resources to make the product. Each village is capable of self-sufficiency. (The steel tools and other products from the civilized world are the major exception). The explanation for the specialization lies, rather, in the sociological aspects of alliance formation. Trade functions as a social catalyst, the starting mechanism by which mutually suspicious groups are repeatedly brought together in friendly meetings. Without these frequent contacts, alliances would be much slower to form and far less stable. A prerequisite to a stable alliance is repeated visiting and feasting, and the trading mechanism serves to bring about these visits.

Clay pots are a good example of how this specialization in trade promotes intervillage relations. The Mömariböwei-teri are a group allied to both Kaobawä's nearby group and the people of a distant Shamatari village who are mortal enemies of Kaobawä. When I first began my fieldwork, I visited the Mömariböwei-teri, about a ten-hour walk away, specifically to ask them about the making of clay pots. They all vigorously denied any knowledge of pot making, saying that they had once known how but had long since forgotten. They added that their allies the Möwaraoba-teri (Sibarariwä's village) made pots and provided them with all they needed. Besides, they said, the clay around their village was not suitable for pots. Later in the year, their alliance with the pot makers cooled, because of a war, and their source was shut off. At the same time, Kaobawä's group began asking them for clay pots. The Mömariböwei-teri promptly "remembered" how to make pots and "discovered" that their clay was suitable, after all. They had merely been creating a local shortage in order to have an excuse to visit an ally. . . .

Alliances may stabilize at any one of three levels: sporadic trading, mutual feasting, or the exchange of women. They are cumulative levels; allies that exchange women also feast and trade together, and allies that feast also trade but do not exchange women. At the lower end of the scale of alliance solidarity lie those villages with which a group is at war, and at the upper end are usually those villages from whom one's group has recently separated – although sometimes the scale is reversed, and a village's mortal enemy is the group from which it has recently split. . . .

There is no rigid geographical correlation between village settlement patterns and the degree of alliance solidarity, but usually immediate neighbors are at least on trading terms and not actively at war. When a war does break out between neighbors, one of them abandons its site and moves to a new location. The nature of the ties between neighboring villages – they may be ties of blood, marriage exchange, reciprocal feasting, or casual trading – depends on many factors, particularly village size, the current state of warfare with more distant groups, and the precise historical ties between neighbors. Whatever the ties, however, each neighbor strives to remain sovereign and independent.

The Yanomamö do not overtly concede that trade is a mechanism for bringing people together repeatedly in order to establish an amicable basis for a more stable alliance. Nor do they acknowledge the relationship between the trading and feasting cycles and village interdependency. In this regard, they are like the Trobriand Islanders of Melanesia in displaying a "functional ignorance" of the adaptive aspects of their trading institutions. Both the Yanomamö and the Trobrianders treat the mechanisms by which people from different groups are induced to visit each other as ends in themselves, not related to the establishment of either economic or political interdependency.

For a Yanomamö, the feast's significance lies in the marvelous quantities of food, the excitement of the dance, and the satisfaction of having others admire and covet the fine decorations he wears – and, if he is so inclined, in the opportunity for a clandestine sexual liaison. The enchantment of the dance issues from the dancer's awareness that, for a brief moment, he is a glorious peacock who commands the admiration of his fellows and that it is his responsibility and his desire to make a spectacular display of his dance steps and gaudy accoutrements. In this brief, ego-building moment, each man, guest or host has the chance to display himself, spinning and prancing about the village periphery, chest puffed out, while all watch, admire, and cheer wildly. The dancer does not say, "We are feasting you so that if we are in trouble you will help us."

For the hosts, the feast serves as a display of their affluence and a challenge for the guests to reciprocate with an equally grandiose feast at a later date. . . . Indeed, some villages provide so much food that the participants compete in drinking enormous quantities of banana soup or peach palm gruel, which they vomit up and then return for more. The plaza rapidly becomes dotted with large pools of vomit, and one must be careful where he walks – and careful not to walk in front of a celebrant who is about to regurgitate. Each good feast calls forth another, and the allies become better acquainted as they reciprocate feasts in the dry season and over the years.

7

THE ASTONISHMENT OF ANTHROPOLOGY

Richard A. Shweder

If there is a piety in cultural anthropology it is the conviction that astonishment deserves to be a universal emotion. Astonishment and the assortment of feelings that it brings with it – surprise, curiosity, excitement, enthusiasm, sympathy – are probably the affects most distinctive of the anthropological response to the difference and strangeness of "others." Anthropologists encounter witchcraft trials, suttee, ancestral spirit attack, fire walking, body mutilation, the dream time, and how do they react? With astonishment. While others respond with horror, outrage, condescension, or lack of interest, the anthropologists flip into their world-revising mood.

Undoubtedly, there is some irony in this pious devotion to the virtues of astonishment. In the postmodern world that cultural anthropology has helped to construct (see, for example, Clifford and Marcus 1986; Clifford 1988; Geertz 1988), everything from science to literal description to one's own subjectivity is self-consciously redefined and revalued as artifice or art. In that world, piety is figured as a form of either innocence or insincerity, both of which stand, quite naturally, in need of defense. The essays *Thinking through Cultures* try to provide one part of that defense of astonishment, by "thinking through cultures" in search of our psychological nature.

The expression "thinking through cultures" is polysemous; one may "think through" other cultures in each of several senses: by means of the other (viewing the other as an expert in some realm of human experience), by getting the other straight (rational reconstruction of the beliefs

From Richard A. Shweder, *Thinking through Cultures: Expeditions in Cultural Psychology*, Cambridge MA: Harvard University Press, 1991, pp. 1–5, 7–11, and 14–19.

Richard A. Shweder, an anthropologist, is Professor of Human Development and Psychology at the University of Chicago.

and practices of the other), by deconstructing and going right through and beyond the other (revealing what the other has suppressed and kept out of sight), witnessing in the context of engagement with the other (revealing one's own perspective on things by dint of a self-reflexive turn of mind). Because the essays are exercises in thinking through cultures in search of the human psyche, it seems appropriate to refer to them as expeditions in cultural psychology. They are expeditions in cultural psychology that, it is to be hoped, exhibit some of the astonishment of anthropology.

The idea of a cultural psychology is the idea that individuals and traditions, psyches and cultures, make each other up. Because the idea of a cultural psychology implies that the processes of consciousness (self-maintenance processes, learning processes, reasoning processes, emotional feeling processes) may not be uniform across the cultural regions of the world, any serious or astonishing treatment of the topic must address the problem of rationality (or psychic unity), as well as several closely related issues, including relativism, romanticism, realism, and the trilogy of modernisms (pre-, post-, and pure).

One of the central myths of the modern period in the West is the idea that the opposition between religion-superstition-revelation and logic-science-rationality divides the world into then and now, them and us. According to this myth the world woke up and became good about three centuries ago when Enlightenment thinkers began to draw some distinctions between things that premodern thinkers had managed to overlook.

Many modernist authors (for example, Ernest Gellner in anthropology, Jean Piaget in psychology) construct an image of the premodern period as a dark age of intellectual confusions: the confusion of language with reality, of physical suffering with moral transgression, of subjectivity with objectivity, of custom with nature. That image of the premodern mind is built out of presupposed separations or distinctions – of language versus reality, subject versus object, custom versus nature – that over the past several decades have been challenged by postmodern scholarship. Today, deep into the postmodern age, there are other stories about rationality and religion waiting to be told.

The problem of rationality (or psychic unity) is one of the central themes of *Thinking through Cultures*. The problem presents itself to anthropologists and other students of cultural psychology in the following form: What inferences about human nature are we to draw from the apparent diversity of human conceptions of reality, and what justification is there for our own conceptions of reality in the light of that apparent diversity?

Nicolas Rescher (1988: 140), in his recent writings on rationality, formulates nicely what is at stake in debates about conceptual diversity. The logic of his formulation goes like this, although I have taken considerable liberties with his wording and added the examples.

Consider the following four propositions. Each will seem plausible to some readers, yet taken together they are incompatible. One or more of them must be rejected, but which?

1   We, the members of our ethnic group, are rationally justified in our conception of things; for example, that when you are dead you are dead, that virtuous people can die young, that souls do not transmigrate, and that authors have a natural inalienable right to publish works critical of revealed truth.
2   They, the members of some other ethnic group, have a different conception of things; for example, that the spirits of your dead ancestors can enter your body and wreak havoc on your life, that widows are unlucky and should be shunned, that a neighbor's envy can make you sick, that souls transmigrate, that nature is a scene of retributive causation and you get the death you deserve, that a parody of scriptural revelation is blasphemous and blasphemers should be punished.
3   They, the members of that other ethnic group, are rationally justified in their conception of things.
4   If others are rationally justified in their conception of things and that conception is different from ours, then we cannot be rationally justified in our conception of things, and vice versa.

The four propositions are mutually incompatible. Accepting any three entails rejection of the fourth. Here one is presented with a fateful choice, for rejecting first one and then another of the four can resolve the inconsistency in a variety of ways.

Rejection of the first proposition is entailed by acceptance of the other three. Those who go searching in other cultural traditions for a lost paradise or age of truth often adopt this stance, which might be described as reverse ethnocentrism or inverse developmentalism. If you are an inverse developmentalist you view your own culture as retrograde, or as oppressive, or as a form of false consciousness, or as a source of illusions. Carlos Castaneda's Don Juan beckons. Colonized peoples sometimes adopt this stance, if they identify strongly with the worldview and practices of the colonizer.

Rejection of the second proposition is entailed by acceptance of the other three. Those who adopt this stance think that all differences are merely apparent, or superficial, or idiomatic. This is the stance associated with the humanistic ecumenical spirit of universalism and the Platonic quest for pure form. From an ecumenical perspective, for example, ancestral spirit attack might be viewed as just a way of speaking about repressed childhood memories or fantasies about malevolent aspects of parents. Or it might be argued, in the name of universalism, that although a queasiness about widows is not part of our public discourse, we, too, manage to isolate them socially and keep them out of sight. In other words, deep down, or viewed in a unitarian light, that faraway place that seemed so different is not so different after all.

Rejection of the third proposition is entailed by acceptance of the other three. This is the stance that underwrites the monotheistic proselytizing spirit of the nineteenth century and the familiar developmental contrasts drawn by Sir Edward Tylor (1958 [1871]) and Sir James Frazer (1890) between magic and science, primitive and modern, superstition and objectivity. . . .

One logical possibility remains: rejection of the fourth proposition. Any defensible anthropological relativism requires the rejection of that proposition and acceptance of the other three. Many of the essays explore that possibility.

Yet is it coherent to claim simultaneously that we are rationally justified in our conception of things (for example, that nature is indifferent to virtuous conduct; that Salman Rushdie should be free to publish unharmed) *and* that others are rationally justified in their conception of things (for example, that nature is just; that Salman Rushdie should be punished), and that this is so even though our conception of things and their conception of things are truly different, and inconsistently so?

The rub, as Rescher and many philosophers are fond of pointing out, is that we could not possibly know that others are rationally justified in their conception of things (proposition 3) if we could not make rational sense of their conception of things "by our lights."

In other words, if we can make rational sense of their conception of things, then their conception of things is not *that* different from ours, for it must make sense in terms that are understandable to us. It is *our* rationality that we explore when we confront *their* conception of things, for how else could we understand them, unless their meanings, beliefs, and modes of justification were in some sense available to us?

Does that mean that claims of genuine difference (proposition 2) must be denied? That would seem to depend on what we mean when we claim that the conceptions others have of things are different from our own.

One thing we just cannot mean is that the other is fundamentally alien to us (see Spiro 1990). Others are not fundamentally alien to us, just inconsistently and importantly different in their conception of things (as expressed in their texts, in their discourse, in their institutions, in their personalities) from our conception of things, at the moment.

Yet the conceptions held by others are available to us, in the sense that when we truly understand their conception of things we come to recognize possibilities latent within our own rationality, or existent in the history of our own reason, and those ways of conceiving of things become salient for us for the first time, or once again. . . .

The problem of rationality (or psychic unity) continues to be an issue in the interpretation of conceptual diversity. It has a distinguished religious and philosophical ancestry. The "problem" is really a gloss for an oft-diagnosed form of intellectual and spiritual uneasiness, which, judging from textual history, East and West, has been a vexation for our kind for a very long time. It is the tension between the claims of tradition for our allegiance versus the claims of our ego to autonomy from the limitations of our customary practice and belief. The philosophical source of the uneasiness is the demand of individual consciousness to be free from the influence of established things. The theological source is the idea that this worldly existence is some kind of negation of pure being.

The idea that existence is a negation of pure being can be traced in the West from Plato through Descartes to various contemporary "structuralisms," which aim to recover the abstract forms, universal grammar or pure being hidden beneath the "superficialities" of any particular person's mental functioning or any particular people's social life.

In the structural traditions the search for an autonomous being or pure consciousness typically proceeds in one of two ways. Descartes made famous a method of erasure (through radical doubt) whereby everything sensuous, subjective, embodied, temporary, local, or tradition-bound is viewed as prejudice, dogma, or illusion, and pure being is reserved for only those things in which an autonomous reason could have absolute confidence, namely, its self and deductive logic.

Others have made famous a method of subtraction, well known in the social sciences through the notions of "convergent validation," "interobserver reliability," and "data aggregation," whereby everything different about different ways of being in the world (or different ways of seeing the world) is treated as error, noise, or bias, and pure being is the abstraction of those common denominators that make people the same.

Yet "prejudice," "dogma," "illusion," "error," "noise," and "bias" are not the only locutions with which to possess or (as the structuralists would have it) dispossess a tradition, and our ability to recognize each other as pure beings does not necessarily arise out of what is left over after we subtract all our differences.

Anatole Broyard, the American writer and literary critic, once remarked, speaking in a very continental voice, that "paranoids are the only ones who notice things anymore." The essays in *Thinking through Cultures* are variations on that theme: that our prejudices make it possible for us to see; that traditions not only obscure but also illuminate; that our differences make us real; that while traditions are particularizing (who could *live* by ecumenism alone?), a peculiar existence can be a selective affirmation of pure being; that the freeing of consciousness goes hand in hand with feeling "astonished" by the variety of ways there are to see and to be. In other words, reason and objectivity are not in opposition to tradition, and they do not lift us out of custom and folk belief. Reason may lift us out of error, ignorance, and confusion. Yet error, ignorance, and confusion are not proper synonyms for tradition, custom, and folk belief. . . .

Romanticism stands out against the view that existence is the negation of pure being, by offering us its alternative, namely, the view that existence is the infusion of consciousness and pure spirit into the material world, thereby narrowing the distance or blurring the boundaries between nature, humanity, and the gods.

Romanticism shares with skeptical empiricism the view that the senses and logic alone cannot bridge that gap between existence and pure being. Left to their own devices, all that the senses and logic can see is a mindless nature, "fallen and dead." Transcendental things are beyond their scope. To make contact with the really real, the inspired (= divinelike) imagination of human beings must be projected out to reality; or, alternatively, the gods must descend to earth.

It is the doctrine of romanticism that existence is best appreciated (that is, understood *and* experienced) as a sensual manifestation of the transcendent, and that time and space, history and local variations in color (and culture), deserve to be examined inspirationally, imaginatively, and artfully for diverse signs of our divinity. . . .

Romanticism is routinely disparaged by its critics as mere "emotivism" or "nihilism" or "solipsism" or "paganism" or "perversity" (or, hard as it may be to believe, as "relativism," which is sometimes used as the code word for all of the above). What the critics fear most is that a rebellion in the name of romance against the subordination of existence to pure being will simply reverse the order of domination, leaving us with rhetoric instead of reason, art instead of reality, sentiment instead of calculation, difference without likeness, the idol without the god. What the critics fear most is a world in which the imagination is not inspired but simply intoxicated, a grotesque world in which the fanciful dominates the real, and subjectivity – worse yet, my special egocentric narcissistic sensibility arrogantly claiming to be divine – becomes the measure of all things. . . .

[T]he criticism misjudges the true project of romanticism. For the aim of romanticism is to revalue existence, not to denigrate pure being; to dignify subjective experience, not to deny reality; to appreciate the imagination, not to disregard reason; to honor our differences, not to underestimate our common humanity.

The negative intent behind the doctrine of romanticism is to expose the pretense that literal truth is artless. The positive intent is to develop theories about how realism – the experience of transcendent things as direct, transparent, or close at hand – is achieved artfully.

The practice of suttee is [so] astonishing, because it is so close to the divine. India is a high civilization. As an anthropologist you know you are working in a high civilization when, after you explain your informants' practices to them, they have their own stored-up accounts of what they are up to, and their explanations are often better, and almost always more imaginative, than your own. Alternatively, the locution "primitive" or "uncivilized" might be reserved for those peoples of the world, if there are any, who seem convinced that it is the examined life that is not worth living. Suttee is no "uncivilized" act. . . .

On September 4, 1987, Roop Kanwar, a beautiful eighteen-year-old, college-educated Rajput woman, received national press coverage in India when she immolated herself in front of a large supportive crowd, with her dead husband resting on her lap. Immediately the scene of the event became a popular pilgrimage site. The cremation ground was enshrined as a romantic memorial to an extraordinary act of devotion and as a place in a sacred geography, that could be pointed to as tangible evidence of the reality of the divine and the descent of the gods.

The country was divided in its response. Everyone agreed that no mortal being could voluntarily stay poised on a funeral pyre during immolation and experience no pain or fright. Critics of suttee argued that it therefore could not have happened as reported – Roop Kanwar must have been forced to the funeral pyre, where she must have been agitated and wanted to flee; or, if it did happen as reported, then it could not have been voluntary – Roop Kanwar must have been drugged or hysterical or crazy. Supporters of suttee argued that therefore Roop Kanwar was no mere mortal – she was infused with the spirit of a goddess or she was a goddess.

Both accounts suggest that at the time of immolation Roop Kanwar was, in some sense, "out of her mind" (the expression connotes both insanity and objectivity), but one account validates and dignifies her act, our world, and the events that go in it, while the other disparages them. For which world or counterworld should we speak? For they are different and inconsistently so.

Suttee is a rare and extraordinary act. Viewed as artful realism . . . suttee works, for those for whom it works, as a representation and confirmation through heroic action of some of the deepest properties of Hinduism's moral world. In that world existence is imbued with divinity. The gods have descended to earth. Since the world is imbued with divinity it is a just world, governed by laws of retributive causation and just retribution for past transgressions and sins. Since the world is a material world it is in transit, an impermanent place through which the divines circulate, at their own rate, in proportion to the limitations of their particular material incarnation and the quality of their moral careers.

Hindu moral doctrine has it that husbands and wives live in the world as gods and goddesses. She is the Laxmi of the house; he is her Narayan. As gods and goddesses their bonds to each other are transcendental and eternal. Yet they are incarnate. They are able to dance and eat and make love and transgress and sin; there is a place for the demonic in a romantic world. And they are able to die, which means that from time to time they must shed their vulnerable human form and be newly born again, male or female, as a lizard, as an owl, as a dog, as a human being. It is the price that must be paid for the romantic possibilities offered by embodiment.

In the Hindu moral world the death of a husband has more than material significance, and its metaphysical meanings run deep. Traditional widows in India spend the balance of their lives absolving themselves of sin (fasting, praying, withdrawing from the world, reading holy texts). In their world of retributive causation, widowhood is a punishment for past transgressions. The fact that your husband died first is a sign telling you that you must now undertake the task of unburdening yourself of guilt, for the sake of your next reincarnation on earth. In such a world the flame on your husband's funeral pyre is appreciated (understood and experienced) as though it was the romantic analogue of the last plane to Lisbon in the movie *Casablanca*. If you are not on the plane it is likely to be a very long time until you see him again, if ever. A shared cremation absolves sins and guarantees eternal union between husband and wife, linked to each other as god and goddess through the cycle of future rebirths.

For those who are in or on the edge of such an inventive world, the extraordinary act of suttee presents itself as an inspiring confirmation of all that metaphysical trafficking between heaven and earth, between humans and gods, between existence and pure being. Indeed, it is conceivable that Roop Kanwar herself understood and experienced her immolation as an astonishing moment when her body and its senses, profane things, became fully sacred, and hence invulnerable to pain, through an act of sacrifice by a goddess seeking eternal union with her god-man.

It is not impossible for us to imagine Roop Kanwar's conception of things. Nor is it difficult to recognize that that particular imaginative conception of things is inconsistently different from our own. The far more challenging issue is whether we can justify the conception of things that I have imagined for her. Can we justify it within the framework of our own rationality, which is the only framework for rationality that we have? Can we *rationally* reject proposition 4 above and endorse the other three? Can we successfully defend the idea (the rejection of proposition

4) that we are rationally justified in our conception of things and that Roop Kanwar is justified in her conception of things, too?

I think we can, and must; yet how we reject proposition 4 will depend, quite crucially, on the conception of reality to which we are committed. How we do it will depend on whether or not we believe that real things (concepts, propositions, gods, the really real) must exist independently of our involvement with them.

If we insist Platonically that the very idea of reality suggests something independent of any one of its particular material realizations as a "thing" in time and space, independent of our involvement with it, independent of our verification procedures, of our presuppositions and theories, of our purposes and interests, then to represent suttee as a rational practice we would have to invoke the notions of conditionalized universals and of time-dependent or space-dependent truths. We would have to say things such as "in India souls reincarnate; in the United States they don't." . . .

Yet the positing of time- and space-dependent truths on earth, and of conditionalized universals subsisting eternally in some Platonic heaven, is not the only way to reject proposition 4. One alternative is to insist on an epistemic conception of truth, reminiscent of the late-eighteenth-century romantic view that transcendent objects spring from the imagination and that there is a spiritual alliance between the mind and the world; they make each other up, as Hilary Putnam has put it (1987: 1). Putnam's basic idea is that "there are external facts," and we can *say what they are*. What we *cannot* say – because it makes no sense – is what the facts are *"independent of all conceptual choices"* (1987: 33).

That romantic conception of an interpenetration or interdependency of objectivity and subjectivity, of pure being and existence, has been variously expressed: as the idea that nothing in particular exists independently of our theoretical interpretation of it; as the idea that our measuring instruments are a part of the reality they measure; as the idea that the world is made up of "intentional" objects, such as "touchdowns" or "weeds" or "commitments" or "in-laws." Intentional objects have real causal force, but only by virtue of our mental representations of them and involvement with them. In all the foregoing Platonic (nonepistemic) and (anti-Platonic) epistemic conceptions of what is real, various apparently inconsistent conceptions of things can coexist because they never really meet head on. They are kept apart by contextualization, either by being made time and space dependent or dependent on our theories, verification techniques, and modes of justification, or by being embedded in some intentional world. They are not contradictions battling with each other in the same world. They are arguments in different worlds, whose "weak" (disconnected) inconsistency (Rescher 1988) just might lead us to appreciate those worlds of difference. When you live in the same world all disagreements are matters of error, igno-rance, or misunderstanding. When you live in different worlds there is far more to a disagreement than meets the eye.

Some may wish to argue that all conceptions of things, even totally inconsistent ones, must inhabit the same global mind; that such a global mind is latent within each of us, or "subsists" in some Platonic heaven; and that it is some shared right of access to that global mind that consti-tutes our common humanity. Those are not unappealing ideas, from which it would seem to follow that psychic unity is not what makes us the same (a universally subsisting global mind stocked with a multitude of disconnected ideas has no causal powers to create an existent psychic uniformity); psychic unity is simply that which makes us imaginable to one another.

If psychic unity is what makes us imaginable to one another, then per-haps the really real truth for us mortal beings is that we can never be everywhere at once (even in a global mind), any more than we can be nowhere in particular. As mere mortals or, if you prefer, as embodied gods, we are always somewhere in particular, giving partial expression to our pure being. Because we are limited in that way, the inconsistency between Roop Kanwar's view of suttee and Allan Bloom's (1987) (or a feminist's, for that matter) is not something we need to resolve; it is something we need to seek, so that through astonishment we may stay on the move between different worlds, and in that way become more complete.

Others may argue that *any* feeling of this-worldly limitation is a con-cession to Platonism, and they may be right. Yet that is a concession I am eager to make, for although existence is not the negation of pure being, any particular existence is partial. Of course if you are an "inno-cent" or a "primitive," convinced that it is the examined life that is not worth living, then you may not be aware that your life is incomplete. But that is precisely why a civilized penchant for transcendence, in the form of a romantic leap into other ways of being, ennobles the spirit and deserves to be in the nature of things.

References

Bloom, A. (1987) *The Closing of the American Mind*, New York: Simon & Schuster.

Clifford, J. (1988) *The Predicament of Culture*, Cambridge MA: Harvard University Press.

Clifford, J. and Marcus, G.E. (eds.) (1986) *Writing Culture*, Berkeley CA: University of California Press.

Frazer, J.G. (1890) *The Golden Bough: A Study in Magic and Religion*, London: Macmillan.

Geertz, C. (1988) *Works and Lives*, Stanford CA: Stanford University Press.

Putnam, H. (1987) *The Many Faces of Realism*, La Salle, IL: Open Court Publishing.

Rescher, N. (1988) *Rationality*, London: Oxford University Press.

Spiro, M.E. (1990) "On the Strange and Familiar in Recent Anthropological Thought," in J. Stigler, R. Shweder, and G. Herdt (eds.) *Cultural Psychology: Essays on Comparative Human Development*, New York: Cambridge University Press.

Tylor, E.B. (1958) [1871] *Primitive Culture*, New York: Harper Torchbooks.

HUMAN RIGHTS, HUMAN DIFFERENCE

Anthropology's contribution to an emancipatory cultural politics

Terence Turner

Human rights pose fundamental problems of both theory and practice for anthropology. The way these questions are dealt with will have important implications for the future of the discipline, both as a theoretical project and as a profession. In addition to the intrinsic theoretical and political importance of the issues they raise, the current surge of concern with human rights among anthropologists has been precipitated by changes in the way anthropology as a discipline relates to its subjects as well as by changes in the subjects themselves. The increased involvement of anthropologists with human rights issues clearly constitutes a cultural and historical phenomenon that calls for anthropological interpretation in its own right. The increasing commitment of the American Anthropological Association to an active role in supporting and protecting human rights has stimulated new theoretical reflection not only on the principles underlying "rights" but on the meaning of the adjective "human" as well. The field of human rights has thus become one in which activist practice has come, in important respects, to lead the development of theory.

The idea of human rights in its received Western formulations is an explicitly universal concept, which presupposes a universal notion of humanity capable of informing the adjective "human" with an operational meaning which can form the basis of "rights." This in turn implies

From Terence Turner, "Human Rights, Human Difference: Anthropology's Contribution to an Emancipatory Cultural Politics," *Journal of Anthropological Research* 53 (1997): 273–79, 285–88 and 290–91.

Terence Turner is Professor of Anthropology at Cornell University.

the existence of some general notion of justice, equity, or a general principle capable of serving as the grounds for specific rights or laws, applicable to all peoples and cultures. Any attempt to derive such a universal principle, with its implications for rights or social ethics, from anthropological knowledge raises the fundamental question of whether it is possible to derive moral or political principles from objective knowledge (to the extent that anthropological knowledge can be so characterized) and, if so, whether anthropological knowledge and theory are up to the job.

... I begin by raising some general anthropological questions concerning the concept of human rights, including the compatibility of universal human rights with cultural relativism. I follow this with ... an anthropological discussion of general features of culture and sociality that might be interpreted to imply principles of human right or rights and review some contributions of recent anthropological human rights activism to this theoretical question. In this latter connection, I refer specifically to the work of the Committee for Human Rights of the American Anthropological Association and its immediate predecessors, the AAA's Commission for Human Rights and the Task Force on Human Rights. As one of their principal charges, these bodies have had the formulation of a general statement on human rights in the light of anthropological knowledge and theory. A programmatic statement, intended both to clarify theoretical issues and to serve as a guide to policy and action on cases of human rights abuses by anthropologists, was completed in 1995 as the preamble to the guidelines for the permanent Committee for Human Rights established in October of that year by the Association (Commission for Human Rights 1995). The theoretical and practical issues with which the present article is concerned were exhaustively discussed in the preparation of this document. The ideas and opinions I set forth in this article were formed primarily through participation in these discussions, in which I took part as a member of all of these bodies.[1]

Are rights human?

The expression "human rights" can be understood to imply that being human automatically or intrinsically confers certain rights. It thus begs the question, from an anthropological point of view, of whether rights can legitimately be considered to be "human," in the sense of a universal attribute of humanity as such. It is not clear, however, in what sense this could be true. Rights are normally understood to consist of specific claims, enforceable against society in general or certain parts of it (e.g., private individuals, institutions, or the state) by persons, corporations, or groups. Such claims may be of various specific kinds: for the ability to exercise certain powers or capacities, to use or have access to certain resources or benefits, to be protected from certain forms of abuse, or to be compensated for damages. The ability to make such claims is often assumed to imply or presuppose the existence of some institutional means of enforcing them, binding on the society that recognizes the rights in question (normally the state or some mechanism such as the feud in stateless societies). The question thus arises of how a universal, homogeneous condition (humanity, if indeed it can be understood as such) can be taken to imply such specific, particular claims as "rights," dependent as they are on such specific, nonuniversal social institutions as states?

For anthropologists, in short, most existing legal and political formulations of human rights seem problematical because of their empirically unexamined and theoretically unproblematized use of the term "human." In the Western tradition (the cultural tradition that has produced the conceptions of rights that form the basis of contemporary human rights discourse), the human is typically conceived as a property of the individual, meaning a social actor inhabiting an individual body. Anthropologists, however, have learned not to regard either social actors or social bodies as unproblematically "individual" in the common Western sense of the term. They have also come to recognize the fundamental role of social relations and groups in producing "human" (i.e., socially integrated and enculturated) individuals. Like many non-Western cultures, anthropology has consequently tended to emphasize the role of collective domains like "culture" or "society" in the construction of individual and collective persons, and thus of humanness. However, the implications of these theoretical perspectives on the nature of the human for notions of human rights – including the vexed question of "collective rights" – remain unclear. Clearly, the precultural, psychobiological constitution of human beings as individuals cannot be interpreted to confer anything as socially and culturally constituted as a "right"; but is there any common aspect of the social and cultural constitution of human beings that can be identified as implying, if not conferring, rights in this sense? The answer to this question, I believe, is "Yes," as I shall try to explain later in this article. First, however, certain related issues must be clarified.

Is a universal principle of right incompatible with cultural relativism?

In confronting this question, anthropologists have to deal with the various forms of cultural relativism that have arisen within their own discipline. Some forms of cultural relativism are overtly incompatible with the idea of universal principles of justice, equity, or rights, but others are consistent with such a notion.

For many anthropologists, of course, "cultural relativism" is not a fully developed theoretical position but, rather, a commitment to suspending moral judgment until an attempt can be made to understand another culture's beliefs and practices in their full cultural, material, and historical contexts. Elvin Hatch, in a perceptive critique of an earlier draft of the present article (see also Hatch 1997) called this sort of nonjudgmental relativist approach the "default mode" of social and political thought and emphasized the political value of the commitment to pluralistic openness it implies as an antidote to the narrow judgmentalism of the conservative and religious right. Davydd Greenwood, in another incisive commentary on the same earlier draft, similarly suggested that cultural relativism should be conceived in this way more as a method than a theory. These points are well taken, but they do not gainsay the need for a theoretically grounded transcultural principle of justice or equity capable of serving as a basis for human rights, nor do they clarify the relation between such a universal criterion and the modest form of cultural relativism they advocate. Such a "default" approach to cultural or ethical relativism only underlines the need for a transcultural criterion, because in itself it gives no guidance for dealing with cases which still appear to constitute violations of elementary justice or human rights even after the acts, practices, or beliefs involved have been analyzed and understood in their cultural context.

There is no question that rights come in a great variety of forms and contents in different societies and cultures. At one extreme of this continuum of variation, some simple stateless societies clearly lack notions of specific "rights," in the sense of specific claims upon, or against, other members of the society or society as a whole, or differentiated social mechanisms for enforcing them. This is one reason why inductive efforts to discover a universal cross-cultural core principle or principles of human rights through a comparative survey of specific rights recognized by all the world's cultures, as advocated for instance by Renteln (1985, 1990), seem unlikely to succeed. Specific rights claims, however, are implicitly (and in many cases explicitly) based on more general principles of fairness, rightness, justice, or equity. It is possible that such general principles might turn out to be shared by cultures and societies with dissimilar rights or even no conception of rights in the strict sense at all. Differing cultural formulations of rights might conceivably be understood as extrapolations under different contextual conditions of such common, transcultural principles of right, equity, or justice. These in turn might be interpreted as arising from some generic aspect or aspects of being human; that is, in the anthropological sense, of becoming enculturated as a member of a particular society and integrated into its system of social relations.

Even if a universal criterion of justice or right could be established by

116

such an empirical survey, this would still not answer the crucial question of the cause of its universality: in other words, what aspect of human species-being makes the principle in question a universal basis of human rights? To answer this question, however, would necessarily involve going beyond cultural relativism in its strong form as a claim that there are no cross-cultural universals. A universal principle of right or justice, grounded in some general attribute of humanness, would become a critical principle, applicable as a standard of moral and political evaluation to all specific cultural formulations of rights. It would in principle also be applicable to cultures lacking any specific forms of rights, in either of two senses: firstly, as a reason for defending the rights of such societies against abuses by other societies or states and, secondly, as a justification for the protection of individuals or groups within a society, even if that society failed to recognize the relevant forms of rights.

Rights are not merely cultural concepts; they are also normative constructs that implicitly or explicitly apply more general moral and jural-political principles to social relations that demand their application in practice by social actors in appropriate contexts. They are, as such, dual constructs, combining general moral and jural principles and specific normative formulations that point beyond the sphere of cultural constructs to that of material social action. This pragmatic aspect of rights may be bracketed and ignored by an anthropological observer interested only in cultural conceptions of rights, but it is unavoidable by an anthropological activist seeking to put rights, or the principles on which they are based, into practice. In this crucial respect, human rights activism drives the development of a more pragmatically grounded anthropological theory of rights.

The problems of judgment and appropriate action remain after the best possible efforts at culturally contextualized, ethically relativist understanding have been made. It may also be suggested that if anthropologically principled grounds for defending the rights of disprivileged or marginalized persons and groups can be articulated, they would provide a stronger basis for defending the human and pragmatic cultural relativist approach advocated by Hatch and Greenwood against right-wing assaults on cultural and social diversity than the humble if practical defense of that approach as a "default method." What is really at issue here is whether anthropologists still believe in the possibility of discovering universal attributes or principles of human species-being that are specific enough to have definite implications for issues like human rights but are nonetheless flexible enough to make due allowance for cultural variation (this is perhaps a more delicate way of asking whether they still believe in anthropology as a discipline committed to discovering what it is to be human).

If anthropological analysis or interpretation can give substantive meaning to the generic fact of being human, then there is no logical reason why this could not be employed as a critical standard in investigating whether the practices and beliefs of particular cultures prevent the realization of such generic aspects of humanness by some of their members (or nonmembers). Such a transcultural critical principle would clearly be incompatible with subjective idealist forms of cultural relativism that hold that the conscious meanings and values of cultural forms for the members of a culture are the only legitimate standard by which the social conduct of its members can be judged. This position leads to the familiar argument that since culture X or society Y lacks any explicit concept of rights, or any notion of common humanity extending to people of different race or ethnicity, it is a violation of their cultural integrity to judge their beliefs or practices toward one another or others by reference to a universal cross-cultural standard. This was the position of Herskovits, in the statement he authored on behalf of the AAA explaining the Association's opposition to the United Nations Universal Declaration of Human Rights in 1947 (American Anthropological Association Executive Board 1947: 539–43). It is noteworthy that Herskovits framed the issue exclusively in terms of the illegitimacy of imposing *Western* values on other cultures, not the application of a transcultural standard on all cultures (although it is reasonably clear that he did not accept the possibility of such a culture-free critical standard).

Relativistic arguments of the Herskovitsian sort, however, fail to deal with the common humanity or species-being of all people, as members of all cultures. Given that all cultures are products of beings of the same (human) species, culture in an abstract sense can be considered a generic attribute of the species as a whole. At this abstract level, it seems reasonable, if currently unfashionable, to posit the existence of universal features of humanness and thus of culture. This in turn opens up the possibility, at least as far as logic is concerned, of universal principles of justice, equity, or reciprocity as constituents of all cultures. There is, after all, no logical incompatibility between a pragmatic cultural relativism, understood as a method of understanding how the specific content of social practices or cultural forms has been conditioned by their relations to their cultural, social and historical context, and universal or transcultural principles considered as constituents of the human capacity for culture.

The mere existence of cultural differences does not logically preclude the possibility of cultural universals, any more than the specific differences among languages preclude the possibility of universal features of language. Discussions of the compatibility of cultural relativism with empirical or theoretical cultural universals should start from the recognition that cultural relativism is itself, paradoxically, a universal claim about the nature of culture in general that presupposes the proposition that all "cultures" are entities of the same type. It is only this implicit assumption that endows cultural differences with the significance they hold for the relativist (otherwise relativism would be reduced to the absurd insistence that cultural differences are merely dissimilarities between different kinds of things, which would make pointing to them both tautological and trivial).

That cultures differ in specific ways thus does not in itself contravene, but rather logically presupposes, the possibility that universal properties or principles of culture might exist at a more general level. The relativist argument that to be human is to be enculturated in a specific culture and social system, different in many respects from all others, does not gainsay that the processes through which people produce their societies and themselves in all their cultural uniqueness might themselves share common features. Processes of social and cultural production and reproduction, rather than cultural traits, values, or norms abstracted from the social processes in which they are produced and used, might thus be considered as the matrix of general attributes of human species-being. "Universal" attributes conceived in this way would be quite compatible with a pragmatic cultural relativism that understands specific cultural differences as the products of activities that mediate universal human capacities to contextually varying circumstances. Such universal capacities might in turn be interpreted as grounds of universal principles of justice, equity, or reciprocity and thus also of jural formulations of rights where they exist. Cultural variation, in sum, is the result of processes that may themselves have universal properties.

At the same time, it is equally true that no such universal human qualities or capacities can be realized in the abstract, but only through the production of specific social and cultural differences. This fundamental anthropological point, however, has only gradually been related to the concept of human rights.

[. . .]

Human rights and human difference: an anthropological principle of right

Largely as a result of the practical experience of the members of the Committee for Human Rights of the AAA, as activists dealing with abuses of the rights of indigenous peoples and other cultural minorities, the issue of difference assumed a central place in the Committee's Draft Declaration on Human Rights. This formulation was intended as a working definition that could provide a basis for action by the Association on cases of human rights violations. The key passage from the Committee's statement on guidelines for action on human rights issues, to which I referred earlier, runs as follows:

> Anthropology as an academic discipline studies the bases and the forms of human diversity and human unity; anthropology as a practice seeks to apply this knowledge to the solution of human problems. As a professional organization of anthropologists, the AAA has long been, and should continue to be, concerned whenever *human difference* is made the basis for a denial of rights – where "human" is understood in its full range of cultural, social, linguistic and biological senses.
>
> (Commission for Human Rights 1995; passage published in Commission for Human Rights 1993; emphasis added)

In the terms of the document, "human difference" is a criterion of human rights because it comprises the concrete specificity of what humans, individually and collectively, have made of themselves, evolutionarily, socially, and culturally. As used in the text, "difference" refers to specific cultural, social, linguistic, or biological features, which are contrasted, as variable and contingent products, to the universal human capacities that enabled their production: in the familiar anthropological phrase, the human "capacity for culture." The "capacity for culture" is essentially the power to produce social existence and thus to determine its meaning and social form. "Difference," as a principle of human rights, denotes the products of the realization of this power. It is thus essentially a principle of empowerment.

"Difference" appears in the statement as a more general criterion than "rights." The latter, while not directly defined, are treated by implication as relatively more specific claims. While difference is explicitly cited in the statement only as an invalid basis for denying rights, rather than a positive principle of right in itself, the implication is that the right to difference may constitute a positive, transcultural basis of human rights. The statement does not specify or imply that the general human capacity for culture, defined as the power to produce culturally significant difference (i.e., to be or make oneself different in some socially significant cultural, social, linguistic, or physical respect), is vested exclusively either in individuals or social groups. Rather, the implication is that it inheres in both. The criterion of difference as formulated in the statement thus implicitly provides a positive conceptual basis for the recognition of the rights of individuals *and* collectivities to realize their mutual potential to produce or realize themselves as meaningfully distinct ("different") beings.

Also implicit in the criterion of "human difference" as a fundamental human right (and explicit in the preceding paragraphs of the statement) is that it is equally present among all human groups and individuals. It is thus inconsistent with claims by any individual or group to have the right to be able to realize its identity or values at the expense of other, different groups or individuals or to prevent their realization of themselves in ways different from its own. It certainly gives no license for the suppression of cultural differences between communal groups or individuals by a state government acting in the name of a supposed collective "right to development," as certain regimes have recently argued. Instead, it provides a positive conceptual basis for the promotion of the rights of individuals *and* collectivities to be able to realize their potential for mutual self-production. At the same time, the criterion of difference is open-ended: it implies that people have a right not only to the different identities they have produced for themselves in the past, but also to those they might produce in the future. It points, as such, not to a concept of culture in terms of inert and historical structures composed of essentialized traits or canons, but to the active historical process of creating cultural (and social and linguistic) meanings, identities, and forms.

As far as the authors of the Guidelines of the Committee for Human Rights of the AAA were concerned, the criterion of difference emerged from the need for a common principle or general rule of thumb to guide action on the cases that were constantly being brought to the Committee and encountered by anthropologists in the field. In contrast to the Enlightenment liberal standard of universal human nature conceived as embodied in self-existing, presocial individuals, the Committee's formulation in terms of human difference is a context-sensitive principle, grounded in pragmatic contexts of contrastive social identity and practice. It equally emphasizes the collective and individual dimensions of "humanness." Collective differences, in other words, are considered to be equally as "human" as individual differences, and all individual rights are considered to imply a collective dimension. At the same time, the criterion of human difference as adopted by the Committee attempts to combine a universal principle with a cultural relativist recognition of the fundamental importance of cultural, social, and individual difference.

Difference, rights, and conflict: principles, politics, and pluralism

To say that people have a right to their differences (as the AAA statement does) does not, on the other hand, imply that they have a right to impose them on one another or to force others to accommodate their different values and social practices at the expense of realizing their own. Nor does it imply that the equal realization by everyone of their different values, social forms, and identities should result in an euharmonic society free of conflicting rights claims by different parties. On the contrary, conflict over rights is to be expected as a by-product of social relations of cooperation and competition among parties to social situations in which each acts to achieve differing needs and values, on the basis of different capacities. In this perspective, the criterion of human difference implies a reconception of the role of social practices and institutions, such as the state, as mediators, arbiters, and regulators of multiple, divergent, and potentially conflicting cultural identities. Advocacy and defense of human rights thus carries over into the complex struggle for pluralist civility, with its intrinsically political corollaries of accommodation and compromise, after the battles for fundamental rights have been fought and won. The defense of the right to difference thus points toward the essential continuity of rights advocacy and political struggles for empowerment, liberation, and civility. The ultimate futility of the attempt to isolate human rights from political issues implies that the human rights movement, and above all anthropologists as human rights theorists and activists, must assume a more broadly political conception of their task. Here my argument reconverges with Kothari's critique:

> Involvement in a politics of transformation on the one hand and a politics of conserving ecologies, cultures and life-styles on the other – alongside preserving the dignity and values associated with the feminine gender and ethnicity – must of necessity become the concern of a broadly defined human rights movement.
>
> (Kothari 1991: 23)

Note

1 Elvin Hatch, as discussant of this paper at the 1995 AAA Invited Session in which it was presented, made several valuable criticisms that I have tried to take into account in the much changed present version. Davydd Greenwood also wrote a challenging and perceptive critique that led me to rethink and reformulate several of my main points. The readers of the draft for the *JAR* made numerous thoughtful criticisms which resulted in major changes. . . .

References

American Anthropological Association Executive Board (AAA) (1947) "Statement on Human Rights" (submitted to the United Nations Commission on Human Rights). *American Anthropologist* (n.s.) 49 (4): 539–43.
Commission for Human Rights of the American Anthropological Association (1993) "Report of the American Anthropological Association Commission for Human Rights." *Anthropology Newsletter* 34: 1, 5.
——(1995) *Guidelines for a Permanent Committee for Human Rights within the American Anthropological Association.*
Hatch, E. (1997) "The Good Side of Relativism." *Journal of Anthropological Research* 53: 371–81.

Kothari, R. (1991) "Human Rights: A Movement in Search of a Theory." In S. Kothari and H. Sethi (eds) *Rethinking Human Rights: Challenges for Theory and Action*. Delhi: Lokayan.

Renteln, A.D. (1985) "The Unanswered Challenge of Relativism and the Consequences for Human Rights." *Human Rights Quarterly* 7(4): 514–40.

——(1990) *International Human Rights: Universalism versus Relativism*. Newbury Park, CA: Sage.

Part III

CHALLENGES TO MORAL OBJECTIVITY

9

THE ARGUMENT FROM RELATIVITY

J.L. Mackie

The argument from relativity has as its premise the well-known variation in moral codes from one society to another and from one period to another, and also the differences in moral beliefs between different groups and classes within a complex community. Such variation is in itself merely a truth of descriptive morality, a fact of anthropology which entails neither first-order nor second-order ethical views.[1] Yet it may indirectly support second-order subjectivism: radical differences between first-order moral judgements make it difficult to treat those judgements as apprehensions of objective truths. But it is not the mere occurrence of disagreements that tells against the objectivity of values. Disagreement on questions in history or biology or cosmology does not show that there are no objective issues in these fields for investigators to disagree about. But such scientific disagreement results from speculative inferences or explanatory hypotheses based on inadequate evidence, and it is hardly plausible to interpret moral disagreement in the same way. Disagreement about moral codes seems to reflect people's adherence to and participation in different ways of life. The causal connection seems to be mainly that way round: it is that people approve of monogamy because they participate in a monogamous way of life rather than that they participate in a monogamous way of life because they approve of monogamy. Of course, the standards may be an idealization of the way of life from which they arise: the monogamy in which people participate may be less complete, less rigid, than that of which it leads them to approve. This is not to say that moral judgements are purely conventional. Of course there have been and are moral heretics and moral

From J.L. Mackie, *Ethics: Inventing Right and Wrong*, London: Penguin Books, 1977, pp. 36–38.

J.L. Mackie was a Fellow of University College, Oxford.

reformers, people who have turned against the established rules and practices of their own communities for moral reasons, and often for moral reasons that we would endorse. But this can usually be understood as the extension, in ways which, though new and unconventional, seemed to them to be required for consistency, of rules to which they already adhered as arising out of an existing way of life. In short, the argument from relativity has some force simply because the actual variations in the moral codes are more readily explained by the hypothesis that they reflect ways of life than by the hypothesis that they express perceptions, most of them seriously inadequate and badly distorted, of objective values.

But there is a well-known counter to this argument from relativity, namely to say that the items for which objective validity is in the first place to be claimed are not specific moral rules or codes but very general basic principles which are recognized at least implicitly to some extent in all society – such principles as provide the foundations of what Sidgwick has called different methods of ethics: the principle of universalizability, perhaps, or the rule that one ought to conform to the specific rules of any way of life in which one takes part, from which one profits, and on which one relies, or some utilitarian principle of doing what tends, or seems likely, to promote the general happiness. It is easy to show that such general principles, married with differing concrete circumstances, different existing social patterns or different preferences, will beget different specific moral rules; and there is some plausibility in the claim that the specific rules thus generated will vary from community to community or from group to group in close agreement with the actual variations in accepted codes.

The argument from relativity can be only partly countered in this way. To take this line the moral objectivist has to say that it is only in these principles that the objective moral character attaches immediately to its descriptively specified ground or subject: other moral judgements are objectively valid or true, but only derivatively and contingently – if things had been otherwise, quite different sorts of actions would have been right. And despite the prominence in recent philosophical ethics of universalization, utilitarian principles, and the like, these are very far from constituting the whole of what is actually affirmed as basic in ordinary moral thought. Much of this is concerned rather with what Hare calls "ideals", or, less kindly, "fanaticism". That is, people judge that some things are good or right, and others are bad or wrong, not because – or at any rate not only because – they exemplify some general principle for which widespread implicit acceptance could be claimed, but because something about those things arouses certain responses immediately in them, though they would arouse radically and irresolvably different responses in others. "Moral sense" or "intuition" is an initially more plausible description of what supplies many of our basic moral judgements than "reason". With regard to all these starting points of moral thinking the argument from relativity remains in full force.

Note

1 A first-order moral view is a view that something is right or wrong, good or bad, etc.; a second-order moral view is a view about the nature and status of the values expressed in first-order views (for example, subjectivism or objectivism) – CWG.

10

KNOWLEDGE, SCIENCE, CONVERGENCE

Bernard Williams

Very often discussions of objectivity come into moral philosophy from an interest in comparing ethical beliefs with knowledge and claims to truth of other kinds, for instance with scientific beliefs. Here a conception of objectivity is naturally associated with such questions as what can make ethical beliefs true, and whether there is any ethical knowledge. It is in this field of comparisons that various distinctions between fact and value are located.

Discussions of objectivity often start from considerations about disagreement. This makes it seem as if disagreement were surprising, but there is no reason why that should be so (the earliest thinkers in the Western tradition found conflict at least as obvious a feature of the world as concord). The interest in disagreement comes about, rather, because neither agreement nor disagreement is universal. It is not that disagreement needs explanation and agreement does not, but that in different contexts disagreement requires different sorts of explanation, and so does agreement. . . .

I believe that in relation to ethics there is a genuine and profound difference to be found, and also – it is a further point – that the difference is enough to motivate some version of the feeling (itself recurrent, if not exactly traditional) that science has some chance of being more or less what it seems, a systematized theoretical account of how the world really is, while ethical thought has no chance of being everything it seems. The

From Bernard Williams, *Ethics and the Limits of Philosophy*, Cambridge MA: Harvard University Press, 1985, pp. 132–36, 140–43, 145–55, 217–19. The text is substantially abridged by CWG, with slight addition by Bernard Williams.

Bernard Williams is Deutsch Professor of Philosophy at the University of California, Berkeley and a Fellow of All Souls College, Oxford.

tradition is right, moreover, not only in thinking that there is such a distinction, but also in thinking that we can come to understand what it is through understanding disagreement. However, it is not a question of how much disagreement there is, or even of what methods we have to settle disagreement, though that of course provides many relevant considerations. The basic difference lies rather in our reflective understanding of the best hopes we could coherently entertain for eliminating disagreement in the two areas. It is a matter of what, under the most favorable conditions, would be the best explanation of the end of disagreement: the explanation – as I shall say from now on – of convergence. . . .

The basic idea behind the distinction between the scientific and the ethical, expressed in terms of convergence, is very simple. In a scientific inquiry there should ideally be convergence on an answer, where the best explanation of the convergence involves the idea that the answer represents how things are; in the area of the ethical, at least at a high level of generality, there is no such coherent hope. The distinction does not turn on any difference in whether convergence will actually occur, and it is important that this is not what the argument is about. It might well turn out that there will be convergence in ethical outlook, at least among human beings. The point of the contrast is that, even if this happens, it will not be correct to think it has come about because convergence has been guided by how things actually are, whereas convergence in the sciences might be explained in that way if it does happen. This means, among other things, that we understand differently in the two cases the existence of convergence or, alternatively, its failure to come about. . . .

One line of objection urges that the idea of "converging on how things are" is available, to some adequate degree, in the ethical case as well [as the scientific]. The place where this is to be seen is above all with the substantive or thick ethical concepts. Many exotic examples of these can be drawn from other cultures, but there are enough left in our own: *coward, lie, brutality, gratitude*, and so forth. They are characteristically related to reasons for action. If a concept of this kind applies, this often provides someone with a reason for action, though that reason need not be a decisive one and may be outweighed by other reasons. Of course, exactly what reason for action is provided, and to whom, depends on the situation, in ways that may well be governed by this and by other ethical concepts, but some general connection with action is clear enough. We may say, summarily, that such concepts are "action-guiding."

At the same time, their application is guided by the world. A concept of this sort may be rightly or wrongly applied, and people who have acquired it can agree that it applies or fails to apply to some new situation. In many cases the agreement will be spontaneous, while in other cases there is room for judgment and comparison. Some disagreement at the margin may be irresoluble, but this does not mean that the use of the concept is not controlled by the facts or by the users' perception of the world. (As with other concepts that are not totally precise, marginal disagreements can indeed help to show how their use *is* controlled by the facts.) We can say, then, that the application of these concepts is at the same time world-guided and action-guiding. How can it be both at once?

The prescriptivist account gives a very simple answer to this question. Any such concept, on that account, can be analyzed into a descriptive and a prescriptive element: it is guided round the world by its descriptive content, but has a prescriptive flag attached to it. It is the first feature that allows it to be world-guided, while the second makes it action-guiding. . . . Prescriptivism claims that what governs the application of the concept to the world is the descriptive element and that the evaluative interest of the concept plays no part in this. All the input into its use is descriptive, just as all the evaluative aspect is output. It follows that, for any concept of this sort, you could produce another that picked out just the same features of the world but worked simply as a descriptive concept, lacking any prescriptive or evaluative force.

Against this, critics have made the effective point that there is no reason to believe that a descriptive equivalent will necessarily be available.[1] How we "go on" from one application of a concept to another is a function of the kind of interest that the concept represents, and we should not assume that we could see how people "go on" if we did not share the evaluative perspective in which this kind of concept has its point. An insightful observer can indeed come to understand and anticipate the use of the concept without actually sharing the values of the people who use it. But in imaginatively anticipating the use of the concept, the observer also has to grasp imaginatively its evaluative point. He cannot stand quite outside the evaluative interests of the community he is observing, and pick up the concept simply as a device for dividing up in a rather strange way certain neutral features of the world. . . .

This possibility, of the insightful but not totally identified observer, bears on an important question, whether those who properly apply ethical concepts of this kind can be said to have ethical knowledge.

Let us assume, artificially, that we are dealing with a society that is maximally homogeneous and minimally given to general reflection; its members simply, all of them, use certain ethical concepts of this sort. (We may call it the "hypertraditional" society.) What would be involved in their having ethical knowledge? According to the best available accounts of propositional knowledge,[2] they would have to believe the judgments they made; those judgments would have to be true; and their judgments would have to satisfy a further condition that the first two conditions must be nonaccidentally linked: granted the way that the people have gone about their inquiries, it must be no accident that the belief they have acquired is a true one, and if the truth on the subject had been otherwise, they would have acquired a different belief, true in those different circumstances. Thus I may know, by looking at it, that the die has come up 6, and this roughly involves the claim that if it had come up 4, I would have come to believe, by looking at it, that it had come up 4 (the alternative situations to be considered have to be restricted to those moderately like the actual one). Taking a phrase from Robert Nozick, we can say that the third requirement – it involves a good deal more elaboration than I have suggested – is that one's belief should "track the truth."

The members of the hypertraditional society apply their thick concepts, and in doing so they make various judgments. If any of those judgments can ever properly be said to be true, then their beliefs can track the truth, since they can withdraw judgments if the circumstances turn out not to be what was supposed, can make an alternative judgment if it would be more appropriate, and so on. They have, each, mastered these concepts, and they can perceive the personal and social happenings to which the concepts apply. If there is truth here, their beliefs can track it. The question left is whether any of these judgments can be true.

An objection can be made to saying that they are. If they are true, the observer can correctly say that they are; letting F stand in for one of their concepts, he can say, "The headman's statement, 'The boy is F,' is true." Then he should be able to say, in his own person, "the boy is F." But he is not prepared to do that, since F is not one of his concepts.

How strong is this objection? It relies on the following principle: A cannot correctly say that B speaks truly in uttering S unless A could also say something tantamount to S. This may seem to follow from a basic principle about truth, the *disquotation principle*,[3] to the effect that P is true if and only if P. But that principle cannot be applied so simply in deciding what can be said about other people's statements. Someone investigating another society might come to understand, for instance, that some terms in the language could be used only by women, or by people of a certain social position. He could understand that some of their statements were true, but not make them himself, since he did not satisfy the conditions.

We can see the case of the ethical concept as only a deeper example of the same thing. In both cases, there is a condition that has to be satisfied if one is to speak in a certain way, a condition satisfied by the locals and not by the observer, and in both cases it is a matter of belonging to a certain culture. When we compare those cases with each other, and both of them with the situation in which vocabulary is affected by the speaker's gender, we can understand why the observer is barred from saying just what the locals say, and we can also see that he is not barred from recognizing that what they say can be true. The disquotation principle, then, does not lead to the conclusion that the locals' statements, involving their thick ethical concepts, cannot be true.

There is another argument for the conclusion that the locals' statements may not be true. This claims that they may be false: not because they can be mistaken in ways that the locals themselves could recognize, but because an entire segment of the local discourse may be seen from outside as involving a mistake. This possibility has been much discussed by theorists. Social anthropologists have asked whether ritual and magical conceptions should be seen as mistaken in our terms, or rather as operating at a different level, not commensurable with our scientific ideas. Whatever may be said more generally, it is hard to deny that magic, at least, is a causal conception, with implications that overlap with scientific conceptions of causality.[4] To the extent this is so, magical conceptions can be seen from the outside as false, and then no one will have known to be true any statement claiming magical influence, even though he may have correctly used all the local criteria for claiming a given piece of magical influence. The local criteria do not reach to everything that is involved in such claims. In cases of this sort, the problem with conceding truth to the locals' statements is . . . that their statements may imply notions similar enough to some of [the observer's] for him to deny what they assert.

We may see the local ethical statements in a way that raises this difficulty. On this reading, the locals' statements imply something that can be put in the observer's terms and is rejected by him: that it is *right*, or *all right*, to do things he thinks it is not right, or all right, to do. Prescriptivism sees things in this way. The local statements entail, together with their descriptive content, an all-purpose *ought*. . . .

Of course, there is a minimal sense in which the locals think it "all right" to act as they do, and they do not merely imply this, but reveal it, in the way they live. To say that they "think it all right" at this level is not to mention any further and disputable judgment of theirs; it is merely to record their practice. Must we agree that there is a judgment, to be expressed by using some universal moral notion, which they accept and the observer may very well reject?

I do not think we have to accept this idea. . . . The basic question is how we are to understand the relations between practice and reflection. The very general kind of judgment that is in question here – a judgment using a very general concept – is essentially a product of reflection, and it comes into question when someone stands back from the practices of the society and its use of these concepts and asks whether this is the right way to go on, whether these are good ways in which to assess actions, whether the kinds of character that are admired are rightly admired. In many traditional societies themselves there is some degree of reflective questioning and criticism, and this is an important fact. It is for the sake of the argument, to separate the issues, that I have been using the idea of the hypertraditional society where there is no reflection.

In relation to this society, the question now is: Does the practice of the society, in particular the judgments that members of the society make, imply answers to reflective questions about that practice, questions they have never raised? . . .

There are two different ways in which we can see the activities of the hypertraditional society. They depend on different models of ethical practice. One of them may be called an "objectivist" model. According to this, we shall see the members of the society as trying, in their local way, to find out the truth about values, an activity in which we and other human beings, and perhaps creatures who are not human beings, are all engaged. We shall then see their judgments as having these general implications, rather as we see primitive statements about the stars as having implications that can be contradicted by more sophisticated statements about the stars. On the other model we shall see their judgments as part of their way of living, a cultural artifact they have come to inhabit (though they have not consciously built it). On this, nonobjectivist, model, we shall take a different view of the relations between that practice and critical reflection. We shall not be disposed to see the level of reflection as implicitly already there, and we shall not want to say that their judgments have, just as they stand, these implications.

The choice between these two different ways of looking at their activities will determine whether we say that the people in the hypertraditional society have ethical knowledge. It is important to be quite clear what ethical knowledge is in question. It is knowledge involved in their making judgments in which they use their thick concepts. We are not considering whether they display knowledge *in using those concepts rather than some others*: this would be an issue at the reflective level. The question "Does the society possess ethical knowledge?" is seriously ambiguous in that way. The collective reference to the society invites us to take the perspective in which its ethical representations are compared with other societies' ethical representations, and this is the reflective level, at which they certainly do not possess knowledge. There is another sense of the question in which it asks whether members of the society could, in exercising their concepts, express knowledge about the world to which they apply them, and the answer to that might be yes.

The interesting result of this discussion is that the answer will be yes if we take the nonobjectivist view of their ethical activities: various members of the society will have knowledge, when they deploy their concepts carefully, use the appropriate criteria, and so on. But on the objectivist view they do not have knowledge, or at least it is most unlikely that they do, since their judgments have extensive implications, which they have never considered, at a reflective level, and we have every reason to believe that, when those implications are considered, the traditional use of ethical concepts will be seriously affected.

The objectivist view, while it denies knowledge to the unreflective society, may seem to promise knowledge at the reflective level. Characteristically, it expects the demands of knowledge to be satisfied only by reflection. No doubt there are some ethical beliefs, universally held and usually vague ("one has to have a special reason to kill someone"), that we can be sure will survive at the reflective level. But they fall far short of any adequate, still less systematic, body of ethical knowledge at that level, and I think that, at least as things are, no such body of knowledge exists. Later I shall suggest that, so far as propositional knowledge of ethical truths is concerned, this is not simply a matter of how things are. Rather, at a high level of reflective generality there could be no ethical knowledge of this sort – or, at most, just one piece.

If we accept that there can be knowledge at the hypertraditional or unreflective level; if we accept the obvious truth that reflection characteristically disturbs, unseats, or replaces those traditional concepts; and if we agree that, at least as things are, the reflective level is not in a position to give us knowledge we did not have before – then we reach the notably un-Socratic conclusion that, in ethics, *reflection can destroy knowledge*. . . .

Some think of the knowledge given by applying ethical concepts as something like perception. But there is a vital asymmetry between the case of the ethical concepts and the perspectival experience of secondary qualities such as colors. This asymmetry shows, moreover, that the distinction between the scientific and the ethical has wider implications. . . .

The main difference is that, in the case of secondary qualities, what explains also justifies; in the ethical case, this is not so. The psychological capacities that underly our perceiving the world in terms of certain secondary qualities have evolved so that the physical world will present itself to us in reliable and useful ways. Coming to know that these qualities constitute our form of perceptual engagement with the world, and that this mode of presentation works in a certain way, will not unsettle the system. In the ethical case, we have an analogy to the perceptual just to this extent, that there is local convergence under these concepts: the judgments of those who use them are indeed, as I put it before, world-guided. This is certainly enough to refute the simplest oppositions of fact and value. But if it is to mean anything for a wider objectivity, everything depends on what is to be said *next*. With secondary qualities, it is the explanation of the perspectival perceptions that enables us, when we come to reflect on them, to place them in relation to the perceptions of other people and other creatures; and that leaves everything more or less where it was, so far as our perceptual judgments are concerned. The question is whether we can find an ethical analogy to that. Here we have to go outside local judgments to a reflective or second-order account of them, and here the analogy gives out.

There is, first, a problem of what the second-order account is to be. An *explanation* of those local judgments and of the conceptual differences between societies will presumably have to come from the social sciences: cultural differences are in question. Perhaps no existing explanation of such things goes very deep, and we are not too clear how deep an explanation might go. But we do know that it will not look much like the explanation of color perception. The capacities it will invoke are those involved in finding our way around in a social world, not merely the physical world, and this, crucially, means *in some social world or other*, since it is certain both that human beings cannot live without a culture and that there are many different cultures in which they can live, differing in their local concepts.

In any case, an explanatory theory is not enough to deal with the problems of objectivity raised by the local ethical concepts. In the case of secondary qualities, the explanation also justifies, because it can show how the perceptions are related to physical reality and how they can give knowledge of that reality, which is what they purport to do. The question with them is: Is this a method of finding our way around the physical world? The theoretical account explains how it is. In the ethical case, this is not the kind of question raised by reflection. If we ask the question "Is this a method of finding our way around the social world?" we would have to be asking whether it was a method of finding our way around some social world or other, and the answer to that must obviously be yes (unless the society were extremely disordered, which is not what we were supposing). The question raised is rather "Is this a good way of living compared with others?"; or, to put it another way, "Is this the best kind of social world?"

When these are seen to be the questions, the reflective account we require turns out to involve reflective *ethical* considerations. These are the considerations that some believe should take the form of an ethical theory. The reflective considerations will have to take up the job of justifying the local concepts once those have come to be questioned. An ethical theory might even, in a weak sense, provide some explanations. It might rationalize some cultural differences, showing why one local concept rather than others was ethically appropriate in particular circumstances. But while it might explain why it was reasonable for people to have these various ethical beliefs, it would not be the sort of theory that could explain why they did or did not have them. It could not do something that explanations of perception can do, which is to generate an adequate theory of error and to account generally for the tendency of people to have what, according to its principles, are wrong beliefs.

If a wider objectivity were to come from all this, then the reflective ethical considerations would themselves have to be objective. This brings us back to the question whether the reflective level might generate its own ethical knowledge. If this is understood as our coming to have propositional knowledge of ethical truths, then we need some account of what "tracking the truth" will be. The idea that our beliefs can track the truth at this level must at least imply that a range of investigators could rationally, reasonably, and unconstrainedly come to converge on a determinate set of ethical conclusions. What are the hopes for such a process? I do not mean of its actually happening, but rather of our forming a coherent picture of how it might happen. If it is construed as convergence on a body of ethical truths which is brought about and explained by the fact that they are truths – this would be the strict analogy to scientific objectivity – then I see no hope for it. In particular, there is no hope of extending to this level the kind of world-guidedness we have been considering in the case of the thick ethical concepts. Discussions at the reflective level, if they have the ambition of considering all ethical experience and arriving at the truth about the ethical, will necessarily use the most general and abstract ethical concepts such as "right," and those concepts do not display world-guidedness . . .

I cannot see any convincing theory of knowledge for the convergence of reflective ethical thought on ethical reality in even a distant analogy to the scientific case.

I do not believe, then, that we can understand reflection as a process that substitutes knowledge for beliefs attained in unreflective practice. We must reject the objectivist view of ethical life as in that way a pursuit of ethical truth. But this does not rule out all forms of objectivism. There is still the project of trying to give an objective grounding or foundation to ethical life. For this, we should look in the direction of ideas about human nature. . . . [I]t would be significant enough if such considerations could give us a schema of an ethical life that would be the best ethical life, the most satisfactory for human beings in general. The question to be answered is: Granted that human beings need to share a social world, is there anything to be known about their needs and their basic motivations that will show us what this world would best be?

I doubt that there will turn out to be a very satisfying answer. It is probable that any such considerations will radically underdetermine the ethical options even in a given social situation. Any ethical life is going to contain restraints on such things as killing, injury, and lying, but those restraints can take very different forms. Again, with respect to the virtues, which is the most natural and promising field for this kind of inquiry, we only have to compare Aristotle's catalogue of the virtues with any that might be produced now to see how pictures of an appropriate human life may differ in spirit and in the actions and institutions they call for. We also have the idea that there are many and various forms of human excellence which will not all fit together into one harmonious whole, so any determinate ethical outlook is going to represent some kind of specialization of human possibilities. That idea is deeply entrenched in any naturalistic or, again, historical conception of human nature – that is, in any adequate conception of it – and I find it hard to believe that it will be overcome by an objective inquiry, or that human beings could turn out to have a much more determinate nature than is suggested by what we already know, one that timelessly demanded a life of a particular kind.

The project of giving to ethical life an objective and determinate grounding in considerations about human nature is not, in my view, very likely to succeed. But it is at any rate a comprehensible project, and I believe it represents the only intelligible form of ethical objectivity at the reflective level. It is worth asking what would be involved in its succeeding. . . .

If the project succeeded, it would not simply be a matter of agreement on a theory of human nature. The convergence itself would be partly in social and psychological science, but what would matter would be a convergence to which scientific conclusions provided only part of the means. Nor, on the other hand, would there be a convergence directly on ethical truths, as in the other objectivist model. One ethical belief might be said to be in its own right an object of knowledge at the reflective level, to the effect that a certain kind of life was best for human beings. But this will not yield other ethical truths directly. The reason, to put it summarily, is that the excellence or satisfactoriness of a life does not stand to beliefs involved in that life as premise stands to conclusion. Rather, an agent's excellent life is characterized by *having* those beliefs, and most of the beliefs will not be about that agent's dispositions or life, or about other people's dispositions, but about the social world. That life will involve, for instance, the agent's using some thick concepts rather than others. Reflection on the excellence of a life does not itself establish the truth of judgments using those concepts or of the agent's other ethical judgments. Instead it shows that there is good reason (granted the commitment to an ethical life) to live a life that involves those concepts and those beliefs.

The convergence that signaled the success of this project would be a convergence of practical reason, by which people came to lead the best kind of life and to have the desires that belonged to that life; convergence in ethical belief would largely be a part and consequence of that process. One very general ethical belief would, indeed, be an object of knowledge at that level. Many particular ethical judgments, involving the favored thick concepts, could be known to be true, but then judgments of this sort (I have argued) are very often known to be true anyway, even when they occur, as they always have, in a life that is not grounded at the objective level. The objective grounding would not bring it about that judgments using those concepts were true or could be known: this was so already. But it would enable us to recognize that certain of them were the best or most appropriate thick concepts to use. Between the two extremes of the one very general proposition and the many concrete ones, other ethical beliefs would be true only in the oblique sense that they were the beliefs that would help us to find our way around in a social world which – on this optimistic program – was shown to be the best social world for human beings.

This would be a structure very different from that of the objectivity of science. There would be a radical difference between ethics and science, even if ethics were objective in the only way in which it intelligibly could be. However, this does not mean that there is a clear distinction between (any) fact and (any) value; nor does it mean that there is no ethical knowledge. There is some, and in the less reflective past there has been more.

Notes

1 Notably John McDowell, "Are Moral Requirements Hypothetical Imperatives?", *Proceedings of the Aristotelian Society*, suppl. vol. 52 (1978); "Virtue and Reason," *Monist*, 62 (1979).
2 The most subtle and ingenious discussion of propositional knowledge I know is that of Robert Nozick in ch. 3 of his *Philosophical Explanations*. Some central features of Nozick's account, notably the use of subjunctive conditionals, had been anticipated by Fred Dretske, as Nozick acknowledges in his note 53 to that chapter (p. 630), which gives references.
3 Alfred Tarski, "The Concept of Truth in Formalized Languages," in *Logic, Semantics, Meta-Mathematics* (Indianapolis: Hackett Publishing Co., 1981). On the present issue, see David Wiggins, "What Would Be a Substantial Theory of Truth?", in Zak van Straaten (ed.), *Philosophical Subjects: Essays Presented to P. F. Strawson* (New York: Oxford University Press, 1980). Wiggins' discussion raises a further issue, whether the observer could even understand what the sentences mean, unless he could apply a disquotational truth formula to them. In this he is influenced by Donald Davidson, "Truth and Meaning," *Synthese*, 17 (1967). The fact that there can be a sympathetic but nonidentified observer shows that it cannot be impossible to understand something although one is unwilling to assert it oneself.
4 See John Skorupski, *Symbol and Theory* (New York: Cambridge University Press, 1976).

11

MORAL RELATIVITY AND TOLERANCE

David B. Wong

Comparing the truth of virtue-centered and rights-centered moralities

1 Identifying the differences

. . . It is time to establish differences between the truth conditions of moral statements based on virtue-centered moralities and truth conditions of moral statements based on rights-centered moralities. To begin the case, we must be more specific about the differences between virtue-centered and rights-centered moralities.

The first point I want to make has been made by others in connection with Greek moralities – that nothing in these moralities corresponds to the modern moral "ought" as it evolved since the Middle Ages. In Greek, remarks MacIntyre, there is originally no clear distinction between "ought" and "owe" (*dein*).[1] The word was used to identify the duties of social roles, originally those in the household and kinship groups, and then the duties of a citizen in the city-state. The word was used, therefore, to designate duties tied to the practices of a particular social and political structure. The same was true of the Chinese "ought" (*ying*). The modern moral "ought" of Western Europe and America, on the contrary, is a word often used to designate duties that transcend any particular social and political structure. . . .

It has been noted also that "ought" does not play such an important role in virtue-centered moralities as compared to the value terms – "good" and more specific evaluative expressions designating virtues –

From David B. Wong, *Moral Relativity*, Berkeley CA: University of California Press, 1984, pp. 160–61, 165–75, 180–90, and 232–34.

David B. Wong is Professor of Philosophy at Brandeis University.

while the modern "ought" has become the primary word for communicating the requirements of morality. This is something we might expect if one of the major differences between virtue-centered and rights-centered moralities is the presence in the former and absence in the latter of a common good shared by all members of the community. Where the common good is present, the focus of moral concern will be the characterization of that common good and the identification of those qualities in people that would be necessary for sustaining the common good. In rights-centered moralities, we would expect those moral terms directly tied with action to be the most frequently used.

But do such differences really result in variations in truth conditions for moral "A ought to do X" statements? Let us focus on what has been thought to be an important conflict between the two kinds of moralities [the value of freedom] . . .

2 Are there differences over the value of freedom?

. . . [I]n ancient Greek morality, emphasis is placed on the freedom to perform a certain range of actions – those falling under the heading of participation in ruling. The protected range of actions does not include the range protected by the modern civil liberties – expression, religion, and so on. Ancient Greek morality, furthermore, restricts the range of agents who have the protected freedom. It belongs to agents who have the capacity to make wise decisions on how to sustain the common good of the community. In Plato's ideal state, these agents composed the class of Guardians. Aristotle excludes from citizenship the mechanic class because its members lack the leisure to participate and because manual labor makes the soul unfit for enlightened virtue.

In Chinese Confucianism, there is no emphasis on the established Western categories of political and civil liberties. This does not mean, however, that Confucians were not concerned with removing barriers to certain actions or to acquiring certain character traits. They were most concerned with removing the barriers to becoming a person of *jen*, to becoming a person with a fully realized social nature who could act in accordance with filial piety and brotherly respect. It is a gross simplification to call this a freedom to conform to moral constraints (filial piety and brotherly respect), for Confucians viewed a life of *jen* as the most rewarding life a person could have. The stereotype of Eastern morality as subordinating the individual to society is not accurate for the reason that individual fulfillment is seen as lying in society.

At the same time, those who respond to the stereotype by replying that there is *no* difference between Western, rights-centered moralities and Chinese morality on the matter of freedom are also wrong. Hsieh Yu-wei argues that Confucianism does value freedom, the freedom to do good and not freedom from constraints of any kind. This includes freedom to choose which prince to serve, which friends, the place where one lives, and to speak when it is right to do so. And, he asks, which morality allows the individual to do what is wrong?[2] The problem with this reply is that it does not take into account how the range of free choice may be widened or narrowed by the definition of the good and the right. Consider the "freedom to speak when it is right to do so." Clearly the range of verbal behavior allowed depends on the range of actions regarded as permissible. . . . Confucius was not inclined to allow much latitude for those who did not participate in a government.

We see, therefore, a significant difference between virtue-centered and rights-centered moralities on the protected range of actions, and that virtue-centered moralities do not display a uniform position on the matter either. To understand the basis of these differences, we must go back to the notion of a common good that occupies the center of virtue-centered moralities and that is absent or subordinated to other values in rights-centered moralities. In Confucianism, the common good is a life of *jen* for all in accordance with righteousness, *li*, filial piety and brotherly respect. In ancient Greek morality, it is the public order, including the political life. In both kinds of virtue-centered moralities, a shared life is seen as the fulfillment of human nature, and thus they do not provide a congenial home for the notion that the individual needs to be protected *against* interference by the group. There is, however, a difference in the conception of the shared life between Chinese and Greek morality. For the Chinese, the family and kinship group remained the centers of man's social existence. For the Greeks, to say that man is a social animal is to say that he is a political one. It is not surprising, then, that the latter were concerned with the political liberties, while the former were not. . . .

3 The case for variation in truth conditions

We now come to the crucial question: given the difference between rights-centered and virtue-centered moralities on the questions of freedom and of the existence of a common good, the sharing of which constitutes each individual's fulfillment, is there a variation in truth conditions between moral statements made on the basis of two kinds of moralities? Consider what absolutists could say about this case. Perhaps this is a case of environmental relativity in which a virtue-centered morality is applicable to some groups or societies, given their conditions, but inapplicable to others, given different conditions.

May and Abraham Edel apply this method of explanation to the Zuni Indians, who have a virtue-centered morality that is focused on a shared life, structured around religious ritual, in much the same way that Chinese social life was structured around the rituals of ancestor worship.

In both cultures, performance of these rituals was an occasion for affirmation of one's place in the community. By performing a role that others in the tradition performed far into the past and that others would perform in the future, one gains a vivid sense of the continuity of community. By performing a role that is coordinated in complex ways with the roles of others to produce a kind of drama symbolizing certain collective attitudes (reverence for the past, acceptance of the contingencies of nature) of the community, one gains a vivid sense of the present unity of the community. The Zuni center their lives around such ritual, and, as is appropriate under a virtue-centered morality, they praise and encourage the development of qualities that enable them to sustain the ritual life. . . .

We see in Zuni culture . . . the same emphasis on the common good of the shared life and the same absence of emphasis on the civil freedoms. There is great moral concern over the removal of barriers to participation in the religious life of the community.

Now the Edels suggest that at least part of the explanation for the emphasis on cooperation and on the value of a close-knit community life is that the Zuni live in an "isolated desert environment, quite permanent, and subject to attack from without."[3] This method of explanation for the adoption of virtue-centered moralities is also exemplified by Richard Solomon's explanation of why the Chinese adopted Confucianism.[4] . . . [H]owever, other cultures have operated under hard material conditions that might motivate a group to adopt a virtue-centered morality, but they have not. The Eskimos of Greenland are an example. Furthermore, Solomon himself notes that in traditional China, urban Chinese of upper- and middle-income levels also adopted Confucianism.

This method of explanation, therefore, will not tell us why virtue-centered moralities are appropriate to a certain set of conditions, while rights-centered moralities are appropriate to another set of conditions. This is the result that would support the subsumption of the differences between the two moralities as a case of environmental relativity. This result is also undermined by comparative studies of different tribal cultures. Margaret Mead devised a classification of social systems as cooperative, competitive, and individualistic on the basis of the proportions of time and energy devoted by groups to ends that were shared, competitive, or individual. The Zuni social system was classified as cooperative because success in that system was intimately tied to the good of the group and one's status did not go up or down with one's own success. In competitive cultures, one's status does go up or down with one's own efforts, and individual achievement tends to be compared on a single scale of success. In the competitive social system of the Manus of the Admiralty Islands, the overriding goal of each is individual success through the accumulation of property. In individualistic social systems, the individual is not even motivated to achieve status in the eyes of others. Instead, each is like a sovereign state. For the Eskimos of Greenland, the ideal man is one who does what he pleases and takes what he wants without fear. Mead found that such differences did not correlate with differences in subsistence level, with classifications of a system as food-gathering, hunting or agricultural, or with the state of technology. She concluded that the dictates of the natural environment were overriden by cultural definition: "The social conception of success and the structural framework into which individual success is fitted are more determinate than the state of technology or the plentifulness of food."[5]

Absolutists may reply that a virtue-centered morality may *in fact* be appropriate only under certain material conditions having to do with material scarcity or threat of attack from the outside, and that when a group adopts such a morality under other conditions, it is making a mistake. Absolutists must then explain, however, what the mistake is, and how a group could have made it. After all, people do seem to derive certain satisfactions from a way of life embodying a virtue-centered morality, including a sense of security and acceptance in relation to one's fellow human beings. . . .

If environmental relativity is not the entire explanation of the crucial differences between virtue-centered and rights-centered moralities, what about the possibility that the difference is a disagreement over a question that is beyond human powers to settle at this time? . . . [I]t is incumbent on those who give this method of explanation to tell why this disagreement is unresolvable while others are not. This would involve identifying what would be the case if each side were right and telling how the available evidence is consistent with either possibility. Kantian absolutists would have to say that the irresolvability lies in a failure to identify which position in the disagreement is compatible with standards of rationality on practical reasoning. . . . But as far as we know, practically all moral disagreements are irresolvable in this sense because no standard of rationality has been found that clearly implies a substantive moral principle.

Aristotelians such as Foot would have to say that the (presently irresolvable) disagreement is over which way of life is the most beneficial for people.[6] Perhaps we cannot resolve the disagreement at this time because of the extreme difficulty of determining which way provides the best *balance* of satisfactions that seem to conflict with each other. On the one hand, participating in a shared life provides certain unique satisfactions. It provides one with a sense of security and acceptance in relation to one's fellow human beings. It avoids the isolation and stress that competitive and individualistic social systems place on people. On the other hand, the latter social systems provide complementary satisfactions – those stemming from fulfillment of needs for achievement and creativity that an individual could identify as his or her own. And a morality that stressed rights and individual freedoms might better provide for such needs. Ruth Benedict remarked in her discussion of the extremely competitive and individualistic life of the Kwakiutl that

> the pursuit of victory can give vigor and zest to human existence. Kwakiutl life is rich and forceful in its own terms. Its chosen goal has its appropriate virtues. . . . Whatever the social orientation, a society which exemplifies it vigorously will develop certain virtues that are natural to the goals it has chosen.[7]

Now Benedict believes that "it is most unlikely that even the best society will be able to stress in one social order all the virtues we prize in human life"; but Aristotelians would dispute that judgment, and it would seem arbitrary to eliminate such a possibility a priori. We may be able to find social systems that provide a better balance of satisfactions than the Zuni or Kwakiutl. For instance, Bernard Mishkin reported that in the Maori social system of New Zealand, community welfare is the primary end, but that that end is achieved through competition among individuals for approval of the community. . . . Perhaps the Maori system provides a better balance of the complementary virtues achieved in the Zuni and Kwakiutl systems. And perhaps such a system is more beneficial to human beings because it does provide a better balance. It remains for us to discover the ideal balance, and perhaps we haven't enough knowledge to do that at present.

This is an interesting reply and it is probably true that some social systems provide a better balance of important, complementary satisfactions. But it must be pointed out that the idea of balance is itself a moral ideal that is not obviously entitled to the title of the only valid ideal. A culture may tend to place much more value on a certain *kind* of satisfaction and may reject the ideal of *balance* between that kind and others, opting to achieve the highest degree of the most important kind (as Aristotle tended to do on occasion with *theoria*). The ideal of balance, furthermore, is in reality a largely formal notion that is compatible with a number of different interpretations and corresponding ways of life. It is not likely that all satisfactions will be given equal value, for instance. Even if we set aside Aristotle's most zealous intellectualist tendencies, we must recognize that he gave *theoria* a relatively high valuation and a prominent place in his ideal of a way of life balanced between the moral and intellectual virtues. In ancient Chinese culture, however, *theoria* was not given such a high valuation, and the corresponding ideal of balance would be different.

Also, one satisfaction upon which ancient Greek culture seems not to have placed any great value is that of being in harmony with the nonhuman world, knowing its rhythms and changes, not to manipulate it but to live with it. In ancient Chinese and in many American Indian cultures, this is an important part of any desirable way of life. Compare the Greek preoccupation in art with the perfect human form to the Chinese landscapes in which human beings are tiny figures tucked into great living mountains. The notion of what is the most beneficial to human beings is too indeterminate to convince us that there is a fact of the matter over which there is a disagreement we cannot resolve at this time. And the question of how to make the notion more determinate is in fact part of the disagreement to be resolved. . . .

Returning to the final absolutist method of explaining diversity of moral belief, it declares one or the other side to be in error or ignorant of crucial facts. Kantian absolutists would fail to give a convincing explanation for the same reasons they would fail to convince us that the difference between virtue-centered and rights-centered moralities is an irresolvable disagreement over a fact of the matter. Aristotelians such as Foot again could have trouble with the indeterminateness of their conception of benefit, and if they made it more determinate – say they proclaimed that the most beneficial way of life was one that provided a certain balance between important satisfactions, they would have to explain why those who seem to have a different interpretation of the most satisfying way of life are mistaken or ignorant. . . .

This is how relativists could argue by elimination to the hypothesis that there is a difference in truth conditions for moral "A ought to do X" statements between virtue-centered and rights-centered moralities. This variation centers on the question of whether one ought to recognize areas of conduct within which the individual does as he or she wishes without moral or legal constraint. Virtue-centered moralities do not protect certain areas that rights-centered moralities do, and to say there is variation in truth conditions is to say that an adherent of virtue-centered morality could truthfully deny a statement to the effect that one ought to recognize these areas of noninterference, while an adherent of rights-centered moralities could truthfully make that statement. . . .

[T]he failure of absolutist theories to explain certain kinds of disagreements and apparent diversity in moral belief . . . is likely to be incurable. Human beings have needs to resolve internal conflicts between requirements and to resolve interpersonal conflicts of interest. Morality is a social creation that evolved in response to these needs. There are constraints on what a morality could be like and still serve those needs. These constraints are derived from the physical environment, from human nature, and from standards of rationality, but they are not enough to eliminate all but one morality as meeting those needs. Moral relativity is an indication of the plasticity of human nature, of the power of ways of life to determine what constitutes a satisfactory resolution of the conflicts morality is intended to resolve. . . .

Tolerance and nonintervention as implications of moral relativity

3 A valid relativist argument for tolerance

. . . [T]he relativist arguments for tolerance that nonphilosophers give are typically vague and incomplete. They are subject to multiple and conflicting interpretations. As Williams and Harrison interpret them, they proceed from the premise of moral relativism directly to tolerance.[8] They have no premise that expresses a particular ethical viewpoint, and thus are, in Harrison's terms, attempts to derive a participant's conclusions from an observer's premises. Harrison and Williams neglect the possibility that the relativist arguments of nonphilosophers also can be interpreted as arguments from moral relativism and one or more ethical premises to tolerance. This interpretation is an expression of the fact that an observer's premises may be relevant to a participant *within the context of his or her ethical viewpoint*. Consider the argument Harrison criticizes: because "neither side can conclusively prove his case," neither has any "right to impose his own views." We can interpret this as containing a suppressed ethical premise, to the effect that it is wrong to impose one's views on another person unless one can justify them to him or her. And when Herskovits argues that we should seek to harmonize goals that do not dovetail with our own, we can interpret him as speaking from an ethic that values interaction between members of different cultures through mutual consent.[9]

To develop an alternative interpretation of these arguments, let us begin with Kant's formula of humanity as an end in itself: that one ought always to treat humanity never simply as a means but always at the same time as an end. In an illustration of how the formula is to be applied, Kant says that the man who makes a false promise to another man is intending to make use of the man merely as a means to an end he does not share. This is so because the man being deceived "cannot possibly agree with . . . [that] way of behaving to him, and so cannot himself share the end of the action."[10]

Thus one implication of the formula is that we should refrain from interfering with the permissible ends of others. The qualification that the ends be permissible is necessary because others may have immoral or unworthy ends that one may justifiably interfere with.

Now the question arises as to how one is able to distinguish permissible from impermissible ends. Kant does not explicitly address this problem, but an answer naturally falls out of his view that the possession of a rational nature is the basis for the status of human beings as ends in themselves.[11] Permissible ends are rational ends – those that accord with the nature of human beings as rational beings. This implies that one should not interfere with the ends of others unless one can justify the interference to be acceptable to them were they fully rational and informed of all relevant circumstances. To do otherwise is to fail to treat them with the respect due rational beings. Let us call this implication of Kant's formula the "justification principle."[12] Kant believes his principle to be objectively valid for all people. Whether or not this is the case, the theme of individual autonomy is a central and pervasive one in the moral traditions of Europe and of cultures descending from Europe. Kant's principle is a plausible expression of that theme.

Let us now consider what follows when his principle is combined with moral relativism. If moral relativism is true, two persons A and B can have conflicting moralities that are equally true and that therefore may be equally justified. Suppose B is required or permitted by his morality to bring about a state of affairs X. A can bring about some other state of affairs Y that precludes the coming about of X.[13] It would be a violation of the justification principle for A to bring about Y, because she could not justify to B the preventing of X. We thus have an argument for A tolerating B's action according to his moral beliefs. This argument is a possible interpretation of the relativist arguments for tolerance given by nonphilosophers. In fact, it makes a plausible interpretation of arguments given by people who have come to believe in moral relativism within the context of a culture that emphasizes individual autonomy.

The force of the argument from the justification principle will vary with the content of A's moral system. Of course, A will not be moved by it at all if her system contains nothing like the justification principle. Suppose it does. Then she must consider whether there is some other principle in it that requires that she prevent B from bringing about X. Assuming that A's moral system is deontological, the existence of such a principle results in a conflict of prima facie duties. A would have to weigh the justification principle against the other principle. . . .

It is quite possible that there is no general procedure for drawing neat boundaries of the sphere of actions with which one is not to interfere. A, however, can still weigh conflicting prima facie duties, according to the moral significance each duty acquires in the particular situation at hand. For one thing, the weight of the duty to refrain from preventing X (relative to that of the other conflicting duty) varies inversely with the degree to which nonconsenting others are harmed or have their freedom restricted. Consider the difference between B engaging in an unusual sexual act with other consenting adults and B's terrorist act of kidnapping and murder. The relative weight of the duty to refrain, furthermore, varies inversely with the probability of occurrence of possible harm or restriction of freedom, together with the clarity with which the harm or restriction can be defined. For an example of a case in which the relative weight is not diminished, consider the claim by some that homosexual activity between consenting adults could undermine the values of the traditional family over a whole society. There is no hard evidence for the probability of such an effect; the idea of exactly what values would be undermined and why their undermining would be harmful is very fuzzy. . . .

4 Problems posed for the argument

Kantians may raise the following problem for the relativist argument from the justification principle: in arguing for that principle, Kant presupposed that there is a single moral system that is valid for all rational human beings; hence it is highly unlikely that anyone will ever have a good reason to assert the conjunction of moral relativism and the justification principle.

The first point to make in dealing with this problem is that the justification principle is interpretable in such a way that the content of what it prescribes is independent of any proposition entailing the falsity of moral relativism. We don't have to be moral absolutists to resolve to refrain from interfering with the permissible ends of others. Second, it is a fact that many have found Kant's principle appealing while remaining unpersuaded by the arguments for it. . . . This leads me to a third point.

It is possible for a moral relativist to have a good reason for holding the justification principle, if not all good reasons for holding a moral principle must follow from the nature of practical reason. . . . Sympathy, compassion, and concern for another for his or her own sake may give rise to reasons for accepting the justification principle. If one desires freedom from the interference of others, one may sympathize with others to whom that freedom is denied, and find satisfaction in helping them to achieve it. Also, the desire to be part of a group in which there is mutual respect and support may motivate adherence to the principles. . . .

Harrison poses other problems for any relativist argument for tolerance. The first problem he poses begins with the claim that almost all significant actions and decisions will be disapproved by someone. If A refrains from preventing X by bringing about Y merely because B disapproves of Y, and if A carries out that policy consistently, she would be paralyzed.[14] This is not a real problem for the relativist argument from the justification principle because it allows for the possibility that the principle may have exceptions or be overridden by another moral principle. The reason presented for tolerance in the argument, furthermore, is not as simple as B's disapproval of Y. The reason is that B is required or permitted by his morality to bring about X, and if A prevents X from occurring this would constitute a violation of the justification principle. Such a reason applies to only a small subset of our significant actions.

Another problem posed by Harrison is that A must weigh her own attitude toward X and Y. If A refrains from preventing X because of B's attitude, and if she believes she is required by her moral system to bring about Y, then isn't she favoring B's over her own? This would be rational, says Harrison, only if A thinks B more liable to be correct in his judgment.[15] If A, however, is persuaded by the relativist argument from the justification principle, she would not be favoring B's attitude over her own. She would be persuaded by her belief in the principle. The conflict is between two principles in A's system, as well as between A and B.

A third problem posed by Harrison is that there is as much reason for B to allow A to override him: "They should both try to allow the other to do what they consider to be wrong."[16] The result would be that no one does anything. In reply, it is relevant to point out an asymmetry between the situations of A and B. A must decide whether to block an anticipated action of B and thus to restrict B's freedom. B must decide whether to offend A's sense of morality by trying to bring about X, but there may be no further result concerning A in particular. Her freedom may not be restricted, and in such a case the justification principle would provide B no reason to allow A's intervention. It is true that if B holds the justification principle, he will have reason to refrain from bringing about X, to the extent that his action will have an adverse effect on A.

But while each may affect the other, one may affect the other in such a way that the justification principle must weigh more heavily in his or her decision-making. For instance, if B engages in homosexual activity with another consenting adult and A must decide whether to prevent such activity through the law, it would seem most likely that the justification principle must weigh more against A's intervention than B's abstinence from homosexual activity. . . .

A final problem is suggested by one of Williams' criticisms of the "anthropologist's heresy": that its central confusion is to try to derive from the view that moral principles are relative to some nonrelative principle governing the attitude of one society toward another. Does the argument for tolerance presented here make the same error? To answer this question, we need to distinguish different ways in which moral principles can be relative. The form of moral relativism assumed here implies that moral principles can be relative in the sense that they can be true and justified in one society but not in another. It implies nothing about the scope of applying moral principles. It does not imply, for instance, that a moral principle such as "It is wrong to interfere with another society's values" must be implicitly relativized, as "It is wrong for our society (but perhaps not for others) to interfere with another society's values." My version of moral relativism is compatible with Williams' claim that a morality often comes to range over all persons and not just over the members of the society in which it originates. A moral principle can have universal scope; that is, it can apply to all moral agents in the sense of directing them to perform certain actions; and it may be *true of* all agents given a certain set of truth conditions that a group or society assigns to the principle; but since there may be more than one set of truth conditions for the principle, it may not be *universally justifiable* to all agents. . . .

The relativist argument from the justification principle concludes with a principle that is nonrelative with respect to the content of truth conditions, not necessarily with respect to justifiability. It is consistent, therefore, with that argument to condemn the intolerant behavior of those in another society even though tolerance may not be justifiable to them. A nice question to raise at this point is whether the argument allows us to try to *prevent* their intolerant behavior. The argument does seem to imply a prima facie duty not to interfere with them, but if we are committed to promoting tolerance, then we must ask whether our interference is a lesser evil than letting them impose their will on others. We would have to weigh conflicting prima facie duties, both derived from the value of tolerance. It would not be a contradiction to conclude that our commitment to that value weighed in favor of interference.

Notes

1 Alasdair MacIntyre, *After Virtue* (Notre Dame: University of Notre Dame Press, 1981), p. 115.
2 Hsieh Yu-wei, "The Status of the Individual in Chinese Ethics," in Charles Moore (ed.) *The Chinese Mind* (Honolulu: University of Hawaii Press, 1967), pp. 307–22.
3 May and Abraham Edel, *Anthropology and Ethics* (Cleveland: Press of Case Western Reserve University, 1968), p. 63.
4 Richard Solomon, *Mao's Revolution and the Chinese Political Culture* (Berkeley: University of California Press, 1971).
5 Margaret Mead, "Interpretive Statements," in Margaret Mead (ed.) *Cooperation and Conflict among Primitive Peoples* (New York: McGraw-Hill), p. 511.
6 See Philippa Foot, *Virtues and Vices* (Berkeley: University of California, 1978).
7 Ruth Benedict, *Patterns of Culture* (New York: Penguin, 1934), p. 229.
8 See Bernard Williams, *Morality: An Introduction to Ethics* (New York: Harper & Row, 1972) and Geoffrey Harrison, "Relativism and Tolerance," in Peter Laslett and James Fishkin (eds.) *Philosophy, Politics and Society* (New Haven: Yale University Press, 1979), pp. 273–90.
9 Melville Herskovits, *Cultural Relativism: Perspectives in Cultural Pluralism* (New York: Vintage, 1972), p. 11.
10 Immanuel Kant, *Groundwork of the Metaphysic of Morals*, trans. H. J. Paton (New York: Harper & Row, 1964), p. 97; 2d edn, p. 68; Prussian edn, p. 430.
11 Kant, *Groundwork*, p. 96; 2d edn, p. 66; Prussian edn, p. 429.
12 A contemporary philosopher who also emphasizes the value of noninterference with the ends of others is Alan Gewirth. He defines the generic right to freedom as a right to control whether or not one will participate in "transac-

tions" with agents. One's participation must be subject to one's own unforced consent, given with knowledge of relevant circumstances and in an emotionally calm state of mind. See his *Reason and Morality* (Chicago: University of Chicago Press, 1978) pp. 135–38. One could formulate a relativist argument for tolerance premised on Gewirth's right to freedom, instead of Kant's justification principle. The conclusions will be much the same, although Gewirth's right to freedom has some different implications. The set of actions that a relevantly informed and calm person would consent to is not necessarily the same as the set that the person would accept were he or she relevantly informed and fully rational.

13 The variable schema is borrowed from Harrison, pp. 278–79, so that some of his arguments may be related easily to the ones to be set out here.
14 Harrison, pp. 280–81.
15 Harrison, p. 281.
16 Harrison, p. 281.

Part IV

DEFENSES OF MORAL OBJECTIVITY

12

MORAL DISAGREEMENT

David O. Brink

[T]he antirealist might claim, disagreement in ethics is pervasive – more pervasive than it is in the natural or social sciences. Indeed, moral disputes are so pervasive and so intractable that the best explanation of this kind of disagreement is that there are no moral facts.

Of course . . . it will not be sufficient that nihilism be *an* explanation of the existence and nature of moral disagreement; it must *clearly be the best* explanation.

The argument from moral diversity or disagreement has been a popular and philosophically influential source of moral skepticism. Mackie's "argument from relativity" is the most perspicuous formulation of the argument from disagreement, so I shall focus on it.[1]

As Mackie recognizes, disagreement does not entail nihilism; we do not infer from the fact that there are disagreements in the natural or social sciences that these disciplines do not concern matters of objective fact. Nor, from the fact that there is a specific dispute in some discipline, do we make what might seem to be the more modest inference that there is no fact of the matter on the particular issue in question. For example, no one concluded from the apparently quite deep disagreement among astronomers a short while ago about the existence of black holes that there was no fact of the matter concerning the existence of black holes. The argument from disagreement must claim that disagreement in ethics is somehow more fundamental than disagreement in other disciplines. Mackie's claim seems to be that realism about a discipline requires that its disputes be resolvable and that although scientific disputes do seem resolvable, many moral disputes do not. For this reason, the best

From David O. Brink, *Moral Realism and the Foundations of Ethics*, Cambridge: Cambridge University Press, 1989, pp. 197–209.

David O. Brink is Associate Professor of Philosophy at the University of California, San Diego.

explanation of the facts about moral disagreement requires the rejection of moral realism.

I think the moral realist should question the premises of this formulation of the argument from disagreement. Does realism about a discipline require that its disputes be resolvable? Certainly, realism about a discipline does not require that all actual cognizers eventually reach agreement. It could be reasonable to expect agreement on a set of facts only if all cognizers were fully informed and fully rational and had sufficient time for deliberation. Thus, if realism about a discipline requires that its disputes be resolvable, this must mean that its disputes must be resolvable *in principle*.

Does realism about a discipline require that its disputes be resolvable even in principle? I think that a realist should resist the assumption that it ought to be possible, in practice or even in principle, to get *any* cognizer to hold true beliefs. All of our beliefs are revisable, at least in principle, and dialectical investigation of our beliefs can identify explanatory tensions in our beliefs and force more or less drastic revision in them if it is carried out thoroughly. In this way, coherentist reasoning can, at least in principle, identify and correct significant and substantial error. But no theory of justification adequate to the task of accounting for justified but fallible belief (e.g., in an external world) can preclude the possibility of *systematic* error. We cannot demonstrate, and should not be expected to be able to demonstrate, the success of evolutionary theory to someone who holds systematically mistaken observational beliefs about the behavior and adaptation of different species. We cannot defend, and should not be expected to be able to defend, historical hypotheses to someone who holds no true psychological generalizations about human behavior. Similarly, there may be people with such hopelessly and systematically mistaken moral beliefs that we cannot, and should not be expected to be able to, convince them of true moral claims. Because the argument from disagreement alleges that the moral realist cannot adequately explain the nature of moral disagreement, we are entitled to see what could be said about moral disagreement and its resolvability *on realist assumptions*. And, as in these nonmoral cases, we can imagine people whose initial starting points are so badly mistaken that there should be no expectation of convincing them of the truth. We can imagine people whose view of themselves and others is so distorted by, say, self-concern or an inability to represent vividly the consequences of their actions that all of their considered moral beliefs will be badly mistaken. Even though these beliefs are revisable, the fact that they are systematically mistaken means that there may be no basis for correcting their errors.

Although this is, I think, a possibility, and one that demonstrates that the realist need not believe it possible, even in principle, to convince any cognizer of true moral claims, it does not undermine the argument from disagreement. For although a nonskeptical realist need not assume that any and every moral dispute is resolvable even in principle, he cannot treat every serious disagreement as one between interlocutors at least one of whom is systematically mistaken. I lose my claim to justified belief the more I simply dismiss opponents as systematically mistaken. It is incumbent on the moral realist, therefore, to claim that *most* moral disputes are resolvable at least in principle.

Is this claim plausible? Mackie supposes that the realist will defend it by trying to explain away apparent moral disagreements as the application by interlocutors of shared moral principles under different empirical conditions. This is the familiar idea that people who live in different social, economic, and environmental conditions might apply the same moral principle to justify quite different policies. An economically underdeveloped country might think that in a society in its economic condition distributive inequalities provide incentives that benefit everyone and that this justifies such inequalities. A more economically advanced country might oppose distributive inequalities on the ground that in societies at its level of affluence distributive inequalities are divisive and so work to everyone's disadvantage. The economically underdeveloped society thinks it should promote certain distributive inequalities, whereas the economically more developed society thinks it should oppose distributive inequalities. This might look like a moral disagreement, but the fact is that the disagreement is only apparent. The one society thinks that inequalities are justified *in economically backward conditions*, while the other society thinks that inequalities are unjustified *in economically favorable conditions*. Not only is there no disagreement here; a common moral principle seems to justify both beliefs. Since this sort of disagreement is only apparent, it poses no problem for the moral realist.

Mackie finds this realist explanation of moral disagreement inadequate for two reasons. First, this explanation of moral disputes commits the moral realist to treating many moral facts as contingent. The apparently conflicting moral beliefs of apparent disputants can only be contingently true, because their compatibility depends on contingent facts about their different environments. Necessity can attach only to the shared moral principles that underlie their apparent disagreement.

It is not entirely clear how this fact about a realist account of apparent disputes is supposed to constitute an objection to moral realism. Mackie seems to assume that the moral realist cannot accept this kind of contingency and is committed to defending the necessity of moral facts. But why?

It cannot be Mackie's view that moral facts are necessary, since he thinks that no moral statements are true. But if Mackie can reject completely belief in the necessity of moral truths, why can't the realist, if she needs to, deny that all moral truths are necessary? Perhaps Mackie thinks that the realist, but not he, is committed to defending common beliefs about morality and that it is a common belief about morality that moral truths are necessary.

But there are several problems with this argument. Although my defense of coherentism commits me to the general reliability of considered moral beliefs, it does not commit me to the reliability of common nonmoral, second-order beliefs about morality. Moreover, I see no reason to think that belief in the necessity of moral truths is a common belief about morality, and, even if it were, there would be good reason to reject it. The ethical naturalist claims that moral facts are constituted by, and thus supervene on, natural and social scientific facts such as economic, social, and psychological facts. The naturalist, therefore, ought to accept happily the claim that "if things had been otherwise [in certain respects], quite different sorts of actions would have been right (see this volume, p. 128)." The contingency of many moral facts is, I think, a happy, rather than an untoward, consequence of the realist's explanation of apparent moral disagreement.

So, the realist's explanation of apparent moral disagreement commits him to the contingency of some moral facts. But this is a perfectly acceptable commitment, since many moral facts are contingent. Moreover, as Mackie recognizes, the realist's explanation of apparent disagreement allows him to treat some moral facts as necessary. Also, how many moral facts the realist must regard as contingent depends, in part, on how often the realist seeks to explain moral disagreement away as only apparent moral disagreement.

This brings us to Mackie's second reason for finding the realist explanation of apparent moral disagreement inadequate. Mackie seems to assume that the realist must offer this explanation as a general account of moral disputes, and he points out, quite rightly, that not all putative disagreements are merely apparent. People do disagree about what is right or wrong in a particular set of circumstances, and the realist must be able to explain why most genuine disputes are resolvable at least in principle.

But the realist can plausibly explain this; Mackie is wrong to restrict the realist to explaining moral disputes away as only apparent. We already noted that it is only *most* genuine disputes that a realist must regard as resolvable in principle. Some interlocutors may be so systematically mistaken that although our dispute with them concerns a matter of objective fact, we cannot, and should not be expected to be able to, convince them of true claims. Other genuine moral disputes are also in a certain sense not resolvable even in principle. For even a moral realist can maintain that some genuine moral disputes have no uniquely correct answers. Moral ties are possible, and considerations, each of which is objectively valuable, may be incommensurable. Disputes over moral ties and incommensurable values are resolvable in principle only in the sense that it ought to be possible in principle to show interlocutors who are not systematically mistaken that their dispute has no unique resolution. Of course, there are limits on how often we may construe disputes as tied or incommensurable and still plausibly defend the existence of objective moral facts and true moral propositions.

The moral realist can plausibly maintain that most moral disputes are genuine, have a unique solution, and can be resolved at least in principle. First, many genuine moral disagreements depend on disagreements over the nonmoral facts. Of these, some depend on culpable ignorance of fact and others do not.

Often, at least one disputant culpably fails to assess the nonmoral facts correctly by being insufficiently imaginative in weighing the consequences for various people of different actions or policies. Culpable failure to be sufficiently imaginative may result from negligence (e.g., laziness), prejudice, self-interest, or social ideology. This sort of error is especially important in moral disputes, since thought experiments, as opposed to actual tests, play such an important part in the assessment of moral theories. Thought experiments play a larger role in moral methodology than they do in scientific methodology, both because it is often (correctly) regarded as immoral to assess moral theories by realizing the relevant counterfactuals, and because the desired test conditions for moral theories are often harder to produce (e.g., the experiments would involve too many variables to control for and the subjects would not always want to cooperate). Because moral disputes that depend on this kind of culpable ignorance of nonmoral fact turn on nonmoral issues that are supposed to be resolvable at least in principle, these moral disputes should themselves be resolvable at least in principle.

Other genuine moral disputes depend on reasonable (nonculpable) but nonetheless resolvable disagreements over the nonmoral facts. The correct answers to controversial moral questions often turn on nonmoral issues about which reasonable disagreement is possible and about which no one may know the answer. Moral disagreement can turn on nonmoral disagreement over such questions as "What (re)distribution of goods would make the worst-off representative person in a society best-off?," "Would public ownership of the means of production in the United States lead to an increase or decrease in the average standard of living?," "What are the most important social determinants of personality?," "What kind of life would Vera's severely mentally retarded child lead (if she brought her pregnancy to term and raised the child), and how would caring for him affect Vera and her family?," "How malleable is human nature?," "Which, if any, religious claims are true?," and "If there is a god, how should its will be ascertained? (e.g., should scripture be read literally?)." However difficult and controversial these issues are, disputes about them are supposed to be resolvable at least in principle. Insofar as moral disputes turn on such issues they too are resolvable in principle.

Other genuine moral disputes do not depend on nonmoral disagreement; they represent antecedent moral disagreement. Mackie's discussion of how moral realism will explain apparent moral disagreement shows that he regards moral disagreement as resolvable if, and only if, there is *antecedent* agreement on general moral principles. But this assumption reflects a one-way view of moral justification, according to which moral principles can justify particular moral judgments but not vice versa, that our defense of a coherence theory of justification entitles us to reject. As coherentism insists, justification consists in *mutual* support between moral principles and judgments about particular cases. Agreement about general moral principles may be exploited to resolve (genuine) disagreement about particular moral cases, and agreement about particular moral cases may be exploited to resolve disagreement about general moral principles. Since no one's moral beliefs are entirely consistent, much less maximally coherent, considerations of coherence force each of us to revise our moral beliefs in particular ways. Ideally, we make trade-offs among the various levels of generality of belief in such a way as to maximize initial commitment, overall consistency, explanatory power, and so on. The fact that we disagree about some moral issues at the beginning of this process of adjustment gives no compelling reason to suppose that this process of adjustment will not, in the limit, resolve our disagreement. Indeed, the nihilist is committed to claiming that there is often no resolution of competing moral claims even in principle. But this is just one claim about what the results of a systematic dialectical moral inquiry among different interlocutors would be, which must stand alongside various nonskeptical claims about what the results would be, and enjoys no privileged a priori position in relation to its competitors. As coherentists and realists about other things, we assume that this kind of coherentist reasoning is in principle capable of resolving quite deep antecedent disagreement in the natural sciences, the social sciences, and philosophy itself. There seems no reason to deny that most moral errors are not also resolvable at least in principle by coherentist reasoning. Certainly, given the burden of proof that the argument from disagreement must bear at this stage of the dialectic, the fact that the realist cannot produce a proof of her claim that most moral error is in principle correctable by coherentist reasoning gives us no reason to doubt this claim.

What of the diachronic character of the argument from disagreement? Does the fact that there seems to have been so little convergence of moral belief over time support the claim that many moral disputes are unresolvable? I do not think these questions raise any difficulties that we have not already addressed, but perhaps they focus issues in a certain way.

We need to distinguish, in our assessments of the amount of current moral consensus and of the prospects for convergence, between two levels of moral thought: (1) popular moral thought, and (2) reflective moral theory. Of course, according to a coherentist moral epistemology, levels (1) and (2) are connected; (2) begins with (1) and is in this respect at least continuous with (1). But coherentism also allows the dialectical investigation of our moral beliefs to force significant revision in those beliefs, and in this way (2) can come to diverge significantly from (1). This difference is important because the prospect of persistent disagreement at level (1) would seem much less troublesome if the prospects for agreement at level (2) were good or if there were plausible realist explanations for why agreement at level (2) should be hard to secure.

There certainly are realist explanations for why there is less convergence to date at level (1) than some might have expected there to be. Moral thinking, as we noted, is subject to various distorting influences such as particular conceptions of self-interest, prejudice, and other forms of social ideology. Because the subject matter of ethics concerns, among other things, the appropriate distribution of the benefits and burdens of social and personal interaction, these distorting influences often afflict moral thinking more than scientific thinking; it is just such issues on which these distorting mechanisms are most likely to operate. (I would not want to underestimate the extent to which such influences have distorted, say, social scientists' claims about the social and economic consequences of particular public policies or psychologists' and biologists' claims about the nature and heritability of intelligence. But these are the sorts of exceptions that prove the rule, and they also help the realist explain the persistence of moral disputes.) And these sources of distortion are hardy perennials.

There are other realist explanations for why agreement should be hard to secure at both levels.

. . . [S]ecular moral theory (level [2]) is in some ways a comparatively underdeveloped area of inquiry. In part, this reflects the influence of religious beliefs on both levels (1) and (2). This is not to say there have not been secular moralists since at least the Greeks, that religious ethics should not be taken seriously, that religious moralists do not make secularly acceptable moral claims, or that secular ethics is incompatible with theism. But it is certainly true that specifically religious doctrines and commitments have at many points shaped and constrained moral thinking. In some periods and places religious constraints on secular moral theory have been direct, taking the form of institutional censorship or sanctions. In other periods and places religious doctrines and commitments have constrained secular moral theory indirectly by affecting level (1). Religious commitments and doctrines have shaped what many people, and not just conscious adherents to these commitments and doctrines, take to be serious moral possibilities (think, for example, about Christian influences on popular views of sexual morality). And this sort of influence is important, since moral progress requires moral debate, and moral debate requires moral imagination. Moreover, insofar as such doctrines and commitments are not rationally defensible but must be held, if at all, as articles of faith, they have not just exerted disproportionate influence on the shape of moral thought but have actually distorted it. For the enterprise of moral theory is simply the attempt to find a rationally defensible system of moral beliefs. Moreover, it is a fundamental moral commitment that in morality's allocation of the benefits and burdens of social and personal interaction, the imposition of burdens on some requires rational justification in order to be morally legitimate. Specifically religious influences on ethics, therefore, have hindered moral progress at both levels (1) and (2), insofar as they have either infected moral thought with nonrational elements or artificially restricted people's moral imaginations. Science was not able to develop properly under similar religious constraints and did not really take off until, among other things, these constraints were largely shed. Perhaps moral thought would benefit from similar autonomy.

In any case, however much it may be due to religious influences, systematic, secular moral theory is a relatively underdeveloped area of inquiry. There are, of course, a number of figures in the history of philosophy who have developed fairly systematic, secular (or secularly acceptable) moral and political theories, many of which are powerful and attractive theories. But notice two things:

First, these figures sum to a very small total (they could perhaps be counted on two or three hands). The number of people who have worked full time to produce systematic moral theories does not even begin to compare with the number of those who have worked full time on theoretical issues in the natural sciences. Although, of course, there have been professional politicians and political strategists for a long time, the idea of a class of people devoting most of their time to the study of issues of moral and political theory is a comparatively recent one. Perhaps more progress is to be hoped for in ethics when systematic moral theory has flourished longer. These considerations provide a realistic explanation of why there has not yet been the right sort of convergence of moral opinion, as well as some reason to be cautiously optimistic about the prospects for convergence at least at level (2).

Second, the theories that have been developed have, with a few exceptions (e.g., Locke and Bentham), had very little and certainly imperfect impact on level (1). Lay persons are typically willing to defer to theorists or theoretical debate on matters scientific, but they seem largely uninterested in profiting from theoretical work that has been done in moral or political theory. (Public debates over abortion, affirmative action, and constitutional litigation concerning civil rights spring to mind.) Of course, it is not surprising that lay persons do not familiarize themselves with all of the philosophical details of existing moral theories. A certain amount of ignorance of theory is necessary if there are to be lay persons; this is as true in ethics as in science. But most lay persons, even those with strong moral sensibilities, seem largely unaware of, or uninterested in, even the outlines of theoretical work in ethics. Nor do I think that this popular ignorance of, or indifference to, moral theory can be justified by appeal to the state of theoretical disagreement in ethics or by appeal to an individual's obligation, as a moral agent, to decide matters for herself. Certainly, an individual's moral views can profit from exposure to ethical theory, even if, indeed, perhaps especially when, theoretical issues are in dispute. And one need not abdicate one's moral agency by consulting others who have thought systematically about the moral issues that concern one. Indeed, moral responsibility would seem to demand that one's moral decision be as informed as possible, and this would seem to argue in favor of consulting moral theory both when moral theory speaks unequivocally and when there is theoretical disagreement.

This makes one wonder how, if at all, the appropriate development in level (2) might affect level (1). Current popular neglect of the moral theory that is available might encourage skepticism about the effect that the development of moral theory might have on popular moral thought. But if this neglect is due in part to the comparatively underdeveloped state of moral theory, perhaps its development would encourage greater interest in, and respect for, the resources of moral theory. True, such development (with its demands on intellectual resources) may itself presuppose a greater interest in moral theory or moral issues. But marginally greater interest in certain moral issues could spur marginally greater interest in moral theory, which could spur moderately greater allocation of intellectual resources toward moral theory, which in turn could spur further interest in moral issues, and so on.

In any event, the prospects for the appropriate kind of convergence at level (2), given the appropriate development of systematic moral theory, would be sufficient reassurance to the moral realist. The fact, if it would be a fact, that the appropriate sort of convergence at level (2) would not produce similar convergence at level (1) should trouble us no more than the fact that agreement among biologists on some form of evolutionary theory does not secure the agreement of all lay persons (e.g., certain fundamentalist Christians).

Moreover, there are realist explanations for not expecting convergence in ethics, at level (1) or level (2), even over fairly long periods of time. To believe that there are moral facts and that moral knowledge is possible, as the realist does, involves no commitment to thinking that moral knowledge is easy to acquire. Insofar as particular moral disputes depend on complex nonmoral issues about economics, social theory, human nature, and the rationality of religious belief that have themselves been the subject of persistent diachronic dispute, realists should expect to find persistent moral disagreement at level (1). And insofar as these persistent nonmoral disputes are themselves intellectually legitimate (e.g., are not to be explained as the product of some distorting mechanism), realists should expect to find persistent moral disagreement at level (2). That is, there are persistent nonmoral disputes that not only provide the realist with replies by analogy (respectable company to keep) but are, in fact, largely responsible for the persistence of many moral disputes.

Finally, it seems false to the facts to suppose there has been no significant convergence of moral belief or moral progress over time, even at level (1). Most people no longer think that slavery, racial discrimination, rape, or child abuse is acceptable. Even those who still engage in these activities typically pay lip service to the wrongness of these activities and conceal the real nature of their activities from others and often themselves. Cultures or individuals who do not even pay lip service to these moral claims are rare, and we will typically be able to explain their moral beliefs as the product of various religious, ideological, or psychological distorting mechanisms. This will seem especially appropriate here, since the relevant changes in moral consciousness have all been changes in the same direction. That is, with each of these practices, in almost all cases where people's moral attitudes toward the practice have undergone informed and reflective change, they have changed in the same way (with these practices, from approval to disapproval and not the other way around). When changes in moral consciousness exhibit this sort of pattern, this is further reason to view the changes as progress. Of course, in viewing these changes in moral consciousness as progress and cultural or individual deviations as mistakes, I am relying at least in part on current moral views. But how could assessments of progress in ethics or the sciences be anything other than theory-dependent in this way? Surely, the sort of realism I have been defending is entitled to appeal to this kind of moral convergence as (defeasible) evidence of moral progress.

So nihilism is not clearly the best explanation of the nature of moral disagreement. The moral realist need only claim that *most genuine* moral disputes are *in principle* resolvable. Not all apparent moral disputes are genuine; some merely reflect the application of antecedently shared moral principles in different circumstances. Not every genuine moral dispute is even in principle resolvable, since some interlocutors may be so systematically mistaken in their moral beliefs that it is not possible to convince them of true claims. Moreover, moral ties are possible and some objective values or magnitudes may be incommensurable. Of those genuine moral disputes that moral realism is committed to regarding as resolvable in principle, some depend on disagreement over nonmoral issues, and others depend on antecedent disagreement over moral issues. Since nonmoral disagreement, whether culpable or not, is ex hypothesi resolvable in principle, moral disagreement that depends on nonmoral disagreement must itself be resolvable at least in principle. Finally, there seems no good reason to deny that genuine moral disputes (among interlocutors who are not systematically morally mistaken) that depend on antecedent moral disagreement are resolvable at least in principle on the basis of coherentist reasoning. These resources allow the realist a plausible account of the nature and significance of synchronic and diachronic moral disagreement.

Note

1 See chapter 9 in this volume – CWG.

13

NON-RELATIVE VIRTUES
An Aristotelian approach[1]

Martha Nussbaum

1

[O]n one central point there is a striking divergence between Aristotle and contemporary virtue theory. To many current defenders of an ethical approach based on the virtues, the return to the virtues is connected with a turn towards relativism – towards, that is, the view that the only appropriate criteria of ethical goodness are local ones, internal to the traditions and practices of each local society or group that asks itself questions about the good. The rejection of general algorithms and abstract rules in favour of an account of the good life based on specific modes of virtuous action is taken . . . to be connected with the abandonment of the project of rationally justifying a single norm of flourishing life for all human beings and a reliance, instead, on norms that are local both in origin and in application. . . .

This is an odd result, as far as Aristotle is concerned. For it is obvious that he was not only the defender of an ethical theory based on the virtues, but also the defender of a single objective account of the human good, or human flourishing. This account is supposed to be objective in the sense that it is justifiable by reference to reasons that do not derive merely from local traditions and practices, but rather from features of humanness that lie beneath all local traditions and are there to be seen whether or not they are in fact recognized in local traditions. And one of

From Martha Nussbaum, "Non-relative Virtues: An Aristotelian Approach," in M. Nussbaum and A. Sen (eds.) *The Quality of Life*, Oxford University Press, 1993, pp. 242–52, 254–57, and 259–69.

Martha Nussbaum is Ernst Freund Distinguished Service Professor of Law and Ethics at the University of Chicago, appointed in the Philosophy Department, the Law School, the Divinity School, and the College; she is an Associate of the Classics Department and an Affiliate of the Committee on Southern Asian Studies.

Aristotle's most obvious concerns was the criticism of existing moral traditions, in his own city and in others, as unjust or repressive, or in other ways incompatible with human flourishing. . . . Aristotle evidently believed that there is no incompatibility between basing an ethical theory on the virtues and defending the singleness and objectivity of the human good. Indeed, he seems to have believed that these two aims are mutually supportive.

The purpose of this paper is to establish that Aristotle did indeed have an interesting way of connecting the virtues with a search for ethical objectivity and with the criticism of existing local norms, a way that deserves our serious consideration as we work on these questions. . . .

2

The relativist, looking at different societies, is impressed by the variety and the apparent non-comparability in the lists of virtues she encounters. Examining the different lists, and observing the complex connections between each list and a concrete form of life and a concrete history, she may well feel that any list of virtues must be simply a reflection of local traditions and values, and that, virtues being (unlike Kantian principles or utilitarian algorithms) concrete and closely tied to forms of life, there can in fact be no list of virtues that will serve as normative for all these varied societies. It is not only that the specific forms of behaviour recommended in connection with the virtues differ greatly over time and place, it is also that the very areas that are singled out as spheres of virtue, and the manner in which they are individuated from other areas, vary so greatly. For someone who thinks this way, it is easy to feel that Aristotle's own list, despite its pretensions to universality and objectivity, must be similarly restricted, merely a reflection of one particular society's perceptions of salience and ways of distinguishing. . . .

But if we probe further into the way in which Aristotle in fact enumerates and individuates the virtues, we begin to notice things that cast doubt upon the suggestion that he simply described what was admired in his own society. . . .

What he does, in each case, is to isolate a sphere of human experience that figures in more or less any human life, and in which more or less any human being will have to make *some* choices rather than others, and act in *some* way rather than some other. . . . Aristotle then asks, what is it to choose and respond well within that sphere? And what is it to choose defectively? The "thin account" of each virtue is that it is whatever being stably disposed to act appropriately in that sphere consists in. There may be, and usually are, various competing specifications of what acting well, in each case, in fact comes to. Aristotle goes on to defend in each case some concrete specification, producing, at the end, a full or "thick" definition of the virtue.

Here are the most important spheres of experience recognized by Aristotle, along with the names of their corresponding virtues.[2]

Sphere	Virtue
1 Fear of important damages, esp. death	Courage
2 Bodily appetites and their pleasures	Moderation
3 Distribution of limited resources	Justice
4 Management of one's personal property, where others are concerned	Generosity
5 Management of personal property, where hospitality is concerned	Expansive hospitality
6 Attitudes and actions with respect to one's own worth	Greatness of soul
7 Attitude to slights and damages	Mildness of temper
8 "Association and living together and the fellowship of words and actions"	
(a) Truthfulness in speech	Truthfulness
(b) Social association of a playful kind	Easy grace (contrasted with coarseness, rudeness, insensitivity)
(c) Social association more generally	Nameless, but a kind of friendliness (contrasted with irritability and grumpiness)
9 Attitude to the good and ill fortune of others	Proper judgement (contrasted with enviousness, spitefulness, etc.)
10 Intellectual life	The various intellectual virtues, such as perceptiveness, knowledge, etc.
11 The planning of one's life and conduct	Practical wisdom

... What I want to insist on here ... is the care with which Aristotle articulates his general approach, beginning from a characterization of a sphere of universal experience and choice, and introducing the virtue-name as the name (as yet undefined) of whatever it is to choose appropriately in that area of experience. On this approach, it does not seem possible to say, as the relativist wishes to, that a given society does not contain anything that corresponds to a given virtue. . . . [E]veryone makes some choices and acts somehow or other in these spheres: if not properly, then improperly. Everyone has *some* attitude, and corresponding behaviour, towards her own death; her bodily appetites and their management; her property and its use; the distribution of social goods; telling the truth; being kind to others; cultivating a sense of play and delight, and so on. No matter where one lives one cannot escape these questions, so long as one is living a human life. But then this means that one's behaviour falls, willy-nilly, within the sphere of the Aristotelian virtue, in each case. If it is not appropriate, it is inappropriate; it cannot be off the map altogether. People will of course disagree about what the appropriate ways of acting and reacting in fact *are*. But in that case, as Aristotle has set things up, they are arguing about the same thing, and advancing competing specifications of the same virtue. The reference of the virtue term in each case is fixed by the sphere of experience – by what we shall from now on call the "grounding experiences." The thin or "nominal" definition of the virtue will be, in each case, that it is whatever being disposed to choose and respond well consists in, in that sphere. The job of ethical theory will be to search for the best further specification corresponding to this nominal definition, and to produce a full definition.

3

. . . [T]he reference of the virtue terms is fixed by spheres of choice, frequently connected with our finitude and limitation, that we encounter in virtue of shared conditions of human existence. The question about virtue usually arises in areas in which human choice is both non-optional and somewhat problematic. . . . Each family of virtue and vice or deficiency words attaches to some such sphere. And we can understand progress in ethics, like progress in scientific understanding, to be progress in finding the correct fuller specification of a virtue, isolated by its thin or nominal definition. This progress is aided by a perspicuous mapping of the sphere of the grounding experiences. . . .

In the Aristotelian approach it is obviously of the first importance to distinguish two stages of the inquiry: the initial demarcation of the sphere of choice, of the "grounding experiences" that fix the reference of the virtue term; and the ensuing more concrete inquiry into what the appropriate choice, in that sphere, *is*. . . .

Here, then, is a sketch for an objective human morality based upon the idea of virtuous action – that is, of appropriate functioning in each human sphere. The Aristotelian claim is that, further developed, it will retain the grounding in actual human experiences that is the strong point of virtue ethics, while gaining the ability to criticize local and traditional

171

moralities in the name of a more inclusive account of the circumstances of human life, and of the needs for human functioning that these circumstances call forth.

4

The proposal will encounter many objections. . . .

The first objection concerns the relationship between singleness of problem and singleness of solution. Let us grant for the moment that the Aristotelian approach has succeeded in coherently isolating and describing areas of human experience and choice that form, so to speak, the *terrain* of the virtues, and in giving thin definitions of each of the virtues as whatever it is that choosing and responding well within that sphere consists in. Let us suppose that the approach succeeds in doing this in a way that embraces many times and places, bringing disparate cultures together into a single debate about the good human being and the good human life. . . . Still, it might be argued, what has been achieved is, at best, a single discourse or debate about virtue. It has not been shown that this debate will have, as Aristotle believes, a single answer. . . . What is given in experience across groups is only the *ground* of virtuous action, the circumstances of life to which virtuous action is an appropriate response. Even if these grounding experiences are shared, that does not tell us that there will be a shared appropriate response.

The second objection goes deeper. For it questions the notion of spheres of shared human experience that lies at the heart of the Aristotelian approach. The approach, says this objector, seems to treat the experiences that ground the virtues as in some way primitive, given, and free from the cultural variation that we find in the plurality of normative conceptions of virtue. . . .

But, the objector continues, such assumptions are naïve. They will not stand up either to our best account of experience or to a close examination of the ways in which these so-called grounding experiences are in fact differently constructed by different cultures. In general, first of all, our best accounts of the nature of experience, even perceptual experience, inform us that there is no such thing as an "innocent eye" that receives an uninterpreted "given." Even sense-perception is interpretative, heavily influenced by belief, teaching, language, and in general by social and contextual features. . . .

[I]n the area of the human good . . . it is only a very naïve and historically insensitive moral philosopher who would say that the experience of the fear of death, or of bodily appetites, is a human constant. Recent anthropological work on the social construction of the emotions,[3] for example, has shown to what extent the experience of fear has learned and culturally variant elements. . . .

[T]he Aristotelian idea that there can be a single, non-relative discourse about human experiences such as mortality or desire is a naïve one. There is no such bedrock of shared experience, and thus no single sphere of choice within which the virtue is the disposition to choose well. So the Aristotelian project cannot even get off the ground.

Now the Aristotelian confronts a third objector, who attacks from a rather different direction. . . . [W]e could imagine a form of human life that does not contain these experiences – or some of them – at all, in any form. Thus the virtue that consists in acting well in that sphere need not be included in an account of the human good. In some cases, the experience may even be a sign of *bad* human life. . . .

Some objectors of the third kind will stop at this point, or use such observations to support the second objector's relativism. But in another prominent form this argument takes a non-relativist direction. . . . The objection to Aristotelian virtue ethics will then be that it limits our social aspirations, encouraging us to regard as permanent and necessary what we might in fact improve to the benefit of all human life. This is the direction in which the third objection to the virtues was pressed by Karl Marx, its most famous proponent. According to Marx's argument, a number of the leading bourgeois virtues are responses to defective relations of production. Bourgeois justice, generosity, etc., presuppose conditions and structures that are not ideal and that will be eliminated when communism is achieved. . . . It is in this sense that communism leads human beings beyond ethics.

The Aristotelian is thus urged to inquire into the basic structures of human life with the daring of a radical political imagination. . . .

5

. . . The first objector is right to insist on the distinction between singleness of framework and singleness of answer. . . . At this point, however, we can make four observations to indicate how the Aristotelian might deal with some of the objector's concerns here. First, the Aristotelian position that I wish to defend need not insist, in every case, on a single answer to the request for a specification of a virtue. The answer might well turn out to be a disjunction. The process of comparative and critical debate will, I imagine, eliminate numerous contenders. . . . But what remains might well be a (probably small) plurality of acceptable accounts. These accounts may or may not be capable of being subsumed under a single account of greater generality. . . .

Second, the general answer to a "What is *X*?" question in any sphere may well be susceptible of several or even of many concrete specifications, in connection with other local practices and local conditions. The normative account where friendship and hospitality are concerned, for example, is likely to be extremely general, admitting of many concrete "fillings." Friends in England will have different customs, where regular social visiting is concerned, from friends in ancient Athens. Yet both sets of customs can count as further specifications of a general account of friendship that mentions, for example, the Aristotelian criteria of mutual benefit and well-wishing, mutual enjoyment, mutual awareness, a shared conception of the good, and some form of "living together."[4] Sometimes we may want to view such concrete accounts as optional alternative specifications, to be chosen by a society on the basis of reasons of ease and convenience. Sometimes, on the other hand, we may want to insist that a particular account gives the only legitimate specification of the virtue in question for that concrete context; in that case, the concrete account could be viewed as a part of a longer or fuller version of the single normative account. . . .

Third . . . the particular choices that the virtuous person, under this conception, makes will always be a matter of being keenly responsive to the local features of his or her concrete context. . . . The Aristotelian virtues involve a delicate balancing between general rules and a keen awareness of particulars, in which process, as Aristotle stresses, the perception of the particular takes priority. It takes priority in the sense that a good rule is a good summary of wise particular choices, and not a court of last resort. Like rules in medicine and navigation, ethical rules should be held open to modification in the light of new circumstances. . . .

What I want to stress here is that Aristotelian particularism is fully compatible with Aristotelian objectivity. The fact that a good and virtuous decision is context-sensitive does not imply that it is right only *relative to*, or *inside*, a limited context, any more than the fact that a good navigational judgement is sensitive to particular weather conditions shows that it is correct only in a local or relational sense. It is right absolutely, objectively, anywhere in the human world, to attend to the particular features of one's context; and the person who so attends and who chooses accordingly is making, according to Aristotle, the humanly correct decision, period. . . .

Thus the Aristotelian virtue-based morality can capture a great deal of what the relativist is after, and still make a claim to objectivity, in the sense we have described. In fact, we might say that the Aristotelian virtues do better than the relativist virtues in explaining what people are actually doing when they scrutinize the features of their context carefully, looking at both the shared and the non-shared features with an eye to what is best. For, as Aristotle says, people who do this are usually searching for the good, not just for the way of their ancestors. They are prepared to defend their decisions as good or right, and to think of those who advocate a different course as disagreeing about what is right, not just narrating a different tradition.

Finally, we should point out that the Aristotelian virtues, and the deliberations they guide, unlike some systems of moral rules, remain always open to revision in the light of new circumstances and new evidence. In this way, again, they contain the flexibility to local conditions that the relativist would desire – but, again, without sacrificing objectivity. . . .

6

We must now turn to the second objection. Here, I believe, is the really serious threat to the Aristotelian position. Past writers on virtue, including Aristotle himself, have lacked sensitivity to the ways in which different traditions of discourse, different conceptual schemes, articulate the world, and also to the profound connections between the structure of discourse and the structure of experience itself. Any contemporary defence of the Aristotelian position must display this sensitivity, responding somehow to the data that the relativist historian or anthropologist brings forward.

The Aristotelian should begin, it seems to me, by granting that with respect to any complex matter of deep human importance there is no "innocent eye," no way of seeing the world that is entirely neutral and free of cultural shaping. . . . The Aristotelian should also grant, it seems to me, that the nature of human world interpretations is holistic and that the criticism of them must, equally, be holistic. . . .

But these two facts do not imply, as some relativists in literary theory and in anthropology tend to assume, that all world interpretations are equally valid and altogether non-comparable, that there are no good standards of assessment and "anything goes." . . . Certain ways in which people see the world can still be criticized exactly as Aristotle criticized them: as stupid, pernicious, and false. The standards used in such criticisms must come from inside human life. . . . And the inquirer must attempt, prior to criticism, to develop an inclusive understanding of the conceptual scheme being criticized, seeing what motivates each of its parts and how they hang together. . . .

The grounding experiences will not, the Aristotelian should concede, provide precisely a single, language-neutral bedrock on which an account of virtue can be straightforwardly and unproblematically based. The description and assessment of the ways in which different cultures have constructed these experiences will become one of the central tasks of Aristotelian philosophical criticism. But the relativist has, so far, shown no reason why we could not, at the end of the day, say that certain ways of conceptualizing death are more in keeping with the totality of our evidence and the totality of our wishes for flourishing life than others. . . .

Despite the evident differences in the specific cultural shaping of the grounding experiences, we do recognize the experiences of people in other cultures as similar to our own. We do converse with them about matters of deep importance, understand them, allow ourselves to be moved by them. . . . This sense of community and overlap seems to be especially strong in the areas that we have called the areas of the grounding experiences. And this, it seems, supports the Aristotelian claim that those experiences can be a good starting point for ethical debate.

Furthermore, it is necessary to stress that hardly any cultural group today is as focused upon its own internal traditions and as isolated from other cultures as the relativist argument presupposes. Cross-cultural communication and debate are ubiquitous facts of contemporary life, and our experience of cultural interaction indicates that in general the inhabitants of different conceptual schemes do tend to view their inter-action in the Aristotelian and not the relativist way. . . . [T]he traditional society is perfectly capable of viewing an external innovation as a device to solve a problem that it shares with the innovating society. . . . The par-ties do in fact search for the good, not the way of their ancestors; only traditionalist anthropologists insist, nostalgically, on the absolute preser-vation of the ancestral. . . .

As we pursue these possibilities, the basic spheres of experience identi-fied in the Aristotelian approach will no longer, we have said, be seen as spheres of *uninterpreted* experience. But we have also insisted that there is much family relatedness and much overlap among societies. . . . Not without a sensitive awareness that we are speaking of something that is experienced differently in different contexts, we can none the less identify certain features of our common humanity, closely related to Aristotle's original list, from which our debate might proceed.

1   *Mortality*. No matter how death is understood, all human beings face it and (after a certain age) know that they face it. This fact shapes every aspect of more or less every human life.
2   *The body*. Prior to any concrete cultural shaping, we are born with human bodies, whose possibilities and vulnerabilities do not as such belong to any culture rather than any other. Any given human being might have belonged to any culture. The experience of the body is culturally influenced; but the body itself, prior to such experience, provides limits and parameters that ensure a great deal of overlap in what is going to be experienced, where hunger, thirst, desire, and the five senses are concerned. It is all very well to point to the cultural component in these experiences. But when one spends time consider-ing issues of hunger and scarcity, and in general of human misery, such differences appear relatively small and refined, and one cannot

fail to acknowledge that "there are no known ethnic differences in human physiology with respect to metabolism of nutrients"[5]. . . .

3 *Pleasure and pain.* In every culture, there is a conception of pain; and these conceptions, which overlap very largely with one another, can plausibly be seen as grounded in universal and precultural experience. . . . [T]he negative response to bodily pain is surely primitive and universal, rather than learned and optional, however much its specific "grammar" may be shaped by later learning.

4 *Cognitive capability.* Aristotle's famous claim that "all human beings by nature reach out for understanding"[6] seems to stand up to the most refined anthropological analysis. . . .

5 *Practical reason.* All human beings, whatever their culture, participate (or try to) in the planning, and managing of their lives, asking and answering questions about how one should live and act. . . .

6 *Early infant development.* Prior to the greater part of specific cultural shaping, though perhaps not free from all shaping, are certain areas of human experience and development that are broadly shared and of great importance for the Aristotelian virtues: experiences of desire, pleasure, loss, one's own finitude, perhaps also of envy, grief, and gratitude. . . . All humans begin as hungry babies, perceiving their own helplessness, their alternating closeness to and distance from those on whom they depend, and so forth. . . .

7 *Affiliation.* Aristotle's claim that human beings as such feel a sense of fellowship with other human beings, and that we are by nature social animals, is an empirical claim; but it seems to be a sound one. . . .

8 *Humour.* There is nothing more culturally varied than humour; and yet, as Aristotle insists, some space for humour and play seems to be a need of any human life. . . .

We do not have a bedrock of completely uninterpreted "given" data, but we do have nuclei of experience around which the constructions of different societies proceed. There is no Archimedean point here, no pure access to unsullied "nature" – even, here, human nature – as it is in and of itself. There is just human life as it is lived. But in life as it is lived, we do find a family of experiences, clustering around certain focuses, which can provide reasonable starting points for cross-cultural reflection. . . .

7

The third objection raises, at bottom, a profound conceptual question: What is it to inquire about the *human* good? What circumstances of existence go to define what it is to live the life of a *human being*, and not some other life? Aristotle likes to point out that an inquiry into the human good cannot, on pain of incoherence, end up describing the good of some other being, say a god – a good that, on account of our circumstances, it is impossible for us to attain. What circumstances then? . . . It seems clear, first of all, that our mortality is an essential feature of our circumstances as human beings. An immortal being would have such a different form of life, and such different values and virtues, that it does not seem to make sense to regard that being as part of the same search for good. Essential, too, will be our dependence upon the world outside us: some sort of need for food, drink, the help of others. On the side of abilities, we would want to include cognitive functioning and the activity of practical reasoning as elements of any life that we would regard as human. Aristotle argues, plausibly, that we would want to include sociability as well, some sensitivity to the needs of and pleasure in the company of other beings similar to ourselves.

But it seems to me that the Marxist question remains, as a deep question about human forms of life and the search for the human good. For one certainly can imagine forms of human life that do not contain the holding of private property – nor, therefore, those virtues that have to do with its proper management. And this means that it remains an open question whether these virtues ought to be regarded as virtues, and kept upon our list. Marx wished to go much further, arguing that communism would remove the need for justice, courage, and most of the bourgeois virtues. I think we might be sceptical here. Aristotle's general attitude to such transformations of life is to suggest that they usually have a tragic dimension. If we remove one sort of problem – say, by removing private property – we frequently do so by introducing another – say, the absence of a certain sort of freedom of choice, the freedom that makes it possible to do fine and generous actions for others. . . .

8

The best conclusion to this sketch of an Aristotelian programme for virtue ethics was written by Aristotle himself . . .

> So much for our outline sketch for the good. For it looks as if we have to draw an outline first, and fill it in later. It would seem to be open to anyone to take things further and to articulate the good parts of the sketch. And time is a good discoverer or ally in such things. That's how the sciences have progressed as well: it is open to anyone to supply what is lacking.
>
> (*Nicomachean Ethics* 1098a20–26)

Notes

1 This paper was originally motivated by questions discussed at the WIDER Conference on Value and Technology, summer 1986, Helsinki. I would like to thank Steve and Frédérique Marglin for provoking some of these arguments, with hardly any of which they will agree. I would also like to thank Dan Brock for his helpful comments, Amartya Sen for many discussions of the issues, and the participants in the WIDER conference for their helpful questions and comments. Earlier versions of the paper were presented at the University of New Hampshire and at Villanova University; I am grateful to the audiences on those occasions for stimulating discussion. An earlier version of the paper was published in *Midwest Studies in Philosophy*, 1988 vol. 13, pp. 32–53.

2 My list here inserts justice in a place of prominence. (In the *Nicomachean Ethics* (*EN*) it is treated separately, after all the other virtues, and the introductory list defers it for that later examination.) I have also added at the end of the list categories corresponding to the various intellectual virtues discussed in *EN* VI, and also to *phronesis*, or practical wisdom, discussed in *EN* VI as well. Otherwise the order and wording of my list closely follows II. 7, which gives the programme for the more detailed analyses from III. 5 to IV.

3 See, for example, Harré (1986); Lutz (1988).

4 See Nussbaum (1986: ch. 12).

5 See Gopalan (1992).

6 *Metaphysics* I.1.

References

Gopalan, C. (1992) "Undernutrition: Measurement and Implications," in S. Osmani (ed.) *Nutrition and Poverty*, Oxford: Clarendon Press.

Harré, R. (ed.) (1986) *The Social Construction of the Emotions*, Oxford: Basil Blackwell.

Lutz, C. (1988) *Unnatural Emotions*, Chicago: University of Chicago Press.

Nussbaum, M. (1986) *The Fragility of Goodness: Luck and Ethics in Greek Tragedy and Philosophy*, Cambridge: Cambridge University Press.

14

IS CULTURAL PLURALISM RELEVANT TO MORAL KNOWLEDGE?

Alan Gewirth

Cultural pluralism is both a fact and a norm. It is a fact that our world, and indeed our society, are marked by a large diversity of cultures delineated in terms of race, class, gender, ethnicity, religion, ideology, and other partly interpenetrating variables. This fact raises the normative question of whether, or to what extent, such diversities should be recognized or even encouraged in policies concerning government, law, education, employment, the family, immigration, and other important areas of social concern.

I shall argue here that moral knowledge can and should be invoked to help answer the normative question. But before I undertake this task, we must take account of two extreme, mutually opposed views about the relation of moral knowledge to cultural pluralism as fact. According to one extreme, the fact of cultural pluralism disproves the existence of moral knowledge. According to the other extreme, the existence of moral knowledge disproves the moral relevance of cultural pluralism. The position I shall defend in this essay is closer to the second extreme than to the first; but some important qualifications will also have to be acknowledged.

I Some preliminary distinctions

To deal with these issues, we must first clarify the meanings of the constituent terms. First, as to "moral," we must recognize a distinction

From Alan Gewirth, "Is Cultural Pluralism Relevant to Moral Knowledge?," *Social Philosophy and Policy* 11 (1994): 22–42.

Alan Gewirth is Edward Carson Waller Distinguished Service Professor at the University of Chicago.

between *positive* and *normative* conceptions of morality. In general, a morality is a set of rules or directives for actions and institutions, especially as these are held to support or uphold what are taken to be the most important values or interests of persons or recipients other than or in addition to the agent. The rules purport to be categorically obligatory in that compliance with them is held to be mandatory for persons. . . .

Within this general characterization, the positive conception of morality consists in rules or directives that are in fact upheld as categorically obligatory. . . .

Contrasted with all such positive conceptions of morality is a normative conception. This consists in the moral precepts or rules or principles that are valid and thus ought to be upheld as categorically obligatory. The validity of morality in its normative conception, at least at the level of its fundamental principles, is independent of what persons or groups may contingently say or believe or do; this is the central difference between positive and normative morality. . . .

Given this initial distinction, we may contrast two different meanings of the phrase "moral knowledge." In one, moral knowledge is empirical knowledge about the various positive moralities. The positive conceptions of morality are appropriately studied by empirical disciplines like sociology, social psychology, anthropology, cultural history, and so forth. . . .

In contrast to such empirical modes of moral knowledge, the phrase "moral knowledge" may also have a quite distinct normative import. In this sense, moral knowledge is rational knowledge of the normative conception of morality, i.e., of what truly is morally right or valid. . . .

Let us now turn to "culture." This is also used in both a normative and a positive sense. In the normative sense, "culture" signifies a certain refined development of standards of excellence. . . . This "humanist" sense of culture stands in contrast to a positive "anthropological" sense whereby "culture" signifies a way of life as it is understood, symbolized, and evaluated by the group that lives it. In this positive sense, a culture is a set both of group practices and of related beliefs, and it includes both mores and positive moralities. Thus, in the positive sense, cultures are plural and relativist, in that different societies uphold diverse values and have different sets of practices and beliefs. . . .

An important question for the normative conception of morality presented above is whether it is also subject to such diversities. I shall advert below to some of the complex issues raised by this question. For the present, it must suffice to say that the normative conception as here envisaged holds that certain rational standards of moral rightness are universally valid. There are not alternative or mutually conflicting valid principles of what genuinely is morally right.

II Is there rational knowledge of normative morality?

On the basis of these preliminary distinctions, let us now inquire into the relevance of cultural pluralism to moral knowledge. . . .

The main challenge is to the very concept of normative morality with its accompanying normative conception of moral knowledge as rational knowledge of what is universally morally right or valid. The opposed contention is that there is no such knowledge because there is no one universally valid set or system of what is morally right; on the contrary, what is morally right varies with, and is relative to, the diversity of cultures, the more general beliefs and practices of different societies. In other words, there are only positive moralities; there is no normative morality in the sense in which this has been contrasted with positive moralities. In this regard, then, the fact of cultural pluralism is held to disprove the existence of rational moral knowledge.

. . . [T]here is an important difference in the *concepts* of positive morality and normative morality. For one thing, the contents of the positive conceptions may conflict with one another, not only from one historical era or culture to another, but also within the same historical era, and not only from one contemporaneous but geographically distinct society to another, but also within the same society. . . .

These conflicts within the positive conceptions of morality insistently show the need for a different, normative conception. For the conflicts raise the normative question, which goes back at least to the Hebrew Bible and to Socrates: Which of these positive moralities, if any, is valid or justified, as against its various rivals? This question adduces a normative concept that is distinct from the positive concept, for it asks not, What is recognized, believed, or accepted? but rather, What is morally right or valid, so that it *ought* to be believed and accepted?

. . . [I]t may still be contended by the moral relativist that what I have been calling "normative" morality is simply one positive, ethnocentric morality as against others: it is only the positive morality of "our own" group or culture as against the positive moralities of "other" cultures. . . . Every, or nearly every, positive morality claims rightness or validity for itself: witness its use of crucial concepts like "ought" and "right." Hence, the intended differentiation between normative and positive conceptions of morality has not yet been established.

This consideration shows that to justify the differentiation we must move to a second level: a level that is not simply conceptual but rather is theoretical and argumentative. The argument in question consists in showing that there is a supreme moral principle which is inherently rational, in that self-contradiction is incurred by any actual or prospective agent who rejects the principle. The system of morality based on this principle is normative, not positive, because even if it is not actually accepted in words, beliefs, or actions, it logically ought to be accepted as universally valid. This "ought" is, in the first instance, rational: it signifies what is logically required by the most elemental and universal principle of reason, the principle of noncontradiction. Because of the connection of reason with knowledge and truth, the supreme principle in question is truly the valid and universal moral principle; it can be known to be so, and all actions and institutions rationally must adhere to it. . . .

The argument[1] depends on the recognition that *action* is the universal and necessary context of all moralities and indeed of all practice. For all positive moralities and other practical precepts, amid their vast differences of specific contents, are concerned, directly or indirectly, with telling persons how they ought to act, especially toward one another. In addition, all persons are actual, prospective, or potential agents, and no person can reject for herself the whole context of agency, except, perhaps, by committing suicide; and even then the steps she takes to achieve this purpose would themselves be actions. The general context of action thus transcends the differences of the various positive cultures and moralities.

Taking off from this universal and morally neutral context, the argument for the supreme principle of morality undertakes to establish two main theses. The first is that every actual or prospective agent logically must accept that she has rights to freedom and well-being as the generic feature and necessary conditions of her action and of generally successful action. If any agent rejects these features, then she rejects the necessary conditions that are proximately involved in her agency, so that she is caught in a contradiction. Freedom is the procedural generic feature of action; it consists in controlling one's behavior by one's unforced choice while having knowledge of relevant circumstances. Well-being is the substantive generic feature of action; it consists in having the general abilities and conditions needed for achieving one's purposes, ranging from life and health to self-esteem and education. The second main thesis of the argument is that the agent logically must also accept that all other actual or prospective agents likewise have rights to freedom and well-being. I also call them "generic rights" because they are rights to have the generic features of action characterize one's behavior. . . .

Reduced to its barest essentials, the argument for the first main thesis is as follows. Freedom and well-being are necessary goods for each agent because they are the generic features and proximate necessary conditions of all his action and generally successful action, and hence are needed for whatever purpose-fulfillment he may seek to attain by acting. Hence, every agent has to accept (1) "I must have freedom and well-being." This "must" is practical-prescriptive in that it signifies the agent's advocacy or endorsement of his having the necessary conditions of his agency. Now by virtue of accepting (1), the agent also has to accept (2) "I have rights to freedom and well-being." For, if he rejects (2), then, because of the correlativity of claim-rights and strict "oughts," he also has to reject (3) "All other persons ought at least to refrain from removing or interfering with my freedom and well-being." By rejecting (3), he has to accept (4) "Other persons may [i.e., It is permissible that other persons] remove or interfere with my freedom and well-being." And by accepting (4), he has to accept (5) "I may not [i.e., It is permissible that I not] have freedom and well-being." But (5) contradicts (1). Since every agent must accept (1), he must reject (5). And since (5) follows from the denial of (2), every agent must reject that denial, so that he must accept (2) "I have rights to freedom and well-being."

I shall give an even briefer summary of the argument for the second main thesis. Since the necessary and sufficient reason for which the agent must hold that he has rights to freedom and well-being is that he is a prospective purposive agent, he logically must accept the generalization (6) "All prospective purposive agents have rights to freedom and well-being."

The supreme moral principle established by these two theses is thus a principle of universal human rights. I call it the Principle of Generic Consistency (PGC), because it combines the formal consideration of *consistency* or avoidance of self-contradiction with the material consideration of the *generic* features and rights of action.

If the above considerations are sound, they show that there is indeed an essential difference between the positive and the normative conceptions of morality, and that the reality of the latter is established by stringently rational argument. So there are moral principles and rules that are universally valid irrespective of positive conceptions of morality and the diversity of positive cultures, and we can know what these valid moral requirements are.

The PGC stands in contrast to kinds of ethical relativism which hold that moral requirements, if valid at all, can be so only in a partial and restricted way, by derivation from various particular cultural or other groups that accept them. . . .

[T]he view has crippling difficulties. It entails, for example, that a "convention or agreement" made by a group of Nazis that requires the killing of Jews is morally right "for" that group, and that all that can be said against it is that "we" ("our" group) disagree with this "convention." But our disagreement would reflect only our own "convention." On this view, there is no way to get beyond the relativism of some group's "convention or agreement."

What is especially damaging about this view, then, is not only that it could sanction the most monstrous violations of human rights, but also, more generally, that it makes it impossible to present rationally grounded moral criticisms, in a non-question-begging way, of the positive moralities of other cultures or societies. . . .

III The epistemic relevance of cultural pluralism to rational moral knowledge

Let us now return to the issue of the relevance of cultural pluralism to rational normative moral knowledge. We may here distinguish two different modes of relevance: *epistemic* and *contentual*. Epistemic relevance concerns the mode of ascertaining the kind of knowledge that I have claimed for the rational normative knowledge of what is morally right. ... [T]he PGC can be known to be valid by purely rational means, and thus independently of the varieties of positive moralities that figure in cultural pluralism.

There is, however, a more extreme interpretation of epistemic relevance that attacks the alleged culture-independence of the cognitive powers of reason itself. According to this interpretation, conceptions of reason or rationality are themselves relative to the diversity of cultures. The "rational" appeal to logical and empirical criteria of deduction and induction which is central to the argument outlined above for the PGC, and which is characteristic of Western culture, has as its counterpoise different conceptions of "reason" that figure in the appeals of various Eastern and other non-European cultures to religious faith, myth, intuition, tradition, and other culturally based conditions as the sources of knowledge and truth. It is contended that there is no non-question-begging way of proving the superiority of one of these conceptions of "reason" over the others. ...

[I]t must suffice for now to note three points in reply. First, because they respectively achieve logical necessity and reflect what is empirically ineluctable, deduction and induction are the only sure ways of avoiding arbitrariness and attaining objectivity. ... Second, concerning the various alleged rivals of deductive and inductive reason, such as religious faith or tradition, one may ask for their reasons in the sense of the justifications for upholding them; and any attempt at such justification must make use of reason in the sense of deduction or induction or both. But the reverse relation does not necessarily obtain. Third, although there have indeed been historical demands that deductive and inductive reason itself pass various justificatory tests set by religious faith, myth, tradition, and so forth, the very scrutiny to determine whether these tests are passed must itself make use of deductive or inductive reason. ... Thus, any attack on deductive and inductive reason or any claim to supersede it by some other human power or criterion must rely on such reason to justify its claims.

It remains the case, then, that with regard to the epistemic relevance of cultural pluralism to normative moral knowledge, the former is irrelevant to the latter. The epistemic diversities of cultural pluralism do not disprove the existence of rational moral knowledge as depicted above.

We can have rational knowledge of what is morally right in a way that is independent of the diversity of various positive cultures with their divergent positive moralities and positive conceptions of "reason" and "knowledge."

IV The contentual relevance of cultural pluralism to rational moral knowledge

Let us now turn to the contentual relevance of cultural pluralism to rational moral knowledge. This involves two interrelated questions: First, what bearing does cultural pluralism have on the contents of rational moral knowledge? Second, what bearing does rational moral knowledge have (especially in the way of requirements or permissions) on the contents of the various positive cultures, and thus of cultural pluralism?

On the first question . . . it is held that [the concept of human rights] is "a Western construct with limited applicability," this limitation deriving not only from "ideological differences" but also from "cultural differences whereby the philosophic underpinnings defining human nature and the relationships of individuals to others and to society are markedly at variance with Western individualism."[2] A prime emphasis of this culture-based objection is that in different cultures the unit of society is not the individual (to whom human rights are ascribed) but rather the group: the family, the clan, the tribe, the kinship circle, the community, the state, and so forth. On this view, then, the proper conception of the self is provided by the communitarian thesis that individuals are constituted or defined by the various biological or cultural groups to which they belong. Hence, if rights are to be invoked at all, it is groups or communities, rather than the individuals of traditional rights theories, who can properly be said to have rights. . . .

To this objection it is added that the very concept of a right is a relatively recent idea, stemming from fourteenth-century Europe, and not to be found in ancient times or in non-Western cultures. . . .

Here I shall just note three points. First, the fact that the idea of human rights has not been accepted in various eras or cultures does not prove that the idea is invalid or that it has limited relevance. For the idea of human rights is a normative, not a positive or empirically descriptive conception; it provides a rationally grounded moral model for how persons and groups ought to be regarded and treated, even if existing systems of interpersonal and political relations depart from it. . . .

Second, it is false that the idea of human rights is exclusively a modern Western conception. . . . [E]ven when the *words* "a right" or equivalent expressions are not used, the *idea* of a right can be found in ancient and medieval sources as well as in non-Western cultures. . . .

Third, on the large issue of the purported "individualism" of the prin-

186

ciple of human rights, I must here content myself with two brief replies. (Further considerations will be adduced below.) First, most moral and other practical precepts are addressed, directly or indirectly, to individuals. Since the argument for human rights proceeds in part from the assumptions common to all practical precepts, regardless of their divergent contents in different cultures, the fact that the precepts are addressed to individuals disproves the contention that the "individualism" of human rights is an ethnocentric limitation. . . .

A second reply to the "individualism" charge is the normative emphasis that the primary point of human rights is to protect individuals from unjustified threats to their freedom and well-being on the part of communities or cultures to which they may belong. . . .

V The contentual relevance of rational moral knowledge to cultural pluralism

Having rejected the contentual relevance of cultural pluralism to rational normative moral knowledge, we must now examine the reverse relevance. This concerns the question of how rational moral knowledge judges the rightness or wrongness, and thus the obligatoriness, permissibility, or impermissibility, of the various contents or components of cultural pluralism. The general point is that moral knowledge, as set forth in the PGC, can rationally adjudicate the moral status of the divergent positive cultures. . . .

Such applications involve a host of complex factors, of two main kinds. First, there must be adequate empirical knowledge of the cultural phenomena that are to be morally judged, especially of the various positive moralities. Such knowledge must include analyses of the causal backgrounds, including beliefs and external conditions, that serve to generate and explain the contents of the divergent positive moralities. Second, there must be careful analysis of just how the PGC applies to these phenomena. . . .

I shall confine myself to two main kinds of normative applications of rational moral knowledge (as represented by the PGC) to the contents of cultural pluralism. The first kind is *mandatory* and *negative*: the PGC shows that many cultures, including their positive moralities, contain morally wrong practices and institutions, so that their contradictory opposites are morally right in the sense of required. The morally wrong positive moralities are epitomized in the twentieth century by the cultures of Nazism and Stalinism, with their monstrous violations of the human rights to both freedom and well-being. So there are drastic limits to "cultural freedom," where this refers to the freedom of various cultures to treat some of their human members in drastically immoral ways. . . .

By virtue of prohibiting such morally wrong cultural practices and institutions, the mandatory normative application of rational moral knowledge also requires that cultures include certain basic protections of freedom and well-being for all the prospective purposive agents among their inhabitants. These protections include not only the prohibition of slavery and other basic harms but also the securing of civil liberties, certain democratic institutions, and provisions for welfare. . . .

[One] difficulty of applying the PGC arises from the nonrational sources of many cultural practices, where "rational" is defined by the canons of deductive and inductive logic with their norms concerning empirical inquiry. What does the PGC require when such infringements of human rights as the killing of innocent persons are justified on the basis of certain nonrational religious ideas? . . . Consider, for example, the Hindu religious practice of suttee, where a widow was required to throw herself on her husband's funeral pyre. Concerning this practice it has been written:

> [S]uttee works, for those for whom it works, as a representation and confirmation through heroic action of some of the deepest properties of Hinduism's moral world. In that world existence is imbued with divinity. The gods have descended to earth. . . . A shared cremation absolves sins and guarantees eternal union between husband and wife, linked to each other as god and goddess through the cycle of future rebirths.[3]

Even if one gives the most benign interpretation of the widow's willingness to commit suicide with this justification, there remains the question of whether her conduct is free or voluntary in the sense that she not only controls her behavior by her unforced choice but has knowledge of relevant circumstances, and is to this extent rational. If one views the religious beliefs in question as having been instilled through a long process of enculturation, with no opportunity provided for their critical (including empirical) assessment, then suttee and similar practices are egregious violations of the rights to freedom and well-being.

Let us now turn to a second kind of normative application of rational moral knowledge to cultural pluralism: an application which is *permissive* and *affirmative*. It is here that the tolerance sometimes invalidly attributed to "cultural relativism" finds a place. All those diverse cultural practices and institutions that do not violate the PGC's essential requirements are morally permitted, and indeed are largely encouraged, to exist. In this way a vast array of freedoms and modes of well-being, what J.S. Mill called "experiments of living,"[4] are shown to be morally legitimate. This tolerance is itself an application of the PGC to cultural pluralism: the differences between cultures are to be respected; one must not try to

force all cultures into the mold of some dominant culture, for such forcing would violate the rights to freedom and well-being of the members of
the various subcultures. . . .

Certain affirmative applications of the PGC as rational moral knowledge to cultural pluralism bear so heavily on the rights to freedom and
well-being that they are more mandatory than permissive. These applications deal not with the ways in which cultural groups may treat their
individual members by violating their human rights, but rather with the
ways in which diverse cultural groups may themselves be treated by the
state or the society at large. What is at issue here is the well-founded contention that the members of various groups – including, within the
United States, African Americans, Native Americans (American
Indians), Hispanic Americans, women, and others – are markedly inferior to the members of other, dominant groups in their effective rights to
freedom and well-being, power, wealth, and status. The members of such
submerged groups are discriminated against by the dominant political,
economic, educational, and other salient institutions of the wider society. As a result, the persons in question suffer from serious material dis-
advantages, but also from deep feelings of inferiority, envy, and injustice.
What the PGC requires here is that cultural pluralism be affirmatively
protected: the right to cultural pluralism is an affirmative as well as a
negative right. The needs of the members of various subcultures within
the dominant culture must be recognized and steps must be taken toward
their fulfillment.

This issue may be conceptualized in two different ways, with two different upshots for the moral protection of cultural pluralism. One way is
to maintain the PGC's direct focus on individual right. Insofar as the
individual members of the submerged cultural groups suffer violations
of their generic rights, action must be taken by the state to remove these
violations. . . .

Against this approach it has been argued, however, that the members
of many submerged groups are so closely linked together by strong ties
of group identity – whether in terms of language, history, religion, tradition, race, class, gender, or other variables – that to deal with them only
as individuals apart from this identity would fail to respect an essential
part of their personhood. On this view, what must be protected is not
only individual rights as such but the rights of groups to maintain their
own culture within the larger society. . . .

Even here, however, the concept of "group rights" admits of at least
two distinct interpretations. On one, more individualist interpretation,
the basis of group rights is in their consequences for the rights of individuals: that individual members of a group achieve effective fulfillment
of their rights to freedom and well-being requires that the group to
which they belong be protected in maintaining its cultural heritage of

language, customs, traditions, and so forth. Only so will the autonomy and dignity of the individual members of the group be respected. On another, more collectivist, communitarian, or even organicist interpretation, the group's maintenance of its cultural identity is intrinsically valuable, among other reasons because certain communal goods cannot be parceled out among the distinct individuals who compose the group, but can be had and enjoyed only collectively. . . .

It is not necessary, however, to take a position on these questions in order to note that the PGC requires emphatic recognition that individuals as members of various suppressed groups have equal rights to freedom and well-being. These rights include acceptance, toleration, and support for diverse cultures so long as these do not transgress the PGC's requirements. . . .

From the above considerations, then, there emerge two general normative relations between cultural pluralism and the moral universalism established by rational argument. Negatively, moral universalism sets the outer limits of the legitimacy of the various practices of cultural pluralism. Affirmatively, within these limits moral universalism encourages and upholds the diverse practices of cultural pluralism, the differences between human beings with regard to values and ways of life.

Notes

1 For a full statement of the argument, together with replies to objections, see Alan Gewirth, *Reason and Morality* (Chicago: University of Chicago Press, 1978), chs. 1–3.
2 Adamantia Pollis and Peter Schwab, *Human Rights and Cultural Perspectives* (New York: Praeger Publishers, 1979), p. 1.
3 Richard A. Shweder, *Thinking Through Cultures* (Cambridge, MA: Harvard University Press, 1991), p. 16 (pp. 108–109 in this volume).
4 See J.S. Mill, *On Liberty* (Indianapolis, IN: Bobbs-Merrill), ch. 3, para. 1.

Part V

NEW DIRECTIONS

15

THE PURSUIT OF THE IDEAL

Isaiah Berlin

II

When I was young I read *War and Peace* by Tolstoy, much too early. The real impact on me of this great novel came only later, together with that of other Russian writers, both novelists and social thinkers, of the mid-nineteenth century. These writers did much to shape my outlook. It seemed to me, and still does, that the purpose of these writers was not principally to give realistic accounts of the lives and relationships to one another of individuals or social groups or classes, not psychological or social analysis for its own sake – although, of course, the best of them achieved precisely this, incomparably. Their approach seemed to me essentially moral: they were concerned most deeply with what was responsible for injustice, oppression, falsity in human relations, imprisonment whether by stone walls or conformism – unprotesting submission to man-made yokes – moral blindness, egoism, cruelty, humiliation, servility, poverty, helplessness, bitter indignation, despair on the part of so many. In short, they were concerned with the nature of these experiences and their roots in the human condition: the condition of Russia in the first place, but, by implication, of all mankind. And conversely they wished to know what would bring about the opposite of this, a reign of truth, love, honesty, justice, security, personal relations based on the possibility of human dignity, decency, independence, freedom, spiritual fulfilment.

Some, like Tolstoy, found this in the outlook of simple people, unspoiled by civilization; like Rousseau, he wished to believe that the moral universe of peasants was not unlike that of children, not distorted

From "The Pursuit of the Ideal," in H. Hardy and R. Hausheer (eds.) *The Proper Study of Mankind: An Anthology of Essays*, London: Pimlico, 1998, pp. 2–16.

Isaiah Berlin was a Fellow of All Souls College and New College, Oxford, and was founding President of Wolfson College, Oxford.

by the conventions and institutions of civilization, which sprang from human vices – greed, egoism, spiritual blindness; that the world could be saved if only men saw the truth that lay at their feet; if they but looked, it was to be found in the Christian gospels, the Sermon on the Mount. Others among these Russians put their faith in scientific rationalism, or in social and political revolution founded on a true theory of historical change. Others again looked for answers in the teachings of the Orthodox theology, or in liberal Western democracy, or in a return to ancient Slav values, obscured by the reforms of Peter the Great and his successors.

What was common to all these outlooks was the belief that solutions to the central problems existed, that one could discover them, and, with sufficient selfless effort, realize them on earth. They all believed that the essence of human beings was to be able to choose how to live: societies could be transformed in the light of true ideals believed in with enough fervour and dedication. . . .

When I became a student at the University of Oxford, I began to read the works of the great philosophers, and found that the major figures, especially in the field of ethical and political thought, believed this too. Socrates thought that if certainty could be established in our knowledge of the external world by rational methods . . . the same methods would surely yield equal certainty in the field of human behaviour – how to live, what to be. This could be achieved by rational argument. Plato thought that an elite of sages who arrived at such certainty should be given the power of governing others intellectually less well endowed, in obedience to patterns dictated by the correct solutions to personal and social problems. The Stoics thought that the attainment of these solutions was in the power of any man who set himself to live according to reason. Jews, Christians, Muslims (I knew too little about Buddhism) believed that the true answers had been revealed by God to his chosen prophets and saints, and accepted the interpretation of these revealed truths by qualified teachers and the traditions to which they belonged.

The rationalists of the seventeenth century thought that the answers could be found by a species of metaphysical insight, a special application of the light of reason with which all men were endowed. The empiricists of the eighteenth century, impressed by the vast new realms of knowledge opened by the natural sciences based on mathematical techniques, which had driven out so much error, superstition, dogmatic nonsense, asked themselves, like Socrates, why the same methods should not succeed in establishing similar irrefutable laws in the realm of human affairs. With the new methods discovered by natural science, order could be introduced into the social sphere as well – uniformities could be observed, hypotheses formulated and tested by experiment; laws could be based on them, and then laws in specific regions of experience could be seen to be entailed by wider laws; and these in turn to be entailed by still wider laws, and so on upwards, until a great harmonious system, connected by unbreakable logical links and capable of being formulated in precise – that is, mathematical – terms, could be established.

The rational reorganization of society would put an end to spiritual and intellectual confusion, the reign of prejudice and superstition, blind obedience to unexamined dogmas, and the stupidities and cruelties of the oppressive regimes which such intellectual darkness bred and promoted. All that was wanted was the identification of the principal human needs and discovery of the means of satisfying them. This would create the happy, free, just, virtuous, harmonious world which Condorcet so movingly predicted in his prison cell in 1794. . . .

III

At some point I realized that what all these views had in common was a Platonic ideal: in the first place that, as in the sciences, all genuine questions must have one true answer and one only, all the rest being necessarily errors; in the second place that there must be a dependable path towards the discovery of these truths; in the third place that the true answers, when found, must necessarily be compatible with one another and form a single whole, for one truth cannot be incompatible with another – that we knew a priori. This kind of omniscience was the solution of the cosmic jigsaw puzzle. In the case of morals, we could then conceive what the perfect life must be, founded as it would be on a correct understanding of the rules that governed the universe.

True, we might never get to this condition of perfect knowledge – we may be too feeble-witted, or too weak or corrupt or sinful, to achieve this. The obstacles, both intellectual and those of external nature, may be too many. Moreover, opinions, as I say, had widely differed about the right path to pursue – some found it in churches, some in laboratories; some believed in intuition, others in experiment, or in mystical visions, or in mathematical calculation. But even if we could not ourselves reach these true answers, or indeed, the final system that interweaves them all, the answers must exist – else the questions were not real. The answers must be known to someone: perhaps Adam in Paradise knew; perhaps we shall only reach them at the end of days; if men cannot know them, perhaps the angels know; and if not the angels, then God knows. The timeless truths must in principle be knowable.

Some nineteenth-century thinkers – Hegel, Marx – thought it was not quite so simple. There were no timeless truths. There was historical development, continuous change; human horizons altered with each new step in the evolutionary ladder; history was a drama with many acts; it was moved by conflicts of forces, sometimes called dialectical, in the realms of both ideas and reality – conflicts which took the form of wars, revolutions, violent upheavals of nations, classes, cultures, movements. Yet after inevitable setbacks, failures, relapses, returns to barbarism, Condorcet's dream would come true. The drama would have a happy ending – man's reason had achieved triumphs in the past, it could not be held back for ever. Men would no longer be victims of nature or of their own largely irrational societies: reason would triumph; universal harmonious co-operation, true history, would at last begin.

. . . The day would dawn when men and women would take their lives in their own hands and not be self-seeking beings or the playthings of blind forces that they did not understand. It was, at the very least, not impossible to conceive what such an earthly paradise could be, and if it was conceivable we could, at any rate, try to march towards it. That has been at the centre of ethical thought from the Greeks to the Christian visionaries of the Middle Ages, from the Renaissance to progressive thought in the last century; and, indeed, is believed by many to this day.

IV

At a certain stage in my reading, I naturally met with the principal works of Machiavelli. They made a deep and lasting impression upon me, and shook my earlier faith. I derived from them not the most obvious teachings – on how to acquire and retain political power, or by what force or guile rulers must act if they are to regenerate their societies, or protect themselves and their states from enemies within or without, or what the principal qualities of rulers on the one hand, and of citizens on the other, must be, if their states are to flourish – but something else. Machiavelli was not a historicist: he thought it possible to restore something like the Roman Republic or Rome of the early Principate. He believed that to do this one needed a ruling class of brave, resourceful, intelligent, gifted men who knew how to seize opportunities and use them, and citizens who were adequately protected, patriotic, proud of their state, epitomes of manly, pagan virtues. That is how Rome rose to power and conquered the world, and it is the absence of this kind of wisdom and vitality and courage in adversity, of the qualities of both lions and foxes, that in the end brought it down. Decadent states were conquered by vigorous invaders who retained these virtues.

But Machiavelli also sets side by side with this the notion of Christian virtues – humility, acceptance of suffering, unworldliness, the hope of salvation in an afterlife – and he remarks that if, as he plainly himself favours, a state of a Roman type is to be established, these qualities will not promote it: those who live by the precepts of Christian morality are bound to be trampled on by the ruthless pursuit of power on the part of men who alone can recreate and dominate the republic which he wants to see. He does not condemn Christian virtues. He merely points out that the two moralities are incompatible, and he does not recognize an overarching criterion whereby we are enabled to decide the right life for men. The combination of *virtù* and Christian values is for him an impossibility. He simply leaves you to choose – he knows which he himself prefers.

The idea that this planted in my mind was the realization, which came as something of a shock, that not all the supreme values pursued by mankind now and in the past were necessarily compatible with one another. It undermined my earlier assumption, based on the *philosophia perennis*, that there could be no conflict between true ends, true answers to the central problems of life.

Then I came across Giambattista Vico's *Scienza nuova.* . . . This opened my eyes to something new. Vico seemed to be concerned with the succession of human cultures – every society had, for him, its own vision of reality, of the world in which it lived, and of itself and of its relations to its own past, to nature, to what it strove for. This vision of a society is conveyed by everything that its members do and think and feel – expressed and embodied in the kinds of words, the forms of language that they use, the images, the metaphors, the forms of worship, the institutions that they generate, which embody and convey their image of reality and of their place in it; by which they live. These visions differ with each successive social whole – each has its own gifts, values, modes of creation, incommensurable with one another: each must be understood in its own terms – understood, not necessarily evaluated.

The Homeric Greeks, the master class, Vico tells us, were cruel, barbarous, mean, oppressive to the weak; but they created the *Iliad* and the *Odyssey*, something we cannot do in our more enlightened day. Their great creative masterpieces belong to them, and once the vision of the world changes, the possibility of that type of creation disappears also. We, for our part, have our sciences, our thinkers, our poets, but there is no ladder of ascent from the ancients to the moderns. If this is so, it must be absurd to say that Racine is a better poet than Sophocles, that Bach is a rudimentary Beethoven, that, let us say, the Impressionist painters are the peak which the painters of Florence aspired to but did not reach. The values of these cultures are different, and they are not necessarily compatible with one another. . . . Machiavelli's Rome did not, in fact, exist. For Vico there is a plurality of civilizations (repetitive cycles of them, but that is unimportant), each with its own unique pattern. Machiavelli conveyed the idea of two incompatible outlooks; and here were societies the cultures of which were shaped by values, not means to ends but ultimate ends, ends in themselves, which differed, not in all respects – for they were all human – but in some profound, irreconcilable ways, not combinable in any final synthesis.

After this I naturally turned to the German eighteenth-century thinker

197

Johann Gottfried Herder. Vico thought of a succession of civilizations, Herder went further and compared national cultures in many lands and periods, and held that every society had what he called its own centre of gravity, which differed from that of others. If, as he wished, we are to understand Scandinavian sagas or the poetry of the Bible, we must not apply to them the aesthetic criteria of the critics of eighteenth-century Paris. The ways in which men live, think, feel, speak to one another, the clothes they wear, the songs they sing, the gods they worship, the food they eat, the assumptions, customs, habits which are intrinsic to them – it is these that create communities, each of which has its own "lifestyle". Communities may resemble each other in many respects, but the Greeks differ from Lutheran Germans, the Chinese differ from both; what they strive after and what they fear or worship are scarcely ever similar.

This view has been called cultural or moral relativism. . . . It is not relativism. Members of one culture can, by the force of imaginative insight, understand (what Vico called *entrare*) the values, the ideals, the forms of life of another culture or society, even those remote in time or space. They may find these values unacceptable, but if they open their minds sufficiently they can grasp how one might be a full human being, with whom one could communicate, and at the same time live in the light of values widely different from one's own, but which nevertheless one can see to be values, ends of life, by the realization of which men could be fulfilled.

"I prefer coffee, you prefer champagne. We have different tastes. There is no more to be said." That is relativism. But Herder's view, and Vico's, is not that: it is what I should describe as pluralism – that is, the conception that there are many different ends that men may seek and still be fully rational, fully men, capable of understanding each other and sympathizing and deriving light from each other, as we derive it from reading Plato or the novels of medieval Japan – worlds, outlooks, very remote from our own. Of course, if we did not have any values in common with these distant figures, each civilization would be enclosed in its own impenetrable bubble, and we could not understand them at all; this is what Spengler's typology amounts to. Intercommunication between cultures in time and space is possible only because what makes men human is common to them, and acts as a bridge between them. But our values are ours, and theirs are theirs. We are free to criticize the values of other cultures, to condemn them, but we cannot pretend not to understand them at all, or to regard them simply as subjective, the products of creatures in different circumstances with different tastes from our own, which do not speak to us at all.

There is a world of objective values. By this I mean those ends that men pursue for their own sakes, to which other things are means. I am not blind to what the Greeks valued – their values may not be mine, but

I can grasp what it would be like to live by their light, I can admire and respect them, and even imagine myself as pursuing them, although I do not – and do not wish to, and perhaps could not if I wished. Forms of life differ. Ends, moral principles, are many. But not infinitely many: they must be within the human horizon. If they are not, then they are outside the human sphere. . . .

What is clear is that values can clash – that is why civilizations are incompatible. They can be incompatible between cultures, or groups in the same culture, or between you and me. You believe in always telling the truth, no matter what: I do not, because I believe that it can sometimes be too painful and too destructive. We can discuss each other's point of view, we can try to reach common ground, but in the end what you pursue may not be reconcilable with the ends to which I find that I have dedicated my life. Values may easily clash within the breast of a single individual; and it does not follow that, if they do, some must be true and others false. Justice, rigorous justice, is for some people an absolute value, but it is not compatible with what may be no less ultimate values for them – mercy, compassion – as arises in concrete cases.

Both liberty and equality are among the primary goals pursued by human beings through many centuries; but total liberty for wolves is death to the lambs, total liberty of the powerful, the gifted, is not compatible with the rights to a decent existence of the weak and the less gifted. An artist, in order to create a masterpiece, may lead a life which plunges his family into misery and squalor to which he is indifferent. We may condemn him and declare that the masterpiece should be sacrificed to human needs, or we may take his side – but both attitudes embody values which for some men or women are ultimate, and which are intelligible to us all if we have any sympathy or imagination or understanding of human beings. Equality may demand the restraint of the liberty of those who wish to dominate; liberty – without some modicum of which there is no choice and therefore no possibility of remaining human as we understand the word – may have to be curtailed in order to make room for social welfare, to feed the hungry, to clothe the naked, to shelter the homeless, to leave room for the liberty of others, to allow justice or fairness to be exercised. . . .

These collisions of values are of the essence of . . . what we are. If we are told that these contradictions will be solved in some perfect world in which all good things can be harmonized in principle, then we must answer, to those who say this, that the meanings they attach to the names which for us denote the conflicting values are not ours. We must say that the world in which what we see as incompatible values are not in conflict is a world altogether beyond our ken; that principles which are harmonized in this other world are not the principles with which, in our daily lives, we are acquainted; if they are transformed, it is into conceptions

not known to us on earth. But it is on earth that we live, and it is here that we must believe and act.

The notion of the perfect whole, the ultimate solution, in which all good things coexist, seems to me to be not merely unattainable – that is a truism – but conceptually incoherent; I do not know what is meant by a harmony of this kind. Some among the Great Goods cannot live together. That is a conceptual truth. We are doomed to choose, and every choice may entail an irreparable loss. Happy are those who live under a discipline which they accept without question, who freely obey the orders of leaders, spiritual or temporal, whose word is fully accepted as unbreakable law; or those who have, by their own methods, arrived at clear and unshakeable convictions about what to do and what to be that brook no possible doubt. I can only say that those who rest on such comfortable beds of dogma are victims of forms of self-induced myopia, blinkers that may make for contentment, but not for understanding of what it is to be human.

V

So much for the theoretical objection, a fatal one, it seems to me, to the notion of the perfect state as the proper goal of our endeavours. But there is in addition a more practical socio-psychological obstacle to this, an obstacle that may be put to those whose simple faith, by which humanity has been nourished for so long, is resistant to philosophical arguments of any kind. It is true that some problems can be solved, some ills cured, in both the individual and social life. We can save men from hunger or misery or injustice, we can rescue men from slavery or imprisonment, and do good – all men have a basic sense of good and evil, no matter what cultures they belong to; but any study of society shows that every solution creates a new situation which breeds its own new needs and problems, new demands. The children have obtained what their parents and grandparents longed for – greater freedom, greater material welfare, a juster society; but the old ills are forgotten, and the children face new problems, brought about by the very solutions of the old ones, and these, even if they can in turn be solved, generate new situations, and with them new requirements – and so on, for ever – and unpredictably.

We cannot legislate for the unknown consequences of consequences of consequences. Marxists tell us that once the fight is won and true history has begun, the new problems that may arise will generate their own solutions, which can be peacefully realized by the united powers of harmonious, classless society. This seems to me a piece of metaphysical optimism for which there is no evidence in historical experience. In a society in which the same goals are universally accepted, problems can be only of means, all soluble by technological methods. That is a society

in which the inner life of man, the moral and spiritual and aesthetic imagination, no longer speaks at all. Is it for this that men and women should be destroyed or societies enslaved? Utopias have their value – nothing so wonderfully expands the imaginative horizons of human potentialities – but as guides to conduct they can prove literally fatal. Heraclitus was right, things cannot stand still.

So I conclude that the very notion of a final solution is not only impracticable but, if I am right, and some values cannot but clash, incoherent also. The possibility of a final solution – even if we forget the terrible sense that these words acquired in Hitler's day – turns out to be an illusion; and a very dangerous one. For if one really believes that such a solution is possible, then surely no cost would be too high to obtain it: to make mankind just and happy and creative and harmonious for ever – what could be too high a price to pay for that? To make such an omelette, there is surely no limit to the number of eggs that should be broken – that was the faith of Lenin, of Trotsky, of Mao, for all I know of Pol Pot. Since I know the only true path to the ultimate solution of the problem of society, I know which way to drive the human caravan; and since you are ignorant of what I know, you cannot be allowed to have liberty of choice even within the narrowest limits, if the goal is to be reached. You declare that a given policy will make you happier, or freer, or give you room to breathe; but I know that you are mistaken, I know what you need, what all men need; and if there is resistance based on ignorance or malevolence, then it must be broken and hundreds of thousands may have to perish to make millions happy for all time. What choice have we, who have the knowledge, but to be willing to sacrifice them all?

Some armed prophets seek to save mankind, and some only their own race because of its superior attributes, but whichever the motive, the millions slaughtered in wars or revolutions – gas chambers, gulag, genocide, all the monstrosities for which our century will be remembered – are the price men must pay for the felicity of future generations. If your desire to save mankind is serious, you must harden your heart, and not reckon the cost. . . .

The one thing that we may be sure of is the reality of the sacrifice, the dying and the dead. But the ideal for the sake of which they die remains unrealized. The eggs are broken, and the habit of breaking them grows, but the omelette remains invisible. Sacrifices for short-term goals, coercion, if men's plight is desperate enough and truly requires such measures, may be justified. But holocausts for the sake of distant goals, that is a cruel mockery of all that men hold dear, now and at all times.

VI

If the old perennial belief in the possibility of realizing ultimate harmony is a fallacy, and the position of the thinkers I have appealed

to – Machiavelli, Vico, Herder, Herzen – is valid, then, if we allow that Great Goods can collide, that some of them cannot live together, even though others can – in short, that one cannot have everything, in principle as well as in practice – and if human creativity may depend upon a variety of mutually exclusive choices: then, as Chernyshevsky and Lenin once asked, "What is to be done?" How do we choose between possibilities? What and how much must we sacrifice to what? There is, it seems to me, no clear reply. But the collisions, even if they cannot be avoided, can be softened. Claims can be balanced, compromises can be reached: in concrete situations not every claim is of equal force – so much liberty and so much equality; so much for sharp moral condemnation, and so much for understanding a given human situation; so much for the full force of the law, and so much for the prerogative of mercy; for feeding the hungry, clothing the naked, healing the sick, sheltering the homeless. Priorities, never final and absolute, must be established.

The first public obligation is to avoid extremes of suffering. Revolutions, wars, assassinations, extreme measures may in desperate situations be required. But history teaches us that their consequences are seldom what is anticipated; there is no guarantee, not even, at times, a high enough probability, that such acts will lead to improvement. We may take the risk of drastic action, in personal life or in public policy, but we must always be aware, never forget, that we may be mistaken, that certainty about the effect of such measures invariably leads to avoidable suffering of the innocent. So we must engage in what are called trade-offs – rules, values, principles must yield to each other in varying degrees in specific situations. Utilitarian solutions are sometimes wrong, but, I suspect, more often beneficent. The best that can be done, as a general rule, is to maintain a precarious equilibrium that will prevent the occurrence of desperate situations, of intolerable choices – that is the first requirement for a decent society; one that we can always strive for, in the light of the limited range of our knowledge, and even of our imperfect understanding of individuals and societies. A certain humility in these matters is very necessary.

This may seem a very flat answer, not the kind of thing that the idealistic young would wish, if need be, to fight and suffer for, in the cause of a new and nobler society. And, of course, we must not dramatize the incompatibility of values – there is a great deal of broad agreement among people in different societies over long stretches of time about what is right and wrong, good and evil. Of course traditions, outlooks, attitudes may legitimately differ; general principles may cut across too much human need. The concrete situation is almost everything. There is no escape: we must decide as we decide; moral risk cannot, at times, be avoided. All we can ask for is that none of the relevant factors be ignored, that the purposes we seek to realize should be seen as elements in a total form of life, which can be enhanced or damaged by decisions.

But, in the end, it is not a matter of purely subjective judgement: it is dictated by the forms of life of the society to which one belongs, a society among other societies, with values held in common, whether or not they are in conflict, by the majority of mankind throughout recorded history. There are, if not universal values, at any rate a minimum without which societies could scarcely survive. Few today would wish to defend slavery or ritual murder or Nazi gas chambers or the torture of human beings for the sake of pleasure or profit or even political good – or the duty of children to denounce their parents, which the French and Russian revolutions demanded, or mindless killing. There is no justification for compromise on this. But on the other hand, the search for perfection does seem to me a recipe for bloodshed, no better even if it is demanded by the sincerest of idealists, the purest of heart. No more rigorous moralist than Immanuel Kant has ever lived, but even he said, in a moment of illumination, "Out of the crooked timber of humanity no straight thing was ever made."[1] To force people into the neat uniforms demanded by dogmatically believed-in schemes is almost always the road to inhumanity. We can only do what we can: but that we must do, against difficulties.

Of course social or political collisions will take place; the mere conflict of positive values alone makes this unavoidable. Yet they can, I believe, be minimized by promoting and preserving an uneasy equilibrium, which is constantly threatened and in constant need of repair – that alone, I repeat, is the precondition for decent societies and morally acceptable behaviour, otherwise we are bound to lose our way. A little dull as a solution, you will say? Not the stuff of which calls to heroic action by inspired leaders are made? Yet if there is some truth in this view, perhaps that is sufficient. An eminent American philosopher of our day once said, "There is no a priori reason for supposing that the truth, when it is discovered, will necessarily prove interesting." It may be enough if it is truth, or even an approximation to it; consequently I do not feel apologetic for advancing this. Truth, said Tolstoy, "has been, is and will be beautiful".[2] I do not know if this is so in the realm of ethics, but it seems to me near enough to what most of us wish to believe not to be too lightly set aside.

Notes

1 *Kant's gesammelte Schriften* (Berlin, 1900–), vol. 8, p. 23, line 22.
2 *Sevastopol in May*, chapter 16.

16

THE RATIONALITY OF
TRADITIONS

Alasdair MacIntyre

Begin by considering the intimidating range of questions about what justice requires and permits, to which alternative and incompatible answers are offered by contending individuals and groups within contemporary societies. Does justice permit gross inequality of income and ownership? Does justice require compensatory action to remedy inequalities which are the result of past injustice, even if those who pay the costs of such compensation had no part in that injustice? Does justice permit or require the imposition of the death penalty and, if so, for what offenses? Is it just to permit legalized abortion? When is it just to go to war? The list of such questions is a long one.

Attention to the reasons which are adduced for offering different and rival answers to such questions makes it clear that underlying this wide diversity of judgments upon particular types of issue [is] a set of conflicting conceptions of justice, conceptions which are strikingly at odds with one another in a number of ways. Some conceptions of justice make the concept of desert central, while others deny it any relevance at all. Some conceptions appeal to inalienable human rights, others to some notion of social contract, and others again to a standard of utility. Moreover, the rival theories of justice which embody these rival conceptions also give expression to disagreements about the relationship of justice to other human goods, about the kind of equality which justice requires, about the range of transactions and persons to which considerations of justice are relevant, and about whether or not a knowledge of justice is possible without a knowledge of God's law. . . .

How ought we to decide among the claims of rival and incompatible

From Alasdair MacIntyre, *Whose Justice? Which Rationality?*, Notre Dame IN: University of Notre Dame Press, 1988, pp. 1–2, 5–7, 350–56 and 358–68.

Alasdair MacIntyre is Professor of Philosophy at Duke University.

accounts of justice competing for our moral, social, and political allegiance?

It would be natural enough to attempt to reply to this question by asking which systematic account of justice we would accept if the standards by which our actions were guided were the standards of rationality. To know what justice is, so it may seem, we must first learn what rationality in practice requires of us. Yet someone who tries to learn this at once encounters the fact that disputes about the nature of rationality in general and about practical rationality in particular are apparently as manifold and as intractable as disputes about justice. To be practically rational, so one contending party holds, is to act on the basis of calculations of the costs and benefits to oneself of each possible alternative course of action and its consequences. To be practically rational, affirms a rival party, is to act under those constraints which any rational person, capable of an impartiality which accords no particular privileges to one's own interests, would agree should be imposed. To be practically rational, so a third party contends, is to act in such a way as to achieve the ultimate and true good of human beings. So a third level of difference and conflict appears. . . .

We inhabit a culture in which an inability to arrive at agreed rationally justifiable conclusions on the nature of justice and practical rationality coexists with appeals by contending social groups to sets of rival and conflicting convictions unsupported by rational justification. . . . Disputed questions concerning justice and practical rationality are thus treated in the public realm, not as matter for rational inquiry, but rather for the assertion and counterassertion of alternative and incompatible sets of premises.

How did this come to be the case? The answer falls into two parts, each having to do with the Enlightenment and with its subsequent history. It was a central aspiration of the Enlightenment, an aspiration the formulation of which was itself a great achievement, to provide for debate in the public realm standards and methods of rational justification by which alternative courses of action in every sphere of life could be adjudged just or unjust, rational or irrational, enlightened or unenlightened. So, it was hoped, reason would displace authority and tradition. Rational justification was to appeal to principles undeniable by any rational person and therefore independent of all those social and cultural particularities which the Enlightenment thinkers took to be the mere accidental clothing of reason in particular times and places. . . .

Yet both the thinkers of the Enlightenment and their successors proved unable to agree as to what precisely those principles were which would be found undeniable by all rational persons. . . . Consequently, the legacy of the Enlightenment has been the provision of an ideal of rational justification which it has proved impossible to attain. And hence in key part derives the inability within our culture to unite conviction and rational justification. . . .

Is there some mode of understanding which could find no place in the Enlightenment's vision of the world by means of which the conceptual and theoretical resources can be provided for reuniting conviction concerning such matters as justice on the one hand and rational inquiry and justification on the other? . . .

What the Enlightenment made us for the most part blind to and what we now need to recover is, so I shall argue, a conception of rational inquiry as embodied in a tradition, a conception according to which the standards of rational justification themselves emerge from and are part of a history in which they are vindicated by the way in which they transcend the limitations of and provide remedies for the defects of their predecessors within the history of that same tradition.

[. . .]

The conclusion to which the argument so far has led is not only that it is out of the debates, conflicts, and inquiry of socially embodied, historically contingent traditions that contentions regarding practical rationality and justice are advanced, modified, abandoned, or replaced, but that there is no other way to engage in the formulation, elaboration, rational justification, and criticism of accounts of practical rationality and justice except from within some one particular tradition in conversation, cooperation, and conflict with those who inhabit the same tradition. . . .

It does not follow that what is said from within one tradition cannot be heard or overheard by those in another. Traditions which differ in the most radical way over certain subject matters may in respect of others share beliefs, images, and texts. Considerations urged from within one tradition may be ignored by those conducting inquiry or debate within another only at the cost, by their own standards, of excluding relevant good reasons for believing or disbelieving this or that or for acting in one way rather than another. Yet in other areas what is asserted or inquired into within the former tradition may have no counterpart whatsoever in the latter. And in those areas where there are subject matters or issues in common to more than one tradition, one such tradition may frame its theses by means of concepts such that the falsity of these upheld within one or more other traditions is entailed, yet at the same time no or insufficient common standards are available by which to judge between the rival standpoints. Logical incompatibility *and* incommensurability may both be present.

Logical incompatibility does of course require that at some level of characterization each tradition identifies that about which it is maintaining its thesis in such a way that both its adherents and those of its rival can recognize that it is one and the same subject matter about which they are making claims. But even so, each of course may have its own peculiar standards by which to judge what is to be accounted one and the same in the relevant respect. So two traditions may differ over the criteria to be applied in determining the range of cases in which the concept of justice has application, yet each in terms of its own standards recognizes that in certain of these cases at least the adherents of the other traditions are applying a concept of *justice* which, if it has application, excludes the application of their own. . . .

Each tradition can at each stage of its development provide rational justification for its central theses in its own terms, employing the concepts and standards by which it defines itself, but there is no set of independent standards of rational justification by appeal to which the issues between contending traditions can be decided.

It is not then that competing traditions do not share some standards. . . . Were it not so, their adherents would be unable to disagree in the way in which they do. But that upon which they agree is insufficient to resolve those disagreements. It may therefore seem to be the case that we are confronted with the rival and competing claims of a number of traditions to our allegiance in respect of our understanding of practical rationality and justice, among which we can have no good reason to decide in favor of any one rather than of the others. Each has its own standards of reasoning; each provides its own background beliefs. To offer one kind of reason, to appeal to one set of background beliefs, will already be to have assumed the standpoint of one particular tradition. But if we make no such assumption, then we can have no good reason to give more weight to the contentions advanced by one particular tradition than to those advanced by its rivals.

Argument along these lines has been adduced in support of a conclusion that if the only available standards of rationality are those made available by and within traditions, then no issue between contending traditions is rationally decidable. To assert or to conclude this rather than that can be rational relative to the standards of some particular tradition, but not rational as such. There can be no rationality as such. Every set of standards, every tradition incorporating a set of standards, has as much and as little claim to our allegiance as any other. Let us call this the relativist challenge, as contrasted with a second type of challenge, that which we may call perspectivist.

The relativist challenge rests upon a denial that rational debate between and rational choice among rival traditions is possible; the perspectivist challenge puts in question the possibility of making truth-claims from within any one tradition. For if there is a multiplicity of rival traditions, each with its own characteristic modes of rational justification internal to it, then that very fact entails that no one tradition can offer those outside it good reasons for excluding the theses of its rivals.

Yet if this is so, no one tradition is entitled to arrogate to itself an exclusive title; no one tradition can deny legitimacy to its rivals. What seemed to require rival traditions so to exclude and so to deny was belief in the logical incompatibility of the theses asserted and denied within rival traditions, a belief which embodied a recognition that if the theses of one such tradition were true, then some at least of the theses asserted by its rivals were false.

The solution, so the perspectivist argues, is to withdraw the ascription of truth and falsity, at least in the sense in which "true" and "false" have been understood so far within the practice of such traditions, both from individual theses and from the bodies of systematic belief of which such theses are constitutive parts. Instead of interpreting rival traditions as mutually exclusive and incompatible ways of understanding one and the same world, one and the same subject matter, let us understand them instead as providing very different, complementary perspectives for envisaging the realities about which they speak to us.

The relativist challenge and the perspectivist challenge share some premises and are often presented jointly as parts of a single argument. . . . I am going to argue that they are fundamentally misconceived and misdirected. Their apparent power derives, so I shall want to suggest, from their inversion of certain central Enlightenment positions concerning truth and rationality. While the thinkers of the Enlightenment insisted upon a particular type of view of truth and rationality, one in which truth is guaranteed by rational method and rational method appeals to principles undeniable by any fully reflective rational person, the protagonists of post-Enlightenment relativism and perspectivism claim that if the Enlightenment conceptions of truth and rationality cannot be sustained, theirs is the only possible alternative. . . .

What neither was or is able to recognize is the kind of rationality possessed by traditions. In part this was and is because of the enmity to tradition as inherently obscurantist which is and was to be found equally among Kantians and Benthamites, neo-Kantians and later utilitarians, on the one hand, and among Nietzscheans and post-Nietzscheans on the other. But in part the invisibility of the rationality of tradition was due to the lack of expositions, let alone defenses, of that rationality. . . .

What I have to do, then, is to provide an account of the rationality presupposed by and implicit in the practice of those inquiry-bearing traditions with whose history I have been concerned which will be adequate to meet the challenges posed by relativism and perspectivism. . . .

The rationality of a tradition-constituted and tradition-constitutive enquiry is in key and essential part a matter of the kind of progress which it makes through a number of well-defined types of stage. Every such form of inquiry begins in and from some condition of pure historical contingency, from the beliefs, institutions, and practices of some particular community which constitute a given. Within such a community authority will have been conferred upon certain texts and certain voices. Bards, priests, prophets, kings, and, on occasion, fools and jesters will all be heard. All such communities are always, to greater or lesser degree, in a state of change. . . .

What takes a given community from a first stage in which the beliefs, utterances, texts, and persons taken to be authoritative are deferred to unquestioningly, or at least without systematic questioning, may be one or more of several types of occurrence. Authoritative texts or utterances may be shown to be susceptible to, by actually receiving, alternative and incompatible interpretations, enjoining perhaps alternative and incompatible courses of action. Incoherences in the established system of beliefs may become evident. Confrontation by new situations, engendering new questions, may reveal within established practices and beliefs a lack of resources for offering or for justifying answers to these new questions. The coming together of two previously separate communities, each with its own well-established institutions, practices, and beliefs, either by migration or by conquest, may open up new alternative possibilities and require more than the existing means of evaluation are able to provide.

What responses the inhabitants of a particular community make in the face of such stimuli toward the reformulation of their beliefs or the remaking of their practices or both will depend not only upon what stock of reasons and of questioning and reasoning abilities they already possess but also upon their inventiveness. . . . Since beliefs are expressed in and through rituals and ritual dramas, masks and modes of dress, the ways in which houses are structured and villages and towns laid out, and of course by actions in general, the reformulations of belief are not to be thought of only in intellectual terms; or rather the intellect is not to be thought of as either a Cartesian mind or a materialist brain, but as that through which thinking individuals relate themselves to each other and to natural and social objects as these present themselves to them.

We are now in a position to contrast three stages in the initial development of a tradition: a first in which the relevant beliefs, texts, and authorities have not yet been put in question; a second in which inadequacies of various types have been identified, but not yet remedied; and a third in which response to those inadequacies has resulted in a set of reformulations, reevaluations, and new formulations and evaluations, designed to remedy inadequacies and overcome limitations. . . .

The development of a tradition is to be distinguished from that gradual transformation of beliefs to which every set of beliefs is exposed, both by its systematic and by its deliberate character. The very earliest stages in the development of anything worth calling a tradition of inquiry are thus already marked by theorizing. And the development of a tradition of inquiry is also to be distinguished from those abrupt general changes in belief which occur when, for example, a community undergoes a mass conversion. . . . Some core of shared belief, constitutive of allegiance to the tradition, has to survive every rupture.

When the third stage of development is reached, those members of a community who have accepted the beliefs of the tradition in their new form – and those beliefs may inform only a limited part of the whole community's life or be such as concern its overall structure and indeed its relationship to the universe – become able to contrast their new beliefs with the old. Between those older beliefs and the world as they now understand it there is a radical discrepancy to be perceived. It is this lack of correspondence, between what the mind then judged and believed and reality as now perceived, classified, and understood, which is ascribed when those earlier judgments and beliefs are called *false*. The original and most elementary version of the correspondence theory of truth is one in which it is applied retrospectively in the form of a correspondence theory of falsity. . . .

[I]t is important to remember that the presupposed conception of mind is not Cartesian. It is rather of mind as activity, of mind as engaging with the natural and social world in such activities as identification, reidentification, collecting, separating, classifying, and naming[;] and all this by touching, grasping, pointing, breaking down, building up, calling to, answering to, and so on. The mind is adequate to its objects insofar as the expectations which it frames on the basis of these activities are not liable to disappointment and the remembering which it engages in enables it to return to and recover what it had encountered previously, whether the objects themselves are still present or not. . . .

Those who have reached a certain stage in that development are then able to look back and to identify their own previous intellectual inadequacy or the intellectual inadequacy of their predecessors by comparing what they now judge the world, or at least part of it, to be with what it was then judged to be. To claim truth for one's present mindset and the judgments which are its expression is to claim that this kind of inadequacy, this kind of discrepancy, will never appear in any possible future situation, no matter how searching the inquiry, no matter how much evidence is provided, no matter what developments in rational inquiry may occur. The test for truth in the present, therefore, is always to summon up as many questions and as many objections of the greatest strength possible; what can be justifiably claimed as true is what has sufficiently withstood such dialectical questioning and framing of objections. . . .

There characteristically comes a time in the history of tradition-constituted inquiries when those engaged in them may find occasion or need to frame a theory of their own activities of inquiry. What kind of theory is then developed will of course vary from one tradition to another. . . .

Nonetheless, to some degree, insofar as a tradition of rational inquiry is such, it will tend to recognize what it shares as such with other traditions, and in the development of such traditions common characteristic, if not universal, patterns will appear.

Standard forms of argument will be developed, and requirements for successful dialectical questioning established. The weakest form of argument, but nonetheless that which will prevail in the absence of any other, will be the appeal to the authority of established belief, merely as established. The identification of incoherence within established belief will always provide a reason for inquiring further, but not in itself a conclusive reason for rejecting established belief, until something more adequate because less incoherent has been discovered. At every stage beliefs and judgments will be justified by reference to the beliefs and judgments of the previous stage, and insofar as a tradition has constituted itself as a successful form of inquiry, the claims to truth made within that tradition will always be in some specifiable way less vulnerable to dialectical questioning and objection than were their predecessors.

The conception of rationality and truth as thus embodied in tradition-constituted inquiry is of course strikingly at odds with both standard Cartesian and standard Hegelian accounts of rationality. Because every such rational tradition begins from the contingency and positivity of some set of established beliefs, the rationality of tradition is inescapably anti-Cartesian. In systematizing and ordering the truths they take themselves to have discovered, the adherents of a tradition may well assign a primary place in the structures of their theorizing to certain truths and treat them as first metaphysical or practical principles. But such principles will have had to vindicate themselves in the historical process of dialectical justification. . . . They are justified insofar as in the history of this tradition they have, by surviving the process of dialectical questioning, vindicated themselves as superior to their historical predecessors. Hence such first principles are not self-sufficient, self-justifying epistemological first principles. . . .

Yet if in what it moves from, tradition-constituted inquiry is anti-Cartesian, in what it moves toward, tradition-constituted inquiry is anti-Hegelian. Implicit in the rationality of such inquiry there is indeed a conception of a final truth, that is to say, a relationship of the mind to its objects which would be wholly adequate in respect of the capacities of that mind. But any conception of that state as one in which the mind could by its own powers know itself as thus adequately informed is ruled out; the Absolute Knowledge of the Hegelian system is from this tradition-constituted standpoint a chimaera. No one at any stage can ever rule out the future possibility of their present beliefs and judgments being shown to be inadequate in a variety of ways.

It is perhaps this combination of anti-Cartesian and anti-Hegelian aspects which seems to afford plausibility to the relativist and the perspectivist challenges. Traditions fail the Cartesian test of beginning from unassailable evident truths; not only do they begin from contingent positivity, but each begins from a point different from that of the others. Traditions also fail the Hegelian test of showing that their goal is some final rational state which they share with all other movements of thought. Traditions are always and ineradically to some degree local, informed by particularities of language and social and natural environment. . . . Those educated or indoctrinated into accepting Cartesian or Hegelian standards will take the positivity of tradition to be a sign of arbitrariness. For each tradition will, so it may seem, pursue its own specific historical path, and all that we shall be confronted with in the end is a set of independent rival histories.

The answer to this suggestion, and indeed more generally to relativism and to perspectivism, has to begin from considering one particular kind of occurrence in the history of traditions, which is not among those so far cataloged. Yet it is in the way in which the adherents of a tradition respond to such occurrences, and in the success or failure which attends upon their response, that traditions attain or fail to attain intellectual maturity. The kind of occurrence is that to which I have given the name "epistemological crisis". . . . Epistemological crises may occur in the history of individuals . . . as well as in that of groups. But they can also be crises in and for a whole tradition.

. . . At any point it may happen to any tradition-constituted inquiry that by its own standards of progress it ceases to make progress. Its hitherto trusted methods of inquiry have become sterile. Conflicts over rival answers to key questions can no longer be settled rationally. Moreover, it may indeed happen that the use of the methods of inquiry and of the forms of argument, by means of which rational progress had been achieved so far, begins to have the effect of increasingly disclosing new inadequacies, hitherto unrecognized incoherences, and new problems for the solution of which there seem to be insufficient or no resources within the established fabric of belief.

This kind of dissolution of historically founded certitudes is the mark of an epistemological crisis. The solution to a genuine epistemological crisis requires the invention or discovery of new concepts and the framing of some new type or types of theory which meet three highly exacting requirements. First, this in some ways radically new and conceptually enriched scheme, if it is to put an end to epistemological crisis, must furnish a solution to the problems which had previously proved intractable in a systematic and coherent way. Second, it must also provide an explanation of just what it was which rendered the tradition, before it had acquired these new resources, sterile or incoherent or both. And third, these first two tasks must be carried out in a way which exhibits some fundamental continuity of the new conceptual and theoretical structures

212

with the shared beliefs in terms of which the tradition of inquiry had been defined up to this point.

The theses central to the new theoretical and conceptual structures, just because they are significantly richer than and escape the limitations of those theses that were central to the tradition before and as it entered its period of epistemological crisis, will in no way be derivable from those earlier positions. Imaginative conceptual innovation will have had to occur. The justification of the new theses will lie precisely in their ability to achieve what could not have been achieved prior to that innovation. . . .

To have passed through an epistemological crisis successfully enables the adherents of a tradition of inquiry to rewrite its history in a more insightful way. And such a history of a particular tradition provides not only a way of identifying the continuities in virtue of which that tradition of inquiry has survived and flourished as one and the same tradition, but also of identifying more accurately that structure of justification which underpins whatever claims to truth are made within it, claims which are more and other than claims to warranted assertibility. The concept of warranted assertibility always has application only at some particular stage in the development of a tradition of inquiry, and a claim that such and such is warrantedly assertible always, therefore, has to make implicit or explicit references to such times and places. The concept of truth, however, is timeless. To claim that some thesis is true is not only to claim for all possible times and places that it cannot be shown to fail to correspond to reality in the sense of "correspond" elucidated earlier, but also that the mind which expresses its thought in that thesis is in fact adequate to its object. The implications of this claim made in this way from within a tradition are precisely what enable us to show how the relativist challenge is misconceived.

Every tradition, whether it recognizes the fact or not, confronts the possibility that at some future time it will fall into a state of epistemological crisis, recognizable as such by its own standards of rational justification, which have themselves been vindicated up to that time as the best to emerge from the history of that particular tradition. . . .

That particular tradition's claims to truth can at some point in this process no longer be sustained. And this by itself is enough to show that if part of the relativist's thesis is that each tradition, since it provides its own standards of rational justification, must always be vindicated in the light of those standards, then on this at least the relativist is mistaken. But whether the relativist has claimed this or not, a further even more important possibility now becomes clear. For the adherents of a tradition which is now in this state of fundamental and radical crisis may at this point encounter in a new way the claims of some particular rival tradition. . . .

When they have understood the beliefs of the alien tradition, they may find themselves compelled to recognize that within this other tradition it is possible to construct from the concepts and theories peculiar to it what they were unable to provide from their own conceptual and theoretical resources, a cogent and illuminating explanation – cogent and illuminating, that is, by their own standards – of why their own intellectual tradition had been unable to solve its problems or restore its coherence. The standards by which they judge this explanation to be cogent and illuminating will be the very same standards by which they have found their tradition wanting in the face of epistemological crisis. But while this new explanation satisfies two of the requirements for an adequate response to an epistemological crisis within a tradition – insofar as it *both* explains why, given the structures of inquiry within that tradition, the crisis had to happen as it did *and* does not itself suffer from the same defects of incoherence or resourcelessness, the recognition of which had been the initial stage of their crisis – it fails to satisfy the third. Derived as it is from a genuinely alien tradition, the new explanation does not stand in any sort of substantive continuity with the preceding history of the tradition in crisis.

In this kind of situation the rationality of tradition requires an acknowledgment by those who have hitherto inhabited and given their allegiance to the tradition in crisis that the alien tradition is superior in rationality and in respect of its claims to truth to their own. What the explanation afforded from within the alien tradition will have disclosed is a lack of correspondence between the dominant beliefs of their own tradition and the reality disclosed by the most successful explanation, and it may well be the only successful explanation which they have been able to discover. Hence the claim to truth for what have hitherto been their own beliefs has been defeated. . . .

It is important to remember at this point that not all epistemological crises are resolved so successfully. Some indeed are not resolved, and their lack of resolution itself defeats the tradition which has issued in such crises, without at the same time vindicating the claims of any other. Thus a tradition can be rationally discredited by and in the light of appeal to its very own standards of rationality in more than one way. These are the possibilities which the relativist challenge has failed to envisage. That challenge relied upon the argument that if each tradition carries within it its own standards of rational justification, then, insofar as traditions of inquiry are genuinely distinct and different from each other, there is no way in which each tradition can enter into rational debate with any other, and no such tradition can therefore vindicate its rational superiority over its rivals. But if this were so, then there could be no good reason to give one's allegiance to the standpoint of any one tradition rather than to that of any other. This argument can now be seen to be unsound. It is first of all untrue, and the preceding argument shows it to be untrue, that traditions, understood as each possessing its own account of and practices of rational justification, therefore cannot defeat or be defeated by other traditions. It is in respect of their adequacy or inadequacy in their responses to epistemological crises that traditions are vindicated or fail to be vindicated. . . .

To this the relativist may reply that I have at least conceded that over long periods of time two or more rival traditions may develop and flourish without encountering more than minor epistemological crises, or at least such as they are well able to cope with out of their own resources. And where this is the case, during such extended periods of time no one of these traditions will be able to encounter its rivals in such a way as to defeat them, nor will it be the case that any one of them will discredit itself by its inability to resolve its own crises. This is clearly true. As a matter of historical fact for very long periods traditions of very different kinds do indeed seem to coexist without any ability to bring their conflicts and disagreements to rational resolution . . .

There is, however, a prior question to be answered by the relativist: Who is in a position to issue such a challenge? For the person who is to do so must during such period of time *either* be him or herself an inhabitant of one of the two or more rival traditions, owning allegiance to its standards of inquiry and justification and employing them in his or her reasoning, *or* be someone outside all of the traditions, him or herself traditionless. The former alternative precludes the possibility of relativism. Such a person, in the absence of serious epistemological crisis within his or her tradition, could have no good reason for putting his or her allegiance to it in question and every reason for continuing in that allegiance. What then of the latter alternative? Can the relativist challenge be issued from some standpoint outside all tradition?

. . . [I]t is an illusion to suppose that there is some neutral standing ground, some locus for rationality as such, which can afford rational resources sufficient for inquiry independent of all traditions. . . . The person outside all traditions lacks sufficient rational resources for inquiry and a fortiori for inquiry into what tradition is to be rationally preferred. He or she has no adequate relevant means of rational evaluation and hence can come to no well-grounded conclusion, including the conclusion that no tradition can vindicate itself against any other. To be outside all traditions is to be a stranger to inquiry: it is to be in a state of intellectual and moral destitution, a condition from which it is impossible to issue the relativist challenge.

The perspectivist's failure is complementary to the relativist's. Like the relativist, the perspectivist is committed to maintaining that no claim to truth made in the name of any one competing tradition could defeat the claims to truth made in the name of its rivals. And this we have already seen to be a mistake, a mistake which commonly arises because the perspectivist foists on to the defenders of traditions some conception of truth other than that which is theirs, perhaps a Cartesian or a Hegelian conception of truth or perhaps one which assimilates truth to warranted assertibility.

The perspectivist, moreover, fails to recognize how integral the conception of truth is to tradition-constituted forms of inquiry. . . . [G]enuinely to adopt the standpoint of a tradition thereby commits one to its view of what is true and false and, in so committing one, prohibits one from adopting any rival standpoint. Hence the perspectivist could indeed *pretend* to assume the standpoint of some one particular tradition of inquiry; he or she could not in fact do so. The multiplicity of traditions does not afford a multiplicity of perspectives among which we can move, but a multiplicity of antagonistic commitments, between which only conflict, rational or nonrational, is possible.

Perspectivism, in this once more like relativism, is a doctrine only possible for those who regard themselves as outsiders, as uncommitted or rather as committed only to acting a succession of temporary parts. From their point of view any conception of truth but the most minimal appears to have been discredited. And from the standpoint afforded by the rationality of tradition-constituted inquiry it is clear that such persons are by their stance excluded from the possession of any concept of truth adequate for systematic rational inquiry. Hence theirs is not so much a conclusion about truth as an exclusion from it and thereby from rational debate.

17

POLITICAL LIBERALISM AND THE IDEA OF AN OVERLAPPING CONSENSUS

John Rawls

Lecture I Fundamental ideas

I begin with a first fundamental question about political justice in a democratic society, namely what is the most appropriate conception of justice for specifying the fair terms of social cooperation between citizens regarded as free and equal, and as fully cooperating members of society over a complete life, from one generation to the next?

We join this first fundamental question with a second, that of toleration understood in a general way. The political culture of a democratic society is always marked by a diversity of opposing and irreconcilable religious, philosophical, and moral doctrines. Some of these are perfectly reasonable, and this diversity among reasonable doctrines political liberalism sees as the inevitable long-run result of the powers of human reason at work within the background of enduring free institutions. Thus, the second question is what are the grounds of toleration so understood and given the fact of reasonable pluralism as the inevitable outcome of free institutions? Combining both questions we have: how is it possible for there to exist over time a just and stable society of free and equal citizens, who remain profoundly divided by reasonable religious, philosophical, and moral doctrines? . . .

From John Rawls, *Political Liberalism*, New York: Columbia University Press, 1993, pp. 3–6, 9–11, 36–38, 54–61, 146–48, 150–51, 154, and 156–58.

John Rawls is Emeritus Professor of Philosophy at Harvard University.

§ 1 Addressing two fundamental questions

1 Focusing on the first fundamental question, the course of democratic thought over the past two centuries or so makes plain that there is at present no agreement on the way the basic institutions of a constitutional democracy should be arranged if they are to satisfy the fair terms of cooperation between citizens regarded as free and equal. This is shown in the deeply contested ideas about how the values of liberty and equality are best expressed in the basic rights and liberties of citizens so as to answer to the claims of both liberty and equality. . . .

As a way to answer our first question, justice as fairness[1] tries to adjudicate between these contending traditions, first, by proposing two principles of justice to serve as guidelines for how basic institutions are to realize the values of liberty and equality; and second, by specifying a point of view from which these principles can be seen as more appropriate than other familiar principles of justice to the idea of democratic citizens viewed as free and equal persons. . . . The two principles of justice (noted above) are as follows:

(a) Each person has an equal claim to a fully adequate scheme of equal basic rights and liberties, which scheme is compatible with the same scheme for all; and in this scheme the equal political liberties, and only those liberties, are to be guaranteed their fair value.
(b) Social and economic inequalities are to satisfy two conditions: first, they are to be attached to positions and offices open to all under conditions of fair equality of opportunity; and second, they are to be to the greatest benefit of the least advantaged members of society.

Each of these principles regulates institutions in a particular domain not only in regard to basic rights, liberties, and opportunities but also in regard to the claims of equality; while the second part of the second principle underwrites the worth of these institutional guarantees. The two principles together, with the first given priority over the second, regulate the basic institutions that realize these values. . . .

4 . . . The aim of justice as fairness, then, is practical: it presents itself as a conception of justice that may be shared by citizens as a basis of a reasoned, informed, and willing political agreement. It expresses their shared and public political reason. But to attain such a shared reason, the conception of justice should be, as far as possible, independent of the opposing and conflicting philosophical and religious doctrines that citizens affirm. In formulating such a conception, political liberalism applies the principle of toleration to philosophy itself. The religious doctrines that in previous centuries were the professed basis of society have gradually given way to principles of constitutional government that all citizens,

whatever their religious view, can endorse. Comprehensive philosophical and moral doctrines likewise cannot be endorsed by citizens generally, and they also no longer can, if they ever could, serve as the professed basis of society.

Thus, political liberalism looks for a political conception of justice that we hope can gain the support of an overlapping consensus of reasonable religious, philosophical, and moral doctrines in a society regulated by it. Gaining this support of reasonable doctrines lays the basis for answering our second fundamental question as to how citizens, who remain deeply divided on religious, philosophical, and moral doctrines, can still maintain a just and stable democratic society. To this end, it is normally desirable that the comprehensive philosophical and moral views we are wont to use in debating fundamental political issues should give way in public life. Public reason – citizens' reasoning in the public forum about constitutional essentials and basic questions of justice – is now best guided by a political conception the principles and values of which all citizens can endorse. That political conception is to be, so to speak, political and not metaphysical.[2]

Political liberalism, then, aims for a political conception of justice as a freestanding view. It offers no specific metaphysical or epistemological doctrine beyond what is implied by the political conception itself. As an account of political values, a freestanding political conception does not deny there being other values that apply, say, to the personal, the familial, and the associational; nor does it say that political values are separate from, or discontinuous with, other values. One aim, as I have said, is to specify the political domain and its conception of justice in such a way that its institutions can gain the support of an overlapping consensus. In this case, citizens themselves, within the exercise of their liberty of thought and conscience, and looking to their comprehensive doctrines, view the political conception as derived from, or congruent with, or at least not in conflict with, their other values. . . .

§ 6 *The idea of a well-ordered society*

2 . . . [T]he political culture of a democratic society is characterized (I assume) by three general facts understood as follows.

The first is that the diversity of reasonable comprehensive religious, philosophical, and moral doctrines found in modern democratic societies is not a mere historical condition that may soon pass away; it is a permanent feature of the public culture of democracy. Under the political and social conditions secured by the basic rights and liberties of free institutions, a diversity of conflicting and irreconcilable – and what's more, reasonable – comprehensive doctrines will come about and persist if such diversity does not already obtain.

This fact of reasonable pluralism must be distinguished from the fact of pluralism as such. It is the fact that free institutions tend to generate not simply a variety of doctrines and views, as one might expect from people's various interests and their tendency to focus on narrow points of view. Rather, it is the fact that among the views that develop is a diversity of reasonable comprehensive doctrines. These are the doctrines that reasonable citizens affirm and that political liberalism must address. They are not simply the upshot of self- and class interests, or of people's understandable tendency to view the political world from a limited standpoint. Instead, they are in part the work of free practical reason within the framework of free institutions. Thus, although historical doctrines are not, of course, the work of free reason alone, the fact of reasonable pluralism is not an unfortunate condition of human life. In framing the political conception so that it can ... gain the support of reasonable comprehensive doctrines, we are not so much adjusting that conception to brute forces of the world but to the inevitable outcome of free human reason.

A second and related general fact is that a continuing shared understanding on one comprehensive religious, philosophical, or moral doctrine can be maintained only by the oppressive use of state power. If we think of political society as a community united in affirming one and the same comprehensive doctrine, then the oppressive use of state power is necessary for political community. In the society of the Middle Ages, more or less united in affirming the Catholic faith, the Inquisition was not an accident; its suppression of heresy was needed to preserve that shared religious belief. The same holds, I believe, for any reasonable comprehensive philosophical and moral doctrine, whether religious or nonreligious. A society united on a reasonable form of utilitarianism, or on the reasonable liberalisms of Kant or Mill, would likewise require the sanctions of state power to remain so. Call this "the fact of oppression."

Finally, a third general fact is that an enduring and secure democratic regime, one not divided into contending doctrinal confessions and hostile social classes, must be willingly and freely supported by at least a substantial majority of its politically active citizens. Together with the first general fact, this means that to serve as a public basis of justification for a constitutional regime, a political conception of justice must be one that can be endorsed by widely different and opposing though reasonable comprehensive doctrines.

3 Since there is no reasonable religious, philosophical, or moral doctrine affirmed by all citizens, the conception of justice affirmed in a well-ordered democratic society must be a conception limited to what I shall call "the domain of the political" and its values. The idea of a well-ordered democratic society must be framed accordingly. I assume, then, that citizens' overall views have two parts: one part can be seen to be, or

to coincide with, the publicly recognized political conception of justice; the other part is a (fully or partially) comprehensive doctrine to which the political conception is in some manner related. . . . The point to stress here is that, as I have said, citizens individually decide for themselves in what way the public political conception all affirm is related to their own more comprehensive views . . .

Lecture II The powers of citizens and their representation

§ 2 The burdens of judgment

1 The first basic aspect of the reasonable, then, is the willingness to propose fair terms of cooperation and to abide by them provided others do. The second basic aspect, as I review now, is the willingness to recognize the burdens of judgment and to accept their consequences for the use of public reason in directing the legitimate exercise of political power in a constitutional regime.

Recall that . . . we noted two general facts about the public culture of a constitutional regime: the fact of reasonable pluralism and the fact that this diversity can be overcome only by the oppressive use of state power. These facts call for explanation. For why should free institutions lead to reasonable pluralism, and why should state power be required to suppress it? Why does not our conscientious attempt to reason with one another lead to reasonable agreement? It seems to do so in natural science, at least in the long run.

There are, of course, various explanations. We might suppose, say, that most people hold views that advance their own more narrow interests; and since their interests are different, so are their views. Or perhaps people are often irrational and not very bright, and this mixed with logical errors leads to conflicting opinions. But while such explanations explain much, they are too easy and not the kind we want. We want to know how reasonable disagreement is possible, for we always work at first within ideal theory. Thus we ask: how might reasonable disagreement come about?

2 One explanation is this. Let's say that reasonable disagreement is disagreement between reasonable persons: that is, between persons who have realized their two moral powers to a degree sufficient to be free and equal citizens in a constitutional regime, and who have an enduring desire to honor fair terms of cooperation and to be fully cooperating members of society.[3] Given their moral powers, they share a common human reason, similar powers of thought and judgment: they can draw inferences, weigh evidence, and balance competing considerations.

The idea of reasonable disagreement involves an account of the sources, or causes, of disagreement between reasonable persons so defined. These sources I refer to as the burdens of judgment.[4] The account of these burdens must be such that it is fully compatible with, and so does not impugn, the reasonableness of those who disagree. What, then, goes wrong? An explanation of the right kind is that the sources of reasonable disagreement – the burdens of judgment – among reasonable persons are the many hazards involved in the correct (and conscientious) exercise of our powers of reason and judgment in the ordinary course of political life.

As reasonable and rational we have to make different kinds of judgments.[5] As rational we have to balance our various ends and estimate their appropriate place in our way of life; and doing this confronts us with grave difficulties in making correct judgments of rationality. On the other hand, as reasonable we must assess the strength of people's claims, not only against our claims, but against one another, or on our common practices and institutions, all this giving rise to difficulties in our making sound reasonable judgments. In addition, there is the reasonable as it applies to our beliefs and schemes of thought, or the reasonable as appraising our use of our theoretical (and not our moral and practical) powers, and here too we meet the corresponding kinds of difficulties. We need to keep in mind these three kinds of judgments with their characteristic burdens.

3 Except for the last two sources below, the ones I mention are not peculiar to the reasonable and the rational in their moral and practical use; items (a) to (d) apply mainly to the theoretical uses of our reason. Also, the list I give is not complete. It covers only the more obvious sources.

(a) The evidence – empirical and scientific – bearing on the case is conflicting and complex, and thus hard to assess and evaluate.
(b) Even where we agree fully about the kinds of considerations that are relevant, we may disagree about their weight, and so arrive at different judgments.
(c) To some extent all our concepts, and not only moral and political concepts, are vague and subject to hard cases; and this indeterminacy means that we must rely on judgment and interpretation (and on judgments about interpretations) within some range (not sharply specifiable) where reasonable persons may differ.
(d) To some extent (how great we cannot tell) the way we assess evidence and weigh moral and political values is shaped by our total experience, our whole course of life up to now; and our total experiences must always differ. Thus, in a modern society with its numerous offices and positions, its various divisions of labor, its many social

groups and their ethnic variety, citizens' total experiences are disparate enough for their judgments to diverge, at least to some degree, on many if not most cases of any significant complexity.

(e) Often there are different kinds of normative considerations of different force on both sides of an issue and it is difficult to make an overall assessment.

(f) Finally . . . any system of social institutions is limited in the values it can admit so that some selection must be made from the full range of moral and political values that might be realized. This is because any system of institutions has, as it were, a limited social space. In being forced to select among cherished values, or when we hold to several and must restrict each in view of the requirements of the others, we face great difficulties in setting priorities and making adjustments. Many hard decisions may seem to have no clear answer. . . .

§ 3 Reasonable comprehensive doctrines

1 The second basic aspect of our being reasonable is, I have said, our recognizing and being willing to bear the consequences of the burdens of judgment. I shall now try to show how this aspect limits the scope of what reasonable persons think can be justified to others, and how this leads to a form of toleration and supports the idea of public reason.

Assume first that reasonable persons affirm only reasonable comprehensive doctrines. Now we need a definition of such doctrines. They have three main features. One is that a reasonable doctrine is an exercise of theoretical reason: it covers the major religious, philosophical, and moral aspects of human life in a more or less consistent and coherent manner. It organizes and characterizes recognized values so that they are compatible with one another and express an intelligible view of the world. Each doctrine will do this in ways that distinguish it from other doctrines, for example, by giving certain values a particular primacy and weight. In singling out which values to count as especially significant and how to balance them when they conflict, a reasonable comprehensive doctrine is also an exercise of practical reason. Both theoretical and practical reason (including as appropriate the rational) are used together in its formulation. Finally, a third feature is that while a reasonable comprehensive view is not necessarily fixed and unchanging, it normally belongs to, or draws upon, a tradition of thought and doctrine. Although stable over time, and not subject to sudden and unexplained changes, it tends to evolve slowly in the light of what, from its point of view, it sees as good and sufficient reasons.

This account of reasonable comprehensive doctrines is deliberately loose. We avoid excluding doctrines as unreasonable without strong grounds based on clear aspects of the reasonable itself. Otherwise our account runs the danger of being arbitrary and exclusive. Political liberalism counts many familiar and traditional doctrines – religious, philosophical, and moral – as reasonable even though we could not seriously entertain them for ourselves, as we think they give excessive weight to some values and fail to allow for the significance of others. A tighter criterion is not, however, needed for the purposes of political liberalism.

2 The evident consequence of the burdens of judgment is that reasonable persons do not all affirm the same comprehensive doctrine. Moreover, they also recognize that all persons alike, including themselves, are subject to those burdens, and so many reasonable comprehensive doctrines are affirmed, not all of which can be true (indeed none of them may be true). The doctrine any reasonable person affirms is but one reasonable doctrine among others. In affirming it, a person, of course, believes it to be true, or else reasonable, as the case may be.

Thus, it is not in general unreasonable to affirm any one of a number of reasonable comprehensive doctrines. We recognize that our own doctrine has, and can have, for people generally, no special claims on them beyond their own view of its merits. Others who affirm doctrines different from ours are, we grant, reasonable also, and certainly not unreasonable. Since there are many reasonable doctrines, the idea of the reasonable does not require us, or others, to believe any specific reasonable doctrine, though we may do so. When we take the step beyond recognizing the reasonableness of a doctrine and affirm our belief in it, we are not being unreasonable.

3 Beyond this, reasonable persons will think it unreasonable to use political power, should they possess it, to repress comprehensive views that are not unreasonable, though different from their own. This is because, given the fact of reasonable pluralism, a public and shared basis of justification that applies to comprehensive doctrines is lacking in the public culture of a democratic society. But such a basis is needed to mark the difference, in ways acceptable to a reasonable public, between comprehensive beliefs as such and true comprehensive beliefs.

Since many doctrines are seen to be reasonable, those who insist, when fundamental political questions are at stake, on what they take as true but others do not, seem to others simply to insist on their own beliefs when they have the political power to do so. Of course, those who do insist on their beliefs also insist that their beliefs alone are true: they impose their beliefs because, they say, their beliefs are true and not because they are their beliefs. But this is a claim that all equally could make; it is also a claim that cannot be made good by anyone to citizens generally. So, when we make such claims others, who are themselves reasonable, must count us unreasonable. And indeed we are, as we want to use state power, the collective power of equal citizens, to prevent the rest from affirming their not unreasonable views.

To conclude: reasonable persons see that the burdens of judgment set limits on what can be reasonably justified to others, and so they endorse some form of liberty of conscience and freedom of thought. It is unreasonable for us to use political power, should we possess it, or share it with others, to repress comprehensive views that are not unreasonable. . . .

Lecture IV The idea of an overlapping consensus

§ 3 *An overlapping consensus not a mere* modus vivendi

3 . . . [S]ome will think that even if an overlapping consensus were sufficiently stable, the idea of political unity founded on an overlapping consensus must still be rejected, since it abandons the hope of political community and settles instead for a public understanding that is at bottom a mere *modus vivendi.* To this objection, we say that the hope of political community must indeed be abandoned, if by such a community we mean a political society united in affirming the same comprehensive doctrine. This possibility is excluded by the fact of reasonable pluralism together with the rejection of the oppressive use of the state power to overcome it. . . .

4 That an overlapping consensus is quite different from a *modus vivendi* is clear. . . . [F]irst, the object of consensus, the political conception of justice, is itself a moral conception. And second, it is affirmed on moral grounds, that is, it includes conceptions of society and of citizens as persons, as well as principles of justice, and an account of the political virtues through which those principles are embodied in human character and expressed in public life. An overlapping consensus, therefore, is not merely a consensus on accepting certain authorities, or on complying with certain institutional arrangements, founded on a convergence of self- or group interests. All those who affirm the political conception start from within their own comprehensive view and draw on the religious, philosophical, and moral grounds it provides. The fact that people affirm the same political conception on those grounds does not make their affirming it any less religious, philosophical, or moral, as the case may be, since the grounds sincerely held determine the nature of their affirmation.

The preceding two aspects of an overlapping consensus – moral object and moral grounds – connect with a third aspect, that of stability. This means that those who affirm the various views supporting the political conception will not withdraw their support of it should the relative strength of their view in society increase and eventually become dominant. So long as these views are affirmed and not revised, the political conception will still be supported regardless of shifts in the distribution of political power. Each view supports the political conception for its own sake, or on its own merits. The test for this is whether the consensus is stable with respect to changes in the distribution of power among views. This feature of stability highlights a basic contrast between an overlapping consensus and a *modus vivendi*, the stability of which does depend on happenstance and a balance of relative forces. . . .

§ 4 An overlapping consensus not indifferent or skeptical

1 I turn to a second objection to the idea of an overlapping consensus on a political conception of justice: namely, that the avoidance of general and comprehensive doctrines implies indifference or skepticism as to whether a political conception of justice can be true, as opposed to reasonable in the constructivist sense. This avoidance may appear to suggest that such a conception might be the most reasonable one for us even when it is known not to be true, as if truth were simply beside the point. In reply, it would be fatal to the idea of a political conception to see it as skeptical about, or indifferent to, truth, much less as in conflict with it. Such skepticism or indifference would put political philosophy in opposition to numerous comprehensive doctrines, and thus defeat from the outset its aim of achieving an overlapping consensus.

We try, so far as we can, neither to assert nor to deny any particular comprehensive religious, philosophical, or moral view, or its associated theory of truth and the status of values. Since we assume each citizen to affirm some such view, we hope to make it possible for all to accept the political conception as true or reasonable from the standpoint of their own comprehensive view, whatever it may be. Properly understood, then, a political conception of justice need be no more indifferent, say, to truth in philosophy and morals than the principle of toleration, suitably understood, need be indifferent to truth in religion. Since we seek an agreed basis of public justification in matters of justice, and since no political agreement on those disputed questions can reasonably be expected, we turn instead to the fundamental ideas we seem to share through the public political culture. From these ideas we try to work out a political conception of justice congruent with our considered convictions on due reflection. Once this is done, citizens may within their comprehensive doctrines regard the political conception of justice as true, or as reasonable, whatever their view allows. . . .

§ 5 A political conception need not be comprehensive

1 A third objection is the following: even if we grant that an overlapping consensus is not a *modus vivendi*, as I have defined it, some may say

that a workable political conception must be general and comprehensive. Without such a doctrine on hand, there is no way to order the many conflicts of justice that arise in public life. The deeper the conceptual and philosophical bases of those conflicts, the objection continues, the more general and comprehensive the level of philosophical reflection must be if their roots are to be laid bare and an appropriate ordering found. It is useless, the objection concludes, to try to work out a political conception of justice expressly for the basic structure apart from any comprehensive doctrine. . . .

3 Here we are bound to ask: how can a political conception of justice express values that, under the reasonably favorable conditions that make democracy possible, normally outweigh whatever other values are likely to conflict with them? One reason is this. As I have said, the most reasonable political conception of justice for a democratic regime will be, broadly speaking, liberal. This means that it protects the familiar basic rights and assigns them a special priority; it also includes measures to insure that all citizens have sufficient material means to make effective use of those basic rights. Faced with the fact of reasonable pluralism, a liberal view removes from the political agenda the most divisive issues, serious contention about which must undermine the bases of social cooperation.

The virtues of political cooperation that make a constitutional regime possible are, then, very great virtues. I mean, for example, the virtues of tolerance and being ready to meet others halfway, and the virtue of reasonableness and the sense of fairness. When these virtues are widespread in society and sustain its political conception of justice, they constitute a very great public good, part of society's political capital. Thus, the values that conflict with the political conception of justice and its sustaining virtues may be normally outweighed because they come into conflict with the very conditions that make fair social cooperation possible on a footing of mutual respect.

4 The other reason political values normally win out is that severe conflicts with other values are much reduced. This is because when an overlapping consensus supports the political conception, this conception is not viewed as incompatible with basic religious, philosophical, and moral values. We need not consider the claims of political justice against the claims of this or that comprehensive view; nor need we say that political values are intrinsically more important than other values and that is why the latter are overridden. Having to say that is just what we hope to avoid, and achieving an overlapping consensus enables us to do so.

To conclude: given the fact of reasonable pluralism, what the work of reconciliation by public reason does, thus enabling us to avoid reliance on general and comprehensive doctrines, is two things: first, it identifies the fundamental role of political values in expressing the terms of fair social cooperation consistent with mutual respect between citizens regarded as free and equal; and second, it uncovers a sufficiently inclusive concordant fit among political and other values seen in a reasonable overlapping consensus.

Notes

1 The conception of justice presented in *A Theory of Justice* (Cambridge MA: Harvard University Press, 1971).
2 The context here serves to define the phrase: "political not metaphysical."
3 The two moral powers are the capacity for a sense of justice and the capacity for a conception of the good – CWG.
4 The idea of the burdens of judgment should not be confused with the idea of the burden of proof in legal cases, whether, say, the burden of proof falls on the plaintiff or the defendant.
5 The reasonable and the rational are distinct and independent ideas for Rawls. The rational concerns a single agent who deliberates about its ends and means to those ends. The reasonable (in the practical sense) concerns persons who seek to live together under fair terms of cooperation – CWG.

18

ESSENCE OF CULTURE AND A SENSE OF HISTORY

A feminist critique of cultural essentialism

Uma Narayan

In recent decades, feminists have stressed the need to think about issues of gender in conjunction with, and not in isolation from, issues of class, race, ethnicity, and sexual orientation, and have forcefully illustrated that differences among women must be understood and theorized in order to avoid essentialist generalizations about "women's problems" (Anzaldúa 1987; hooks 1981; Lugones and Spelman 1983). The feminist critique of gender essentialism does not merely charge that essentialist claims about "women" are overgeneralizations, but points out that these generalizations are hegemonic in that they represent the problems of privileged women (most often white, Western, middle-class, heterosexual women) as paradigmatic "women's issues." . . .

In fora committed to the development of transnational and global feminist perspectives, feminists have often specifically reiterated the need to take account of national and cultural differences among women, in order to avoid essentializing analyses that pay inadequate attention to the concerns of women in Third World contexts. I am sympathetic to such feminist criticisms of gender essentialism and to the claim that feminist theories and political agendas need to be responsive to the diversity of women's lives, both within and across national contexts. However, I believe that this feminist injunction to attend to "differences among women" sometimes takes questionable forms. I will argue that feminist efforts to avoid gender essentialism sometimes result in pictures of

From Uma Narayan, "Essence of Culture and a Sense of History: A Feminist Critique of Cultural Essentialism," *Hypatia* 13 (1998): 86–106.

Uma Narayan is Assistant Professor of Philosophy at Vassar College.

culture differences among women that constitute what I shall call "cultural essentialism." . . .

Gender essentialism and cultural essentialism

One important instance in which the injunction to attend to differences among women can lead to problems is when this project is carried out in a manner that avoids essentialism about women by replicating essentialist notions of "cultural differences" between "Western" and "Non-western" cultures. The project of attending to differences among women across a variety of national and cultural contexts then becomes a project that endorses and replicates problematic and colonialist assumptions about the cultural differences between "Western culture" and "non-Western cultures" and the women who inhabit them. . . .

Although often motivated by the injunction to take differences among women seriously, such moves fracture the universalist category "Woman" only slightly, because culture-specific essentialist generalizations differ from universalistic essentialist generalizations only in degree or scope, and not in kind. The resulting portraits of "Western women," "Third World women," "African women," "Indian women," "Muslim women," or the like, as well as the pictures of the "cultures" that are attributed to these various groups of women, often remain fundamentally essentialist. They depict as homogeneous groups of heterogeneous people whose values, interests, ways of life, and moral and political commitments are internally plural and divergent. . . .

There are a number of similarities between gender essentialism and cultural essentialism. While gender essentialism often proceeds to assume and construct sharp binaries about the qualities, abilities, or locations of "men" and "women," cultural essentialism assumes and constructs sharp binaries between "Western culture" and "non-Western cultures" or between "Western culture" and particular "Other" cultures. . . . With both gender essentialism and cultural essentialism, discourses about "difference" often operate to conceal their role in the production and reproduction of such "differences," presenting these differences as something pre-given and prediscursively "real" that the discourses of difference merely describe rather than help construct and perpetuate.

While gender essentialism often conflates socially dominant norms of femininity with the problems, interests, and locations of actual particular women, cultural essentialism often conflates socially dominant cultural norms with the actual values and practices of a culture. While gender essentialism often equates the problems, interests and locations of some socially dominant groups of men and women with those of "all men" and "all women," cultural essentialism often equates the values, worldviews, and practices of some socially dominant groups with those of "all members of the culture." For instance, Mary Daly's chapter on "Indian suttee" (1978) reproduces an essentialist picture of "Indian culture" both by ignoring that *sati* was not a practice ever engaged in by "all Indians" and by effacing the history of criticisms and challenges posed to this practice by various groups of Indians (Narayan 1997).

. . . Why is it that attempts to avoid gender essentialism sometimes generate rather than deter cultural essentialism? I believe that part of the explanation lies in the prevalence of an incomplete understanding of the relationship between "gender essentialism" and "cultural imperialism." The gender essentialism perpetuated by relatively privileged subjects, including Western feminists, is understood to be a form of "cultural imperialism," whereby privileged subjects tend to construct their "cultural Others" in their own image, taking their particular locations and problems to be those of "all women." This account ignores the degree to which cultural imperialism often proceeds by means of an "insistence on Difference," by a projection of Imaginary "differences" that constitute one's Others as Other, rather than via an "insistence on Sameness." . . .

Reducing "cultural imperialism" to the problem of "the imposition of Sameness" conceals the importance of the role that sharply contrasting essentialist pictures of "cultural differences" between "Western culture" and its various "Others" played during colonial times, both in various justifications for colonial rule and in the scripts of various nationalist movements that challenged and sought to overthrow colonialism, pictures that resurface in postcolonial attempts at engaging with issues of cultural difference. . . .

This frequently reiterated contrast between "Western" and "non-Western" cultures was a politically motivated colonial construction. The self-proclaimed "superiority" of "Western culture" functioned as the rationale and mandate for colonialism. The colonial self-portrait of "Western culture" had, however, only a faint resemblance to the moral, political, and cultural values that *actually pervaded* life in Western societies. Thus liberty and equality could be represented as paradigmatic "Western values," hallmarks of its civilizational superiority, at the very moment when Western nations were engaged in slavery, colonization, expropriation, and the denial of liberty and equality not only to the colonized but to large segments of Western subjects, including women. Profound *similarities* between Western culture and many of its Others, such as hierarchical social systems, huge economic disparities between members, and the mistreatment and inequality of women, were systematically ignored in this construction of "Western culture."

The colonial picture of the sharp contrasts between "Western culture" and its Others also resulted in seriously distorted representations of various "colonized cultures," often as a result of the prejudiced and ideologically motivated stereotypes held by Western colonizers but *also* as a result of anti-colonial nationalist movements embracing and trying to revalue the imputed facets of their own "culture" embedded in these stereotypes. Thus, while the British imputed "spiritualism" to Indian culture to suggest lack of readiness for the this-worldly project of self-rule, many Indian nationalists embraced this definition in order to make the anticolonialist and nationalist argument that "our culture" was both distinctive from and superior to "Western culture." . . .

While culturally essentialist feminist representations of "Third World cultures" sometimes depict the practices and values of *privileged* groups as those of the "culture as a whole" (as Daly does in her discussion of *sati*), equally essentialist representations are produced when the "representative Third World woman" is modeled on *marginalized and underprivileged* Third World women. The latter sort of representation effaces Third World heterogeneity as effectively as the former, and bears the marks of a curious asymmetry, in that the most underprivileged of Western women are seldom cast as "representative of Western culture." . . .

Cultural essentialism often poses a pressing problem for feminist agendas in Third World contexts, given that essentialist constructions of particular Third World "cultures" often play a powerful ongoing role in political movements that are inimical to women's interests in various parts of the Third World. These essentialist portraits of culture often depict culturally dominant norms of femininity, and practices that adversely affect women, as central components of "cultural identity." They often equate women's conformity to the status quo with "the preservation of culture" and cast feminist challenges to norms and practices affecting women as "cultural betrayals." . . . When essentialist definitions of Third World cultures are cloaked in the virtuous mantle of resistance to Western cultural imperialism, Third World feminists and others who contest prevailing norms and practices are discursively set up in the roles of "cultural traitors" and "stooges of Western imperialism." In addition, essentialist pictures of "national culture and traditions" often operate to justify the exploitation, domination, and marginalization of religious and ethnic minorities, and members of socially subordinate castes and the poor; and they are used to dismiss a variety of political demands for justice, equality, rights, or democracy as symptoms of the "cultural corruption" wrought by "Western ideas" (Howard 1993, Mayer 1995). . . .

Culturally essentialist maneuvers and feminist challenges

. . . A useful general strategy for resisting cultural essentialism is the cultivation of a critical stance that "restores history and politics" to prevailing ahistorical pictures of "culture." Essentialist pictures of culture

232

represent "cultures" as if they were natural givens, entities that existed neatly distinct and separate in the world, entirely independent of our projects of distinguishing between them. This picture tends to erase the reality that the "boundaries" between "cultures" are human constructs, underdetermined by existing variations in worldviews and ways of life; representations that are embedded in and deployed for a variety of political ends. Essentialist representations of culture eclipse the reality that the labels or designations that are currently used to demarcate or individuate particular "cultures" themselves have a historical provenance, and that what they individuate or pick out as "one culture" often changes over time.

Antiessentialist feminists can counter this static picture of culture by insisting on a historical understanding of the contexts in which what are currently taken to be "particular cultures" came to be seen and defined as such. For example, while a prevailing picture of "Western culture" has its beginning in ancient Greece and perhaps culminating in the contemporary United States, a historical perspective would register that the ancient Greeks did not define themselves as part of "Western culture," an appellation that seems to have arisen only with the advent of European colonialism, and that "American culture" was initially as likely to be distinguished from "European culture" as assimilated to it qua "Western culture." . . .

An antiessentialist perspective would also realize that many of the texts, artifacts, and practices ranging from ancient to modern times that are classified today as parts of "Indian culture" are "held together" by a label whose historical vintage is the British colonial period. This label is connected to the historical unification of an assortment of political territories into "British India," a union that enabled the nationalist challenge to colonialism to emerge as "Indian" and to stake its claim to self-government on the basis of a "national culture" (Narayan 1995). Thus, an antiessentialist understanding of culture should emphasize that the labels that "pick out" particular "cultures" are not simple descriptions we employ to single out already distinct entities. Rather, they are fairly arbitrary and shifting designations, connected to various political projects that had different reasons for insisting upon the distinctiveness of one culture from another. . . .

Moreover, this historical sensibility also needs to be attentive to the historical and political processes by which particular values and practices have come to be imputed as *central* or *definitive* of a particular "culture." . . . Instead of seeing the centrality of particular values, traditions, or practices to any particular culture as *given*, we need to trace the historical and political processes by which these values, traditions, or practices have *come to be deemed* central constitutive components of a particular culture.

The feminist usefulness of both these moves is best illustrated by a concrete example. I will focus on the practice of *sati* (suttee), the immolation of widows on the funeral pyres of their husbands, which was constructed as a central component of "Indian culture" in colonial times, and is deployed in the political rhetoric of contemporary Hindu fundamentalists as an icon of the "good Indian woman," even as widow immolation has all but disappeared as a practice. An important question that feminists need to ask about *sati* is how and why this particular practice, which is not engaged in by the vast majority of Hindu communities let alone all Indian ones, and which was the exceptional rather than routine fate of widows even in the few communities that practiced it, came to be regarded as a "central Indian tradition." The answer lies in complex nineteenth-century debates on the practice between British colonials and Indian elites that constituted *sati* as a "central and authentic Indian tradition." ... As a result of this debate, *sati* came to acquire, for both British and Indians, for its supporters as well as opponents on both sides, an "emblematic status" – becoming a larger-than-life symbol of "Indian culture" in a way that *radically transcended* the reality of its limited practice. Even for many Indian reformers opposed to the actual practice, *sati* became a lofty symbol of "ideal Indian womanhood," indicating a feminine nobility and devotion to family deemed uncharacteristic of Western women. . . .

Ahistorical essentialist pictures of cultures also obscure the degree to which what is seen as constitutive of a particular "culture" and as central to projects of "cultural preservation" *changes over time*. Thus, essentialist notions of culture often rely on a picture that presents cultures not only as "givens" but as "unchanging givens." Obscuring the reality of historical change and the political contestations with which it is entwined promotes a static and "fixed" picture of particular cultures, whereby their "values, practices, and traditions," as well as their sense of what their culture amounts to and what its "preservation" entails, appear immune to history. . . .

Many Third World feminist analyses are vitally useful in drawing attention to how dominant members of a culture often willingly change or discard what were previously regarded as "important cultural practices," and willingly change or surrender various facets of such practices when it suits them, but resist and protest other cultural changes. The changes that are resisted tend to be changes that pose a threat to aspects of the dominant members' social power, and are often changes pertaining to the status and welfare of women. For instance, Olayinka Koso-Thomas's work reveals that in Sierra Leone, virtually all the elaborate initiation rites and training that were traditional preliminaries to female circumcision, and that lasted from one to two years, have fallen by the wayside because people no longer have the time, money or social infrastructure for them. However, the practice of excision itself, abstracted from the whole context of practices in which it used to be embedded, is still seen as a crucial component of "preserving tradition," obscuring the degree to which other aspects of the tradition have been given up (Koso-Thomas 1987: 23). I believe that feminist contestations of what are designated as "traditional cultural practices" need to be alert to such *synecdochic moves* whereby "parts" of a practice come to stand in for a whole, because such substitutions invariably conceal various concrete social changes. . . .

Feminist attention to such aspects of cultural change can help call attention to a general process that I call "selective labeling," whereby those with social power conveniently designate certain changes in values and practices as consonant with "cultural preservation" while designating other changes as "cultural loss" or "cultural betrayal" (Narayan 1997). The deployment of "selective labeling" plays a powerful role in the facilitation of essentialist notions of culture because it allows changes that are approved by socially dominant groups to appear consonant with the preservation of essential values or core practices of a culture, while depicting changes that challenge the status quo as threats to "cultural preservation." . . .

Sensitivity to "selective labeling" can also enable feminists in different national contexts to draw attention to the extensive changes that have occurred *in the lives of women and in practices affecting women* that were once regarded as problematic but have come to be regarded as acceptable cultural modifications by large segments of the population. For instance, public education for women, initially seen as culturally problematic by various segments of the Indian elites, became transformed, in the course of roughly two generations, into something not only permissible but virtually the norm for the daughters of these families. . . .

"Progressive" versions of cultural essentialism

. . . [F]undamentalists are not the only ones who subscribe to and deploy essentialist pictures of culture. Essentialist notions of culture are held by people who occupy a wide range of places on the political spectrum. Progressive Western and Third World subjects, too, sometimes uncritically endorse essentialist notions of what "Western culture" or a particular "Third World culture" amounts to. . . . I would argue, for instance, that feminist discourses that have asserted "women's equality" to be a "Western value" whose extension to Third World contexts is "a culturally imperialist theme imposed by the First World" . . . risk replicating essentialist notions of "culture."

Another example of cultural essentialism emanating from progressive parts of the political spectrum can be found in the contention, by feminists and others, that "human rights" are a "Western concept" whose extension to Third World contexts constitute an illegitimate "imposition of Western values." . . .

The assertion that "equality" and "human rights" are "Western values" is surely complicated by the historical reality that Western doctrines of equality and rights coexisted for decades with support for slavery and colonialism, and that equality and rights were denied to women; to racial, religious, and ethnic minorities within Western nations; and to virtually all subjects of colonized territories. It is only as a result of political struggles by these various excluded groups in both Western and non-Western contexts that doctrines of equality and rights have slowly come to be perceived as applicable to them, too. Thus, one could argue that doctrines of equality and rights, rather than being pure "products of Western imperialism" were often important products of such struggles *against Western imperialism*. Notions of equality and rights have often been significant in these struggles, and have long since embedded themselves in the vocabularies of Third World political struggles. Claims that "equality" and "rights" are "Western values" risk effacing the vital role that such notions have played and continue to play in those movements (Mayer 1995; Narayan 1993). In general, the *origins* of a practice or concept seldom limit its *scope of relevance*. Borrowing the ideas, practices, artifacts, and technologies of Others, assimilating them, and transforming them are ubiquitous processes, and hardly unique to Third World contexts. . . .

Feminist claims that "equality" and "rights" are "Western values" also risk echoing the rhetoric of two groups of people who, despite their other differences, share the characteristic of being no friends of feminist agendas. The first are what I shall call "Western cultural supremacists," whose agenda of constructing flattering portraits of "Western culture" proceeds by claiming ideas of equality, rights, democracy, and so on as "Western ideas" that prove the West's moral and political superiority to all "Other" cultures (Bloom 1987; Schlesinger 1992). The second are Third World fundamentalists who share the views of Western cultural supremacists that all such notions are "Western ideas." Fundamentalists deploy these views to justify the claim that such ideas are "irrelevant foreign notions" used only by "Westernized and inauthentic" Third World subjects and to cloak their violations of rights and suppression of democratic processes in the mantle of cultural preservation (Howard 1993; Mayer 1995).

Certainly, Third World feminists have legitimate concerns about how some Western feminists understand and unpack notions of "women's equality." And they have legitimate worries that some Western feminist human rights agendas might ignore or slight the problems and concerns of various groups of women in their national contexts. However, such conflicts and differences are often not well captured by characterizing them as differences between "Western" and "Third World" understandings of these concepts. . . .

I believe feminists are often better served by analyses that concretely show the particular ways that specific interpretations of rights or equality might be inadequate than by interpretations that criticize these notions for being "Western."

Furthermore, notions such as rights and equality are seriously contested within both Western and Third World contexts, with the result that there is hardly one "Western" or "Third World" or "Indian" vision of these concepts (Kiss 1997). Differences about the significance, implications, and applications of these terms exist within Western and Third World national contexts, as well as cut across them. . . . [P]olitically detrimental and politically valuable understandings of human rights have existed in both Western and Third World contexts. . . .

Feminists must keep in mind that a value or practice's being "non-Western" (either in terms of its origin or its context of prevalence) does not mean that it is anti-imperialist or anti-colonial, let alone compatible with feminist agendas. Feminists must also remember that a value or practice's being "Western" in its origins does not mean that it can play no part in the service of anticolonial or postcolonial feminist agendas. . . .

Cultural relativism and cultural essentialism

Many feminists are tempted to regard relativism as "a weapon against intellectual tyranny" because they share Lorraine Code's sense that it is "demonstrably preferable to imperialist alternatives that recognize no limits" (Code 1998). Many feminists regard relativism as an antidote to "affirmations of universal sameness" that permits those who are privileged "to claim to have access to the one true story" (Code 1998). Relativism appears to be a useful deterrent to Western feminist inclinations to speak for or about women situated elsewhere or differently as though they were "just like us." . . .

However, as my discussion in the first section of this essay indicates, I am reluctant simply to *equate* this problem that constitutes a central concern for contemporary feminist analysis, with the phenomenon of "cultural imperialism" as such. Part of what gives me pause in making this equation is my sense that "cultural imperialism" as it functioned in colonial times had a quite different logic, which *denied rather than affirmed* that one's Others were "just like oneself." I do not wish to deny that the agendas of the colonizing powers required some projection of "Sameness" on colonized peoples. . . . However, even these projections of Sameness involved seeing Others as only "deficient examples of the same" (Lange 1998). Without this difference of "deficiency," the colonized populations' need for the colonial tutelage of Western nations would be undermined. . . .

The colonial willingness and eagerness to speak "for and about Others," and the colonialists' conviction that "theirs was the one true story," was, I believe, intimately interwoven with views that insisted on the colonized Others' *difference from*, and *inferiority to*, the Western subject. . . . Once it is recognized that "assumptions of difference" have been deployed for cultural imperialist ends no less expeditiously than "assumptions of sameness," the temptation to relativism that is motivated by a desire to avoid cultural imperialism ought, I believe, to considerably weaken. . . .

My analysis underscores how much colonial mandates, as well as the political visions of contemporary Third World fundamentalisms, rely on a picture that focuses on "essential differences" between Western and particular Third World cultures. Insofar as versions of relativism subscribe to these colonial pictures of "essential differences" between cultures, relativism becomes a danger rather than an asset to feminist agendas. My previous analysis demonstrates how representations of particular Third World "cultures" that appeal to relativist notions that "our values and ways of life are distinct from those of Western Others, and constitute our national identity and authenticity" can be at least as detrimental to the interests of many Third World women as any "affirmations of universal sameness." . . .

Such relativist pictures of cultural differences are, I believe, both empirically inaccurate and inimical to the interests of postcolonial feminists. Rather than embracing relativism, an anti-imperialist postcolonial feminism is better served by critically interrogating scripts of "cultural difference" that set up sharp binaries between "Western" and various "non-Western" cultures. Such interrogation will reveal both sides of the binary to be, in large measure, *totalizing idealizations*, whose Imaginary status has been concealed by a colonial and postcolonial history of ideological deployments of this binary. . . .

I would argue that what postcolonial feminists need to do is not to endorse "cultural relativism" but to resist various forms of cultural essentialism, *including relativist versions*. In addition to the strategies I previously mentioned, feminists need to resist cultural essentialism by pointing to the internal plurality, dissension and contestation over values, and ongoing changes in practices in virtually all communities that comprise modern nation-states. This critique of cultural essentialism would reject the idea that there is anything that can solidly and uncontroversially be defined as "Indian culture" or "African culture," or "Western culture" for that matter. It would proceed by challenging a "picture of the world" that some versions of cultural relativism assume to be true: that there are *neat packages called "different cultures," each of which is internally consistent and monolithic, and which disagrees only with "Other cultures."*

The position I am endorsing does not deny the existence of "cultural differences" *per se*. It would be foolish to deny that there are practices in certain contexts that are absent in others, and values that are endorsed in some quarters that are not endorsed in others. Rather, the position I endorse denies that "actual cultural differences" correspond very neatly to the "packages" that are currently individuated as "separate cultures" or manifest themselves as evenly distributed across particular "cultures." . . .

While critical of particular pictures of "cultural differences" that underlie certain forms of cultural relativism, my counter-picture does not suffice to answer many important questions that arise in philosophical discussions about relativism. It remains agnostic, for instance, on the question of whether there is one neat and complete universal set of values that ought to command everyone's assent, but optimistic about the prospects for making many of the values that inform progressive politics and feminist agendas meaningful and efficacious in a variety of global contexts. . . .

I believe that antiessentialism about gender and about culture does not entail a simple-minded opposition to *all generalizations*, but entails instead a commitment to examine both their empirical accuracy and their political utility or risk. It is seldom possible to articulate effective political agendas, such as those pertaining to human rights, without resorting to a certain degree of abstraction, which enables the articulation of salient similarities between problems suffered by various individuals and groups. On the other hand, it seems arguably true that there is no need to portray female genital mutilation as an "African cultural practice" or dowry murders and dowry related harassment as a "problem of Indian women" in ways that eclipse the fact that not *all* "African women" or "Indian women" confront these problems, or confront them in identical ways, or in ways that efface local contestations of these problems.

The antiessentialist perspective I advocate does not endorse the view that the existence of cultural and other "differences" renders equally suspect each and every sort of generalization or universalistic claim. Kwame Anthony Appiah makes a useful point when he reminds us that "it is characteristic of those who pose as antiuniversalists to use the term universalism as if it meant *pseudouniversalism*. . . . What they truly object to – and who would not? – is Eurocentric hegemony posing as universalism" (Appiah 1992: 58). I would add that many of the essentialist pictures of "Indian culture" and the like that I critique are forms of what one might call "pseudoparticularism" – equally hegemonic representations of "particular cultures" whose "particularism" masks the reality that they are problematic generalizations about complex and internally differentiated contexts. Besides, even the injunction to attend to a variety of "differences" can hardly avoid the universalistic cast of a general prescription, and no political agenda can avoid general normative assessments of the salience and weight of particular kinds of "differences."

Given the significant dangers that varieties of cultural essentialism pose to feminist agendas, I believe that the development of a feminist perspective that is committed to antiessentialism both about "women" and about "cultures" is an urgent and important task for a postcolonial feminist perspective. Such a perspective must distinguish and extricate feminist projects of attending to differences among women from problematically essentialist colonial and postcolonial understandings of "cultural differences" between Western culture and its "Others." This essay is a contribution to the project of thinking about how contemporary feminists can resist reified and essentialist pictures of "cultures" and of "cultural contrasts" between "Western culture" and "Third World cultures," and submit them to critical interrogation.[1]

Note

1 I would like to thank Jennifer Church, Sandra Harding, Jim Hill, Tina Sheth, and Susan Zlotnick for their generous assistance with various drafts of this paper.

References

Anzaldúa, Gloria (1987) *Borderlands/La Frontera: The New Mestiza*. San Francisco: Aunt Lute Books.

Appiah, Kwame Anthony (1992) *In My Father's House: Africa in the Philosophy of Culture*. New York: Oxford University Press.

Bloom, Allan (1987) *The Closing of the American Mind*. New York: Simon & Schuster.

Code, Lorraine (1998) "How to think globally: Stretching the limits of imagination." *Hypatia* 13(2): 73–85.

Daly, Mary (1978) "Indian suttee: The ultimate consummation of marriage." In *Gyn/Ecology: The MetaEthics of Radical Feminism*. Boston: Beacon Press.

hooks, bell (1981) *Feminist Theory: From Margin to Center*. Boston: South End Press.

Howard, Rhoda (1993) "Cultural absolutism and the nostalgia for community." *Human Rights Quarterly* 15: 315–38.

Kiss, Elizabeth (1997) "Alchemy or fool's gold: Assessing feminist doubts about rights." In Mary Lyndon Shanley and Uma Narayan (eds.) *Reconstructing Political Theory: Feminist Perspectives*. University Park: Pennsylvania State University Press.

Koso-Thomas, Olayinka (1987) *The Circumcision of Women: A Strategy for Eradication*. London: Zed Books.

Lange, Lynda (1998) "Burnt offerings to rationality: A feminist reading of the construction of indigenous peoples in Enrique Dussel's theory of modernity." *Hypatia* 13(3).

Lugones, María C., and Elizabeth V. Spelman (1983) "Have we got a theory for you! Feminist theory, cultural imperialism, and the demand for 'The Woman's Voice'." *Women's Studies International Forum*, 6(6): 573–81.

Mayer, Ann Elizabeth (1995) *Islam and Human Rights: Tradition and Politics*. Boulder CO: Westview Press.

Narayan, Uma (1993) "What do rights have to do with it?: Reflections on what distinguishes 'traditional non-Western' frameworks from contemporary rights-based systems." *Journal of Social Philosophy* 24(2): 186–99.

—— (1995) "Eating cultures: Incorporation, identity and 'Indian food'." *Social Identities* 1(1): 63–88.

—— (1997) *Dislocating Cultures: Identities, Traditions and Third World Feminism*. New York: Routledge.

Schlesinger, Arthur M. Jr. (1992) *The Disuniting of America: Reflections on a Multicultural Society*. New York: W.W. Norton.

BIBLIOGRAPHY

Abramson, K. (1999) "Hume on Cultural Conflicts of Values," *Philosophical Studies* (USA) 93: 173–83.

Adams, R.M. (1993) "Religious Ethics in a Pluralistic Society," in G. Outka and J.P. Reeder, Jr. (eds.) *Prospects for a Common Morality*, Princeton NJ: Princeton University Press.

Afshari, R. (1994) "An Essay on Islamic Cultural Relativism in the Discourse of Human Rights," *Human Rights Quarterly* 16: 235–76.

Altham, J.E.J. and Harrison, R. (eds.) (1995) *World, Mind, and Ethics: Essays on the Ethical Philosophy of Bernard Williams*, Cambridge: Cambridge University Press.

American Anthropological Association Commission for Human Rights (1993) "Report of the American Anthropological Association Commission for Human Rights," *Anthropology Newsletter* 34: 1, 5.

American Anthropological Association Executive Board (1947) "Statement on Human Rights," *American Anthropologist* 49: 539–43.

An-Na'im, A.A. (1987) "Religious Minorities under Islamic Law and the Limits of Cultural Relativism," *Human Rights Quarterly* 9: 1–18.

—— (1990a) "Islam, Islamic Law and the Dilemma of Cultural Legitimacy for Universal Human Rights," in C.E. Welch, Jr. and V.A. Leary (eds.) *Asian Perspectives on Human Rights*, Boulder CO: Westview Press.

—— (1990b) "Problems of Universal Cultural Legitimacy for Human Rights," in A.A. An-Na'im and F.M. Deng (eds.) *Human Rights in Africa*, Washington DC: The Brookings Institute.

An-Na'im, A.A. and Deng, F.M. (eds.) (1990) *Human Rights in Africa: Cross-Cultural Perspectives*, Washington DC: The Brookings Institute.

Annas, J. (1986) "Doing without Objective Values: Ancient and Modern Strategies," in M. Schofield and G. Striker (eds.) *The Norms of Nature: Studies in Hellenistic Ethics*, Cambridge: Cambridge University Press.

—— (1989) "MacIntyre on Traditions," *Philosophy & Public Affairs* 18: 388–404.

Annas, J. and Barnes, J. (1985) *The Modes of Scepticism: Ancient Texts and Modern Interpretations*, Cambridge: Cambridge University Press.

Aquinas, T. (1964–75) *Summa Theologiae*, trans. T. Gilby, *et al.*, New York: McGraw-Hill.

—— (1964) *Commentary on the Nicomachean Ethics*, trans. C.I. Litzinger, O.P., Chicago: Henry Regnery.

Archard, D. (ed.) (1996) *Philosophy and Pluralism*, Cambridge: Cambridge University Press.

Aristotle (1985) *Nicomachean Ethics*, trans. T. Irwin, Indianapolis IN: Hackett Publishing Company.

Arrington, R.L. (1983) "A Defense of Ethical Relativism," *Metaphilosophy* 14: 225–39.

—— (1989) *Rationalism, Realism, and Relativism: Perspectives in Contemporary Moral Epistemology*, Ithaca NY: Cornell University Press.

Baier, A. (1985a) "Theory and Reflective Practices," in Baier, *Postures of the Mind: Essays on Mind and Morals,* Minneapolis MN: University of Minnesota Press.

—— (1985b) "Doing without Moral Theory?," in Baier, *Postures of the Mind: Essays on Mind and Morals,* Minneapolis MN: University of Minnesota Press.

Baier, K. (1989) "Justice and the Aims of Political Philosophy," *Ethics* 99: 771–90.

Bambrough, R. (1979) *Moral Scepticism and Moral Knowledge*, London: Routledge & Kegan Paul.

Barnes, J. (1988–90) "Scepticism and Relativity," *Philosophical Studies* (Ireland) 32: 1–31.

—— (1990) *The Toils of Scepticism*, Cambridge: Cambridge University Press.

Barnett, C.R. (1988) "Is There a Scientific Basis in Anthropology for the Ethics of Human Rights?," in T.E. Downing and G. Kushner (eds.) *Human Rights and Anthropology*, Cambridge MA: Cultural Survival.

Barnett, H.G. (1948) "On Science and Human Rights," *American Anthropologist* 50: 352–55.

Bauer, J.R. and Bell, D.A. (eds.) (1999) *The East Asian Challenge for Human Rights*, Cambridge: Cambridge University Press.

Baylis, F. and Downie, J. (1997) "Child Abuse and Neglect: Cross-Cultural Considerations," in H.L. Nelson (ed.) *Feminism and Families*, New York: Routledge.

Beardsmore, R.W. (1969) *Moral Reasoning*, New York: Schocken Books.

Beis, R.H. (1964) "Some Contributions of Anthropology to Ethics," *Thomist* 28: 174–224.

Benedict, R. (1934a) *Patterns of Culture*, Boston MA: Houghton Mifflin.

—— (1934b) "Anthropology and the Abnormal," *Journal of General Psychology* 10: 59–80.

Benhabib, S. (1992) *Situating the Self: Gender, Community and Postmodernism in Contemporary Ethics*, New York: Routledge.

—— (1995) "Cultural Complexity, Moral Interdependence, and the Global Dialogical Community," in M.C. Nussbaum and J. Glover (eds.) *Women, Culture, and Development: A Study of Human Capabilities*, Oxford: Clarendon Press.

Benn, S.I. (1984) "Persons and Values: Reasons in Conflict and Moral Disagreement," *Ethics* 95: 20–37.

Bennett, J.W. (1949) "Science and Human Rights: Reason and Action," *American Anthropologist* 51: 329–36.

Bennigson, T. (1996) "Irresolvable Disagreement and the Case against Moral Realism," *Southern Journal of Philosophy* 34: 411–37.

243

—— (1998) "Can We Establish that It is Wrong for Men to Shoot Their Wives when Dinner Is Late?" Unpublished lecture given at a meeting of the American Philosophy Association.

Berlin, I. (1969) *Four Essays on Liberty*, London: Oxford University Press.

—— (1998) *The Proper Study of Mankind: An Anthology of Essays*, H. Hardy and R. Hausheer (eds.), New York: Farrar, Straus & Giroux.

Berlin, I. and Williams, B. (1994) "Pluralism and Liberalism: A Reply," *Political Studies* 42: 306–9.

Beyleveld, D. (1991) *The Dialectical Necessity of Morality: An Analysis and Defense of Alan Gewirth's Argument to the Principle of Generic Consistency*, Chicago: University of Chicago Press.

Bidney, D. (1953) "The Concept of Value in Modern Anthropology," in A.L. Kroeber (ed.) *Anthropology Today: An Encyclopedic Inventory*, Chicago: University of Chicago Press.

—— (1959) "The Philosophical Presuppositions of Cultural Relativism and Cultural Absolutism," in Leo R. Ward (ed.) *Ethics and the Social Sciences*, Notre Dame IN: University of Notre Dame Press.

Blackburn, S. (1985) "Errors and the Phenomenology of Value" in T. Honderich (ed.) *Morality and Objectivity: A Tribute to J.L. Mackie*, London: Routledge & Kegan Paul.

—— (1993) *Essays in Quasi-Realism*, New York: Oxford University Press.

Bloom, I.J., Martin, P., and Proudfoot, W.L. (eds.) (1996) *Religious Diversity and Human Rights*, New York: Columbia University Press.

Boas, F. (1938) "An Anthropologist's Credo," *Nation* 147: 201–4.

—— (1974) *The Shaping of American Anthropology 1883–1911: A Franz Boas Reader*, G.W. Stocking, Jr. (ed.), New York: Basic Books.

Bohman, J. (1995) "Public Reason and Cultural Pluralism: Political Liberalism and the Problem of Moral Conflict," *Political Theory* 23: 253–79.

Bok, S. (1993) "What Basis for Morality? A Minimalist Approach," *The Monist* 76: 349–59.

—— (1995) *Common Values*, Columbia MO: University of Missouri Press.

Borofsky, R. (ed.) (1994) *Assessing Cultural Anthropology*, New York: McGraw-Hill.

Boyd, R.N. (1988) "How to Be a Moral Realist," in G. Sayre-McCord (ed.) *Essays on Moral Realism*, Ithaca NY: Cornell University Press.

Brandt, R.B. (1954) *Hopi Ethics: A Theoretical Analysis*, Chicago IL: University of Chicago Press.

—— (1959) *Ethical Theory: The Problems of Normative and Critical Ethics*, Englewood Cliffs NJ: Prentice-Hall.

—— (1984) "Relativism Refuted?," *The Monist* 67: 297–307.

Brems, E. (1997) "Enemies or Allies? Feminism and Cultural Relativism as Dissident Voices in Human Rights Discourse," *Human Rights Quarterly* 19: 136–64.

Breslauer, D.S. (1993) *Judaism and Human Rights in Contemporary Thought*, Westport CT: Greenwood Press.

Brink, D.O. (1984) "Moral Realism and the Sceptical Arguments from Disagreement and Queerness," *Australasian Journal of Philosophy* 62: 111–25.

—— (1989) *Moral Realism and the Foundations of Ethics*, Cambridge: Cambridge University Press.

Brown, S.C. (ed.) (1984) *Objectivity and Cultural Divergence*, Royal Institute of Philosophy Lecture Series 17, supplement to *Philosophy*, Cambridge: Cambridge University Press.

Bunch, C. (1992) "A Global Perspective on Feminist Ethics and Diversity," in E.B. Cole and S. Coultrap-McQuin (eds.) *Explorations in Feminist Ethics: Theory and Practice*, Bloomington IN: Indiana University Press.

Bunting, H. (1996) "A Single True Morality? The Challenge of Relativism," in D. Archard (ed.) *Philosophy and Pluralism*, Cambridge: Cambridge University Press.

Carrithers, M. (1992) *Why Humans Have Cultures: Explaining Anthropology and Diversity*, Oxford: Oxford University Press.

Cavell, S. (1979) *The Claim of Reason: Wittgenstein, Skepticism, Morality, and Tragedy*, Oxford: Clarendon Press.

Cerna, C.M. (1994) "Universality of Human Rights and Cultural Diversity: Implementation of Human Rights in Different Socio-Cultural Contexts," *Human Rights Quarterly* 16: 740–52.

Chagnon, N. (1992) *Yanomamö: The Last Days of Eden*, San Diego CA: Harcourt Brace & Co.

Chang, R. (ed.) (1997) *Incommensurability, Incomparability, and Practical Reason*, Cambridge MA: Harvard University Press.

Code, L. (1995) "Must a Feminist Be a Relativist After All?," in Code, *Rhetorical Spaces: Essays on Gendered Locations*, New York: Routledge.

—— (1998) "How to Think Globally: Stretching the Limits of Imagination," *Hypatia* 13: 73–85.

Cohen, J. (1993) "Moral Pluralism and Political Consensus," in D. Copp, J. Hampton and J.E. Roemer (eds.) *The Idea of Democracy*, Cambridge: Cambridge University Press.

—— (1994) "Pluralism and Proceduralism," *Chicago-Kent Law Review* 69: 589–618.

Cook, J.W. (1999) *Morality and Cultural Differences*, New York: Oxford University Press.

Cooke, M. (1997) "Are Ethical Conflicts Irreconcilable?," *Philosophy & Social Criticism* 23: 1–19.

Cooper, D. (1978) "Moral Relativism," *Midwest Studies in Philosophy* 3: 97–108.

Crowder, G. (1994) "Pluralism and Liberalism," *Political Studies* 42: 293–305.

Dahl, N.O. (1991) "Justice and Aristotelian Practical Reason," *Philosophy and Phenomenological Research* 51: 153–57.

D'Andrade, R. (1995) "Moral Models in Anthropology," *Current Anthropology* 36: 399–408.

Darwall, S. (1998) "Expressivist Relativism?," *Philosophy and Phenomenological Research* 58: 161–69

Davidson, D. (1982) "On the Very Idea of a Conceptual Scheme," in J.W. Meiland and M. Krausz (eds.) *Relativism: Cognitive and Moral*, Notre Dame IN: University of Notre Dame Press.

Davies, B. (1992) *The Thought of Thomas Aquinas*, Oxford: Clarendon Press.

De Bary, W.T. (1998) *Asian Values and Human Rights: A Confucian Communitarian Perspective,* Cambridge MA: Harvard University Press.

DeCew, J.W. (1990) "Moral Conflicts and Ethical Relativism," *Ethics* 101: 27–41.

Dees, R.H. (1994) "Living with Contextualism," *Canadian Journal of Philosophy* 24: 243–60.

Devine, P. E. (1987) "Relativism, Abortion, and Tolerance," *Philosophy and Phenomenological Research* 43: 131–38.

Donnelly, J. (1984) "Cultural Relativism and Universal Human Rights," *Human Rights Quarterly* 6: 400–19.

—— (1989) *Universal Human Rights in Theory and Practice*, Ithaca NY: Cornell University Press.

—— (1990) "Traditional Values and Universal Human Rights: Caste in India," in C.E. Welch, Jr. and V.A. Leary (eds.) *Asian Perspectives on Human Rights*, Boulder CO: Westview Press.

Donoho, D.L. (1991) "Relativism Versus Universalism in Human Rights: The Search for Meaningful Standards," *Stanford Journal of International Law* 27: 345–91.

Donovan, P. (1986) "Do Different Religions Share Common Moral Ground?," *Religious Studies* 22: 367–75.

Doolan, G. (1999) "The Relation of Culture and Ignorance to Culpability in Thomas Aquinas," *The Thomist* 63: 105–24.

Downing, L.A. and Thigpen, R.B. (1986) "Beyond Shared Understandings," *Political Theory* 14: 451–72.

Downing, T.E. and Kushner, G. (eds.) (1988) *Human Rights and Anthropology*, Cambridge MA: Cultural Survival.

Drydyk, J. (1997) "Globalization and Human Rights," in J. Drydyk and P. Peens (eds.) *Global Justice, Global Democracy*, Winnipeg: Society for Socialist Studies and Halifax: Fawned Publishing.

Duncker, K. (1939) "Ethical Relativity? (An Enquiry into the Psychology of Ethics)," *Mind* 48: 39–53.

Dustin, C.A. (1995) "The Untruth in Relativism," *International Journal of Philosophical Studies* 3: 17–53.

Dworkin, R. (1996) "Objectivity and Truth: You'd Better Believe It," *Philosophy & Public Affairs* 25: 87–139.

Dwyer, K. (1991) *Arab Voices: The Human Rights Debate in the Middle East*, Berkeley CA: University of California Press.

Edel, A. (1955) *Ethical Judgment: The Use of Science in Ethics*, Glencoe IL: Free Press.

—— (1970) "On a Certain Value-Dimension in Analyses of Moral Relativism," *Journal of Philosophy* 67: 584–88.

Edel, M. and Edel, E. (1959) *Anthropology and Ethics*, Springfield IL: Charles C. Thomas.

—— (1963) "The Confrontation of Anthropology and Ethics," *Monist* 47: 489–505.

Ekennia, J.N. (1996) "Committed Dialogue as a Response to Pluralism," *International Philosophical Quarterly* 36: 85–95.

Engelhardt, H.T., Jr. (1997) "The Foundations of Bioethics: Liberty and Life with Moral Diversity," *Reason Papers* 22: 101–8.

Ewing, A.C. (1953) *Ethics*, New York: Free Press.

Farley, M.A. (1993) "Feminism and Universal Morality," in G. Outka and J.P.

Reeder, Jr. (eds.) *Prospects for a Common Morality*, Princeton NJ: Princeton University Press.

Fay, B. (1996) *Contemporary Philosophy of Social Science: A Multicultural Approach*, Oxford: Blackwell.

Ferguson, B.R. (1995) *Yanomami Warfare: A Political History*, Sante Fe NM: School of American Research Press.

Finnis, J. (1980) *Natural Law and Natural Rights*, Oxford: Clarendon Press.

—— (1998) *Aquinas: Moral, Political, and Legal Theory*, Oxford: Oxford University Press.

Fleischacker, S. (1992) *Integrity and Moral Relativism*, Leiden: E.J. Brill.

Fogelin, R. (1985) "The Logic of Deep Disagreements," *Informal Logic* 7: 1–8.

Foot, P. (1978a) "Moral Arguments," in *Virtues and Vices and Other Essays in Moral Philosophy*, Oxford: Basil Blackwell.

—— (1978b) "Moral Beliefs," in *Virtues and Vices and Other Essays in Moral Philosophy*, Oxford: Basil Blackwell.

—— (1982) "Moral Relativism," in J.W. Meiland and M. Krausz (eds.) *Relativism: Cognitive and Moral*, Notre Dame IN: University of Notre Dame Press.

Forster, M.N. (1998) "On the Very Idea of Denying the Existence of Radically Different Conceptual Schemes," *Inquiry* 41: 133–85.

Fowl, S.E. (1991) "Could Horace Talk with the Hebrews? Translatability and Moral Disagreement in MacIntyre and Stout," *Journal of Religious Ethics* 19: 1–20.

Freeman, D. (1983) *Margaret Mead and Samoa: The Making and Unmaking of an Anthropological Myth*, Cambridge MA: Harvard University Press.

Freeman, S. (1994) "Political Liberalism and the Possibility of a Just Constitution," *Chicago-Kent Law Review* 69: 619–68.

French, P.A. (1992) *Responsibility Matters*, Lawrence KS: University Press of Kansas.

Friedrich, H. (1991) *Montaigne*, trans. Dawn Eng, Berkeley CA: University of California Press.

Frisch, M.J. (1998) "A Critical Appraisal of Isaiah Berlin's Philosophy of Pluralism," *Review of Politics* 60: 421–33.

Galipeau, C.J. (1994) *Isaiah Berlin's Liberalism*, Oxford: Clarendon Press.

Garcia, J.L.A. (1988) "Relativism and Moral Divergence," *Metaphilosophy* 19: 264–81.

Garmon, M. (1995) "Neither Absolutism nor Relativism," *Metaphilosophy* 26: 347–59.

Gaut, B. (1993) "Moral Pluralism," *Philosophical Papers* 22: 17–40.

Geertz, C. (1973) *The Interpretation of Cultures: Selected Essays*, New York: Basic Books.

—— (1983) *Local Knowledge: Further Essays in Interpretive Anthropology*, New York: Basic Books.

—— (1986) "The Uses of Diversity," in S. McMurrin (ed.) *The Tanner Lectures on Human Values*, vol. 7, Cambridge: Cambridge University Press.

—— (1989) "Anti Anti-Relativism," in M. Krausz (ed.) *Relativism: Interpretation and Confrontation*, Notre Dame IN: University of Notre Dame Press.

Gewirth, A. (1978) *Reason and Morality*, Chicago IL: University of Chicago Press.

—— (1982) *Human Rights: Essays on Justification and Applications*, Chicago IL: University of Chicago Press.

—— (1994) "Is Cultural Pluralism Relevant to Moral Knowledge?," *Social Philosophy and Policy* 11: 22–42. Also in E.F. Paul, F.D. Miller, Jr., and J. Paul (eds.) (1994) *Cultural Pluralism and Moral Knowledge*, Cambridge: Cambridge University Press.

Gibbard, A. (1990) *Wise Choices, Apt Feelings: A Theory of Normative Judgment*, Cambridge MA: Harvard University Press.

Gilligan, C. (1982) *In a Different Voice*, Cambridge MA: Harvard University Press.

—— (1987) "Moral Orientation and Moral Development," in E.F. Kittay and D.T. Meyers (eds.) *Women and Moral Theory*, Totowa NJ: Rowman & Littlefield.

Ginsberg, M. (1953) "On the Diversity of Morals," *Journal of the Royal Anthropological Institute* 83: 117–35.

Glover, J. (1995) "The Research Program of Development Ethics," in M.C. Nussbaum and J. Glover (eds.) *Women, Culture, and Development: A Study of Human Capabilities*, Oxford: Clarendon Press.

Goldman, A.H. (1987) "Red and Right," *Journal of Philosophy* 84: 349–62.

Gowans, C.W. (ed.) (1987) *Moral Dilemmas*, New York: Oxford University Press.

—— (1994) *Innocence Lost: An Examination of Inescapable Moral Wrongdoing*, New York: Oxford University Press.

Gray, J. (1996) *Isaiah Berlin*, Princeton NJ: Princeton University Press.

Greenawalt, K. (1995) *Private Consciences and Public Reasons*, New York: Oxford University Press.

Gustafson, C. and Juviler, P. (eds.) (1999) *Religion and Human Rights: Competing Claims?* Armonk NY: M.E. Sharp.

Gutmann, A. (1993) "The Challenge of Multiculturalism in Political Ethics," *Philosophy & Public Affairs* 22: 171–206.

Gutmann, A. and Thompson, D. (1990) "Moral Conflict and Political Consensus," *Ethics* 101: 64–88.

—— (1996) *Democracy and Disagreement*, Cambridge MA: Harvard University Press.

Haan, N., Bellah, R.N., Rabinow, P., and Sullivan, W.M. (eds.) (1983) *Social Science as Moral Inquiry*, New York: Columbia University Press.

Hampshire, S. (1983) *Morality and Conflict,* Cambridge MA: Harvard University Press.

—— (1989) *Innocence and Experience*, Cambridge MA: Harvard University Press.

Hampton, J. (1993) "The Moral Commitments of Liberalism," in D. Copp, J. Hampton and J.E. Roemer (eds.) *The Idea of Democracy*, Cambridge: Cambridge University Press.

—— (1994) "The Common Faith of Liberalism," *Pacific Philosophical Quarterly* 75: 186–216.

Hankinson, R.J. (1995) *The Skeptic*, London: Routledge.

Hanson, F.A. (1975) *Meaning in Culture*, London: Routledge & Kegan Paul.

Harbour, F.V. (1995). "Basic Moral Values: A Shared Core," *Ethics & International Affairs* 9: 155–70.

Hare, R.M. (1963) *Freedom and Reason*, Oxford: Clarendon Press.

Harman, G. (1977) *The Nature of Morality: An Introduction to Ethics*, New York: Oxford University Press.

—— (1991) "Moral Diversity as an Argument for Moral Relativism," in D. Odegard and C. Stewart (eds.) *Perspectives on Moral Relativism*, Milliken, Ontario: Agathon Books.

—— (1996) "Moral Relativism" in G. Harman and J.J. Thompson (eds.) *Moral Relativism and Moral Objectivity*, Cambridge MA: Blackwell.

—— (1998a) "Précis of Part One of *Moral Relativism and Moral Objectivity*," *Philosophy and Phenomenological Research* 58: 161–69.

—— (1998b) "Response to Critics," *Philosophy and Phenomenological Research* 58: 207–13.

Harrison, G. (1976) "Relativism and Tolerance," *Ethics* 86: 122–35.

Harrison, J. (1976) *Hume"s Moral Epistemology*, Oxford: Clarendon Press.

Hatch, E. (1983) *Culture and Morality: The Relativity of Values in Anthropology*, New York: Columbia University Press.

—— (1997) "The Good Side of Relativism," *Journal of Anthropological Research* 53: 371–81.

Heald, G. (1988) "A Comparison between American, European, and Japanese Values" in B. Almond and B. Wilson (eds.) *Values: A Symposium*, Atlantic Highlands NJ: Humanities Press.

Henkin, L. (1990) *The Age of Rights*, New York: Columbia University Press.

Herodotus (1987) *The History*, trans. David Grene, Chicago IL: University of Chicago Press.

Herskovits, M.J. (1948) *Man and His Works: The Science of Cultural Anthropology*, New York: A.A. Knopf.

—— (1972) *Cultural Relativism: Perspectives in Cultural Pluralism*, F. Herskovits (ed.), New York: Random House.

Heyd, D. (ed.) (1996) *Toleration: An Elusive Virtue*, Princeton NJ: Princeton University Press.

Hollis, M. and Lukes, S. (eds.) (1982) *Rationality and Relativism*, Cambridge MA: MIT Press.

Horton, J. and Mendus, S. (eds.) (1994) *After MacIntyre: Critical Perspectives on the Work of Alasdair MacIntyre*, Notre Dame IN: University of Notre Dame Press.

Howard, R.E. (1986) *Human Rights in Commonwealth Africa*, Totowa NJ: Rowman & Littlefield.

—— (1990) "Group versus Individual Identity in the African Debate on Human Rights," in A.A. An-Na'im and F.M. Deng (eds.) *Human Rights in Africa: Cross-Cultural Perspectives*, Washington DC: The Brookings Institute.

Howell, S. (ed.) (1997) *The Ethnography of Moralities*, London: Routledge.

Hume, D. (1967) *A Treatise of Human Nature*, L.A. Selby-Bigge (ed.), Oxford: Clarendon Press.

—— (1998) *An Enquiry Concerning the Principles of Morals*, T.L. Beauchamp (ed.), Oxford: Oxford University Press.

Huntington, S.P. (1996) *The Clash of Civilizations and the Remaking of World Order*, New York: Simon & Schuster.

Hurley, S.L. (1985) "Objectivity and Disagreement," in T. Honderich (ed.)

Morality and Objectivity: A Tribute to J.L. Mackie, London: Routledge & Kegan Paul.

—— (1989) *Natural Reasons: Personality and Polity*, New York: Oxford University Press.

—— (1993) "Commentary on Martha Nussbaum: Non-Relative Virtues: An Aristotelian Approach," in M. Nussbaum and A. Sen (eds.) *The Quality of Life*, Oxford: Clarendon Press.

Ilesanmi, S.O. (1995) "Human Rights Discourse in Modern Africa: A Comparative Religious Ethical Perspective," *Journal of Religious Ethics* 23: 293–322.

Inada, K.K. (1990) "A Buddhist Response to the Nature of Human Rights," in C.E. Welch, Jr. and V.A. Leary (eds.) *Asian Perspectives on Human Rights*, Boulder CO: Westview Press.

James, S.A. (1994) "Reconciling International Human Rights and Cultural Relativism: The Case of Female Circumcision," *Bioethics* 8: 1–26.

Johnson, W.G. (1988) "Explaining Diversity in Moral Thought: A Theory," *Southern Journal of Philosophy* 26: 115–33.

Jung, K.D. (1994) "Is Culture Destiny? The Myth of Asia's Anti-Democratic Values," *Foreign Affairs* 73: 189–94.

Kekes, J. (1993) *The Morality of Pluralism*, Princeton NJ: Princeton University Press.

—— (1994) "Pluralism and the Value of Life," in E.F. Paul, F.D. Miller, Jr., and J. Paul (eds.) *Cultural Pluralism and Moral Knowledge*, Cambridge: Cambridge University Press.

Kittay, E.F. and Meyers, D.T. (eds.) (1987) *Women and Moral Theory*, Totowa NJ: Rowman & Littlefield.

Kluckhohn, C. (1955) "Ethical Relativity: *Sic et Non*," *Journal of Philosophy* 52: 663–77.

—— (1962) *Culture and Behavior,* R. Kluckhohn (ed.), New York: Macmillan.

Kohls, J. and Buller, P. (1994) "Resolving Cross-cultural Ethical Conflict: Exploring Alternative Strategies," *Journal of Business Ethics* 13: 31–38.

Kolnai, A. (1978) "Moral Consensus," in Kolnai, *Ethics, Value and Reality*, Indianapolis IN: Hackett Publishing Company.

Krausz, M. (ed.) (1989) *Relativism: Interpretation and Confrontation*, Notre Dame IN: University of Notre Dame Press.

Krausz, M. and Meiland, J.W. (eds.) (1982) *Relativism: Cognitive and Moral*, Notre Dame IN: University of Notre Dame Press.

Kukathas, C. (1994) "Explaining Moral Variety," in E.F. Paul, F.D. Miller, Jr., and J. Paul (eds.) *Cultural Pluralism and Moral Knowledge*, Cambridge: Cambridge University Press.

Küng, H. (ed.) (1996) *Yes to a Global Ethic: Voices from Religion and Politics*, New York: Continuum.

Küng, H. and Kuschel, K-J. (eds.) (1995) *A Global Ethic: The Declaration of the Parliament of the World's Religions*, New York: Continuum.

Kupperman, J. (1986) "Wong's Relativism and Comparative Philosophy – A Review of *Moral Relativity*," *Philosophy East and West* 36: 169–76.

Ladd, J. (1957) *The Structure of a Moral Code: A Philosophical Analysis of Ethical Discourse Applied to the Ethics of the Navaho Indian*, Cambridge MA: Harvard University Press.

—— (1963) "The Issue of Relativism," *Monist* 47: 585–609.

—— (ed.) (1985) *Ethical Relativism*, Lanham MD: University Press of America.

Larmore, C.E. (1987) *Patterns of Moral Complexity*, Cambridge: Cambridge University Press.

—— (1994) "Pluralism and Reasonable Disagreement," in E.F. Paul, F.D. Miller, Jr., and J. Paul (eds.) *Cultural Pluralism and Moral Knowledge*, Cambridge: Cambridge University Press.

—— (1996) *The Morals of Modernity*, Cambridge: Cambridge University Press.

Lazari-Pawlowska, I. (1970) "On Cultural Relativism," *The Journal of Philosophy* 67: 577–84.

Lean, M.E. (1970) "Aren't Moral Judgments 'Factual'?," *Personalist* 51: 259–85.

Leary, V.A. (1990) "The Effect of Western Perspectives on International Human Rights," in A.A. An-Na'im and F.M. Deng (eds.) *Human Rights in Africa*, Washington DC: The Brookings Institute.

Li, X. (1995) "Gender Inequality in China and Cultural Relativism," in M.C. Nussbaum and J. Glover (eds.) *Women, Culture, and Development: A Study of Human Capabilities*, Oxford: Clarendon Press.

Linton, R. (1952) "Universal Ethical Principles: An Anthropological View," in R.N. Anshen (ed.) *Moral Principles of Action: Man's Ethical Imperative*, New York: Harper.

Little, D. (1990) "A Christian Perspective on Human Rights," in A.A. An-Na'im and F.M. Deng (eds.) *Human Rights in Africa*, Washington DC: The Brookings Institute.

—— (1999) "Rethinking Human Rights: A Review Essay on Religion, Relativism, and Other Matters," *Journal of Religious Ethics* 27: 151–77.

Little, D., Kelsay, J., and Sachedina, A.A. (eds.) (1988) *Human Rights and the Conflict of Cultures: Western and Islamic Perspectives on Religious Liberty*. Columbia SC: University of South Carolina Press.

Lizot, J. (1985) *Tales of the Yanomami: Daily Life in the Venezuelan Forest*, trans. E. Simon, Cambridge: Cambridge University Press.

Locke, J. (1959) *An Essay Concerning Human Understanding*, A.C. Fraser (ed.), New York: Dover Publications.

—— (1991) "A Letter Concerning Toleration," trans. Popple, in J. Horton and S. Mendus (eds.) *John Locke: A Letter Concerning Toleration in Focus*, London: Routledge.

Loeb, D. (1998) "Moral Realism and the Argument from Disagreement," *Philosophical Studies* 90: 281–303.

Louch, A.R. (1963) "Anthropology and Moral Explanation," *Monist* 47: 610–24.

Lovin, R.W. and Reynolds, F.E. (1992) "Ethical Naturalism and Indigenous Cultures: Introduction," *Journal of Religious Ethics* 20: 267–78.

Lukes, S. (1974) "Relativism: Cognitive and Moral," *Aristotelian Society Supplementary Volume* 48: 165–89.

—— (1991) *Moral Conflict and Politics*, Oxford: Clarendon Press.

—— (1994) "The Singular and the Plural: On the Distinctive Liberalism of Isaiah Berlin," *Social Research* 61: 687–717.

Lyons, D. (1976) "Ethical Relativism and the Problem of Incoherence," *Ethics* 86: 107–21.

MacBeath, A. (1952) *Experiments in Living: A Study of the Nature and*

Foundation of Ethics or Morals in the Light of Recent Work in Social Anthropology, London: Macmillan.

McClintock, T.L. (1963) "The Argument for Ethical Relativism from the Diversity of Morals," *Monist* 47: 528–44.

—— (1969) "The Definition of Ethical Relativism," *Personalist* 50: 435–47.

McDowell, J. (1986) "Critical Notice of *Ethics and the Limits of Philosophy*," *Mind* 95: 377–86.

McInerny, R. (1993) "Ethics," in N. Kretzmann and E. Stump (eds.) *The Cambridge Companion to Aquinas*, Cambridge: Cambridge University Press.

MacIntyre, A. (1984: second edition) *After Virtue*, Notre Dame IN: University of Notre Dame Press.

—— (1988) *Whose Justice? Which Rationality?*, Notre Dame IN: University of Notre Dame Press.

—— (1989) "Relativism, Power, and Philosophy," in M. Krausz (ed.) *Relativism: Interpretation and Confrontation*, Notre Dame IN: University of Notre Dame Press.

—— (1990) *Three Rival Versions of Moral Inquiry: Encyclopedia, Genealogy, and Tradition*, Notre Dame IN: University of Notre Dame Press.

—— (1991) "Reply to Dahl, Baier and Schneewind," *Philosophy and Phenomenological Research* 51: 169–78.

—— (1994) "Moral Relativism, Truth and Justification," in L. Gormally (ed.) *Moral Truth and Moral Tradition: Essays in Honor of Peter Geach and Elizabeth Anscombe*, Dublin: Four Courts Press.

Mackie, J.L. (1977) *Ethics: Inventing Right and Wrong*, London: Penguin Books.

—— (1980) *Hume's Moral Theory*, London: Routledge & Kegan Paul.

McKnight, C.J. (1996) "Pluralism, Realism, and Truth," in D. Archard (ed.) *Philosophy and Pluralism*, Cambridge: Cambridge University Press.

McNaughton, D. (1988) *Moral Vision: An Introduction to Ethics*, Oxford: Basil Blackwell.

McPherran, M.L. (1990) "Pyrrhonism's Arguments against Value," *Philosophical Studies* (USA) 60: 127–42.

Marfording, A. (1997) "Cultural Relativism and the Construction of Culture: An Examination of Japan," *Human Rights Quarterly* 19: 431–48.

Matilal, B.K. (1989) "Ethical Relativism and Confrontation of Cultures," in M. Krausz (ed.) *Relativism: Interpretation and Confrontation*, Notre Dame IN: University of Notre Dame Press.

Mead, M. (1928) *Coming of Age in Samoa*, New York: William Morrow.

—— (1935) *Sex and Temperament in Three Primitive Societies*, London: Routledge.

Mendus, S. (ed.) (1988) *Justifying Toleration: Conceptual and Historical Perspectives*, Cambridge: Cambridge University Press.

Messer, E. (1993) "Anthropology and Human Rights," *Annual Review of Anthropology* 22: 221–49.

—— (1997) "Pluralist Approaches to Human Rights," *Journal of Anthropological Research* 53: 293–317.

Mill, J.S. (1956) *On Liberty*, C.V. Shields (ed.), Indianapolis IN: Bobbs-Merrill.

Miller, R.W. (1985) "Ways of Moral Learning," *Philosophical Review* 94: 507–56.

—— (1992) *Moral Differences: Truth, Justice and Conscience in a World of Conflict*, Princeton NJ: Princeton University Press.

Milne, A.J.M. (1986) *Human Rights and Human Diversity: An Essay in the Philosophy of Human Rights*, Albany NY: State University of New York Press.

Milo, R.D. (1986) "Moral Deadlock," *Philosophy* 61: 453–71.

Modood, T. (1982–83) "Differences in Moral Reasoning," *Philosophical Studies* (Ireland) 29: 157–85.

Monshipouri, M. (1998) *Islamism, Secularism, and Human Rights in the Middle East*, Boulder CO: Rienner.

Montaigne, M. [1958] (1965) *The Complete Essays of Montaigne*, trans. D.M. Frame, Stanford CA: Stanford University Press.

Moody-Adams, M.M. (1990) "On the Alleged Methodological Infirmity of Ethics," *American Philosophical Quarterly* 27: 225–35.

—— (1997) *Fieldwork in Familiar Places: Morality, Culture, and Philosophy*, Cambridge MA: Harvard University Press.

—— (1998) "The Virtues of Nussbaum's Essentialism," *Metaphilosophy* 29: 263–72.

Moon, D. (1993) *Constructing Community: Moral Pluralism and Tragic Conflict*, Princeton NJ: Princeton University Press.

Morgan, K.P. (1991) "Strangers in a Strange Land: Feminists Visit Relativists," in D. Odegard and C. Stewart (eds.) *Perspectives on Moral Relativism*, Milliken, Ontario: Agathon Books.

Mulhall, S. (1994) *Stanley Cavell: Philosophy's Recounting of the Ordinary*, Oxford: Clarendon Press.

Nagel, T. (1986) *The View from Nowhere*, New York: Oxford University Press.

—— (1987) "Moral Conflict and Political Legitimacy," *Philosophy & Public Affairs* 16: 215–40.

Nagengast, C. (1997) "Women, Minorities, and Indigenous Peoples: Universalism and Cultural Relativity," *Journal of Anthropological Research* 53: 349–69.

Narayan, U. (1997) *Dislocating Cultures: Identities, Traditions, and Third-World Feminism*, New York: Routledge.

—— (1998) "Essence of Culture and a Sense of History: A Feminist Critique of Cultural Essentialism," *Hypatia* 13: 86–106.

Narveson, J. (1987) "Critical Notice of *Moral Relativity*," *Canadian Journal of Philosophy* 17: 235–58.

Nielsen, K. (1966) "Ethical Relativism and the Facts of Cultural Relativity," *Social Research* 33: 531–51.

—— (1971) "Anthropology and Ethics," *Journal of Value Inquiry* 5: 253–66.

—— (1974) "On the Diversity of Moral Beliefs," *Cultural Hermeneutics* 2: 281–303.

Nietzsche, F. (1966) *Beyond Good and Evil*, trans. W. Kaufmann, New York: Random House.

—— (1994) *On the Genealogy of Morality*, trans. C. Diethe, K. Ansell-Pearson (ed.), Cambridge: Cambridge University Press.

Noddings, N. (1984) *Caring: A Feminine Approach to Ethics and Moral Education*, Berkeley CA: University of California Press.

Norton, D.F. (1982) *David Hume: Common-Sense Moralist, Sceptical Metaphysician*, Princeton NJ: Princeton University Press.

—— (1993) "Hume, Human Nature, and the Foundations of Morality," in D.F. Norton (ed.) *The Cambridge Companion to Hume*, Cambridge: Cambridge University Press.

Norton, D.L. (1996) *Imagination, Understanding, and the Virtue of Liberality*, Lanham MD: Rowman & Littlefield.

Nussbaum, M.C. (1993) "Non-relative Virtues: An Aristotelian Approach," in M. Nussbaum and A. Sen (eds.) *The Quality of Life*, Oxford: Clarendon Press.

—— (1994) *The Therapy of Desire: Theory and Practice in Hellenistic Ethics*, Princeton NJ: Princeton University Press.

—— (1995a) "Human Capabilities, Female Human Beings," in M.C. Nussbaum and J. Glover (eds.) *Women, Culture, and Development: A Study of Human Capabilities*, Oxford: Clarendon Press.

—— (1995b) "Aristotle on Human Nature and the Foundations of Ethics," in J.E.J. Altham and R. Harrison (eds.) *World, Mind, and Ethics: Essays on the Ethical Philosophy of Bernard Williams*, Cambridge: Cambridge University Press.

—— (1998) "Political Animals: Luck, Love, and Dignity," *Metaphilosophy* 29: 273–87.

—— (1999a) "Women and Cultural Universals," in Nussbaum, *Sex and Social Justice*, New York: Oxford University Press.

—— (1999b) "Religion and Women's Human Rights," in Nussbaum, *Sex and Social Justice*, New York: Oxford University Press.

—— (1999c) "Judging Other Cultures: The Case of Genital Mutilation," in Nussbaum, *Sex and Social Justice*, New York: Oxford University Press.

—— (forthcoming) *Women and Human Development: The Capabilities Approach*, Cambridge: Cambridge University Press.

Nussbaum, M.C. and Glover, J. (eds.) (1995) *Women, Culture, and Development: A Study of Human Capabilities*, Oxford: Clarendon Press.

Odegard, D. and Stewart, C. (eds.) (1991) *Perspectives on Moral Relativism*, Milliken, Ontario: Agathon Books.

Okin, S.M. (1994) "Gender Inequality and Cultural Differences," *Political Theory* 22: 5–24.

—— (1995) "Inequalities between the Sexes in Different Cultural Contexts," in M.C. Nussbaum and J. Glover (eds.) *Women, Culture, and Development: A Study of Human Capabilities*, Oxford: Clarendon Press.

—— (1998) "Feminism, Women's Human Rights, and Cultural Differences" *Hypatia* 13: 32–52.

Outka, G. and Reeder, J.P. (eds.) (1993) *Prospects for a Common Morality*, Princeton NJ: Princeton University Press.

Paul, E.F., Miller, F.D., Jr., and Paul, J. (eds.) (1994) *Cultural Pluralism and Moral Knowledge*, Cambridge: Cambridge University Press.

Perry, M.J. (1997) "Are Human Rights Universal? The Relativist Challenge and Related Matters," *Human Rights Quarterly* 19: 461–509.

—— (1998) *The Idea of Human Rights: Four Inquiries*, New York: Oxford University Press.

Phillips, D.Z. and Mounce, H.O. (1970) *Moral Practices*, New York: Schocken Books.

Plato (1961) *Theaetetus*, trans. F.M. Cornford, in E. Hamilton and H. Cairns (eds.) *The Collected Dialogues of Plato*, Princeton NJ: Princeton University Press.

Pollis, A. (1996) "Cultural Relativism Revisited: Through a State Prism," *Human Rights Quarterly* 18: 316–44.

Pollis, A. and Schwab, P. (1980) "Human Rights: A Western Construct with Limited Applicability," in A. Pollis and P. Schwab (eds.) *Human Rights: Cultural and Ideological Perspectives*, New York: Praeger Publishers.

Popkin, R.H. (1979) *The History of Skepticism from Erasmus to Spinoza*, Berkeley CA: University of California Press.

Post, S.G. and Leisey, R.G. (1995) "Analogy, Evaluation, and Moral Disagreement," *Journal of Value Inquiry* 29: 45–55.

Postow, B.C. (1979) "Dishonest Relativism," *Analysis* 39: 45–48.

Quinn, W. (1993) "Reflection and the Loss of Moral Knowledge: Williams on Objectivity," in Quinn, *Morality and Action*, Cambridge: Cambridge University Press.

Railton, P. (1993) "What the Non-Cognitivist Helps Us to See the Naturalist Must Help Us to Explain," in J. Haldane and C. Wright (eds.) *Reality, Representation, and Projection*, New York: Oxford University Press.

—— (1996) "Moral Realism: Prospects and Problems," in W. Sinnott-Armstrong and M. Timmons (eds.) *Moral Knowledge? New Readings in Moral Epistemology*, New York: Oxford University Press.

Ramos, A.R. (1987) "Reflecting on the Yanomami: Ethnographic Images and the Pursuit of the Exotic," *Cultural Anthropology* 2: 284–309.

Rawls, J. (1971) *A Theory of Justice*, Cambridge MA: Harvard University Press.

—— (1987) "The Idea of an Overlapping Consensus," *Oxford Journal of Legal Studies* 7: 1–25.

—— (1989) "The Domain of the Political and Overlapping Consensus," *The New York University Law Review* 64: 233–55.

—— (1993) "The Law of Peoples," in S. Shute and S. Hurley (eds.) *On Human Rights: The Oxford Amnesty Lectures 1993*, New York: Basic Books.

—— (1993) *Political Liberalism*, New York: Columbia University Press.

—— (1997) "The Idea of Public Reason Revisited," *University of Chicago Law Review* 64: 765–807.

Raz, J. (1994a) "Facing Diversity: The Case of Epistemic Abstinence," in Raz, *Ethics in the Public Domain*, Oxford: Clarendon Press.

—— (1994b) "Liberalism, Scepticism, and Democracy," in Raz, *Ethics in the Public Domain*, Oxford: Clarendon Press.

Redfield, R. (1953) *The Primitive World and Its Transformations*, Ithaca NY: Cornell University Press.

—— (1957) "The Universally Human and the Culturally Variable," *Journal of General Education* 10: 150–60.

Regis, E., Jr. (ed.) (1984) *Gewirth's Ethical Rationalism: Critical Essays with a Reply by Alan Gewirth*, Chicago IL: University of Chicago Press.

Renteln, A.D. (1985) "The Unanswered Challenge of Relativism and the Consequences for Human Rights," *Human Rights Quarterly* 7: 514–40.

—— (1988) "Relativism and the Search for Human Rights," *American Anthropologist* 90: 56–71.

—— (1990) *International Human Rights: Universalism Versus Relativism*, Newbury Park CA: Sage Publications.

Rescher, N. (1993) *Pluralism: Against the Demand for Consensus*, Oxford: Clarendon Press.

—— (1997) *Objectivity: The Obligations of Impersonal Reason*, Notre Dame IN: University of Notre Dame Press.

Richardson, H.S. (1990) "The Problem of Liberalism and the Good," in R.B. Douglass and G.M. Mara (eds.) *Liberalism and the Good*, New York: Routledge.

Rorty, A.O. (1990) "Varieties of Pluralism in a Polyphonic Society," *Review of Metaphysics* 44: 3–20.

—— (1992) "The Advantages of Moral Diversity," *Social Philosophy & Policy* 9: 38–62.

—— (1994) "The Hidden Politics of Cultural Identification," *Political Theory* 22: 152–66.

—— (1995) "The Many Faces of Morality," *Midwest Studies in Philosophy* 20: 67–82.

Rorty, R. (1979) *Philosophy and the Mirror of Nature*, Princeton NJ: Princeton University Press.

Ross, W.D. (1930) *The Right and the Good*, Oxford: Clarendon Press.

Rotenstreich, N. (1977) "On Ethical Relativism," *Journal of Value Inquiry* 11: 81–103.

Rouner, L.S. (ed.) (1988) *Human Rights and the World's Religions*, Notre Dame IN: University of Notre Dame Press.

Rousseau, J.J. (1975) "The Creed of the Savoyard Priest," in *The Essential Rousseau*, trans. L. Bair, New York: Meridian.

Russell, B. (1984) "Moral Relativism and Moral Realism," *Monist* 67: 435–51.

Salmon, M.H. (1997) "Ethical Considerations in Anthropology and Archaeology, or Relativism and Justice for All," *Journal of Anthropological Research* 53: 47–63.

Scanlon, T.M. (1995) "Moral Theory: Understanding and Disagreement," *Philosophy and Phenomenological Research* 55: 343–56.

——(1998) *What We Owe to Each Other*, Cambridge MA: Harvard University Press.

Schacht, R. (1983) *Nietzsche*, London: Routledge.

—— (ed.) (1994) *Nietzsche, Genealogy, Morality: Essays on Nietzsche's Genealogy of Morals*, Berkeley CA: University of California Press.

Scheper-Hughes, N. (1984) "The Margaret Mead Controversy: Culture, Biology, and Anthropological Inquiry," *Human Organization*: 43: 85–93.

—— (1995) "The Primacy of the Ethical: Propositions for a Militant Anthropology," *Current Anthropology* 36: 409–20.

Schiffer, S. (1990) "Meaning and Value," *Journal of Philosophy* 87: 602–18.

Schirmer, J. (1988) "The Dilemma of Cultural Diversity and Equivalence in Universal Human Rights Standards," in T.E. Downing and G. Kushner (eds.) *Human Rights and Anthropology*, Cambridge MA: Cultural Survival.

Schmidt, P. H. (1955) "Some Criticisms of Cultural Relativism," *Journal of Philosophy* 52: 780–91.

Schneewind, J.B. (1991) "MacIntyre and the Indispensability of Tradition," *Philosophy and Phenomenological Research* 51: 165–68.

—— (1998) *The Invention of Autonomy: A History of Modern Moral Philosophy*, Cambridge: Cambridge University Press.

Seabright, P. (1988) "Objectivity, Disagreement, and Projectibility," *Inquiry* 31: 25–51.

Sextus Empiricus (1994) *Outlines of Scepticism*, trans. J. Annas and J. Barnes, Cambridge: Cambridge University Press.

—— (1997) *Against the Ethicists*, trans. R. Bett, Oxford: Clarendon Press.

Shafer-Landau, R. (1994) "Ethical Disagreement, Ethical Objectivism and Moral Indeterminacy," *Philosophy and Phenomenological Research* 54: 331–44.

Sherwin, S. (1991) "Feminism and Moral Relativism," in D. Odegard and C. Stewart (eds.) *Perspectives on Moral Relativism*, Milliken, Ontario: Agathon Books.

Shrage, L. (1994) *Moral Dilemmas of Feminism: Prostitution, Adultery, and Abortion*, New York: Routledge.

Shute, S. and Hurley, S. (eds.) (1993) *On Human Rights: The Oxford Amnesty Lectures 1993*, New York: Basic Books.

Shweder, R.A. (1989) "Post-Nietzschean Anthropology: The Idea of Multiple Objective Worlds," in M. Krausz (ed.) *Relativism: Interpretation and Confrontation*, Notre Dame IN: University of Notre Dame Press.

—— (1991) *Thinking through Cultures: Expeditions in Cultural Psychology*, Cambridge MA: Harvard University Press.

—— (1996) "The View from Manywheres," *Anthropology Newsletter* 37: 1, 4–5.

Shweder, R.A. and Levine, R.A. (eds.) (1984) *Culture Theory: Essays on Mind, Self, and Emotion*, Cambridge: Cambridge University Press.

Shweder, R.A., Much, N.C., Mahapatra, M. and Park, L. (1997) "The 'Big Three' of Morality (Autonomy, Community, Divinity) and the 'Big Three' Explanations of Suffering," in A.M. Brandt and P. Rozin (eds.) *Morality and Health*, New York: Routledge.

Silver, M. (1994) "Irreconcilable Moral Disagreement," in L. Foster and P. Herzog (eds.) *Defending Diversity: Contemporary Philosophical Perspectives on Pluralism and Multiculturalism*, Amherst MA: University of Massachusetts Press.

Sinnott-Armstrong, W. (1996) "Moral Skepticism and Justification," in W. Sinnott-Armstrong and M. Timmons (eds.) *Moral Knowledge? New Readings in Moral Epistemology*, New York: Oxford University Press.

Skorupski, J. (1996) "Value-Pluralism," in D. Archer (ed.) *Philosophy and Pluralism*, Cambridge: Cambridge University Press.

Snare, F.E. (1980) "The Diversity of Morals," *Mind* 89: 353–69.

—— (1984) "The Empirical Bases of Moral Scepticism," *American Philosophical Quarterly* 21: 215–25.

Solum, L.B. (1994) "Inclusive Public Reason," *Pacific Philosophical Quarterly* 75: 217–31.

Sosa, E. (1998) "Objectivity without Absolutes: Reflections on Determinacy and Relativism." Unpublished lecture delivered at Fordham University.

Spiro, M.E. (1986) "Cultural Relativism and the Future of Anthropology," *Cultural Anthropology* 1: 259–86.

—— (1992a) "A Critique of Cultural Relativism with Special Reference to

Epistemological Relativism," in Spiro, *Anthropological Other or Burmese Brother*, New Brunswick NJ: Transaction Publishers.

—— (1992b) "On the Strange and Familiar in Recent Anthropological Thought," in Spiro, *Anthropological Other or Burmese Brother*, New Brunswick NJ: Transaction Publishers.

Sreenivasan, G. (1998) "Interpretation and Reason," *Philosophy & Public Affairs* 27: 142–71.

Stace, W.T. (1962) *The Concept of Morals*, New York: Macmillan.

Stevenson, C.L. (1944) *Ethics and Language*, New Haven CT: Yale University Press.

—— (1963) "The Nature of Ethical Disagreement," in Stevenson, *Facts and Values: Studies in Ethical Analysis*, New Haven CT: Yale University Press.

Steward, J.H. (1948) "Comments on the Statement on Human Rights," *American Anthropologist* 50: 351–52.

Stewart, D. (1859) *The Philosophy of the Active and Moral Powers of Man*, in Stewart, *The Collected Works*, vol. VI, W. Hamilton (ed.), Edinburgh: Thomas Constable.

Stewart, R.M. and Thomas, L.L. (1991) "Recent Work on Ethical Relativism," *American Philosophical Quarterly* 28: 85–100.

Stocker, M. (1990) *Plural and Conflicting Values*, Oxford: Clarendon Press.

Stocking, G.W., Jr. (1992) *The Ethnographer's Magic and Other Essays in the History of Anthropology*, Madison WI: University of Wisconsin Press.

Stout, J. (1988) *Ethics after Babel: The Languages of Morals and Their Discontents*, Boston MA: Beacon Press.

—— (1993) "On Having a Morality in Common," in G. Outka and J.P. Reeder, Jr. (eds.) *Prospects for a Common Morality*, Princeton NJ: Princeton University Press.

Sturgeon, N.L. (1994) "Moral Disagreement and Moral Relativism," in E.F. Paul, F.D. Miller, Jr., and J. Paul (eds.) *Cultural Pluralism and Moral Knowledge*, Cambridge: Cambridge University Press.

Sumner, W.G. (1906) *Folkways: A Study of the Sociological Importance of Usages, Manners, Customs, Mores, and Morals*, Boston MA: Ginn.

Sunstein, C.R. (1996) *Legal Reasoning and Political Conflict*, New York: Oxford University Press.

Swidler, A. (ed.) (1982) *Human Rights in Religious Traditions*, New York: The Pilgrim Press.

Tasioulas, J. (1998) "Relativism, Realism, and Reflection," *Inquiry* 41: 377–410.

Taylor, C. (1989) *Sources of the Self: The Making of Modern Identity*, Cambridge MA: Harvard University Press.

—— (1993) "Explanation and Practical Reason," in M. Nussbaum and A. Sen (eds.) *The Quality of Life*, Oxford: Clarendon Press.

Taylor, P.W. (1958) "Social Science and Ethical Relativism," *Journal of Philosophy* 55: 32–44.

—— (1963) "The Ethnocentric Fallacy," *Monist* 47: 563–84.

Tennekes, J. (1971) *Anthropology, Relativism and Method: An Inquiry into the Methodological Principles of a Science of Culture*, Assen: Koninklijke Van Gorcum.

Tersman, F. (1998) "Crispin Wright on Moral Disagreement," *Philosophical Quarterly* 48: 359–65.

Thurman, R.A.F. (1988) "Social and Cultural Rights in Buddhism," in L.S. Rouner (ed.) *Human Rights and the World's Religions*, Notre Dame IN: University of Notre Dame Press.
—— (1996) "Human Rights and Human Responsibilities: Buddhist Views of Individualism and Altruism," in I.J. Bloom, J.P. Martin, and W.L. Proudfoot (eds.) *Religious Diversity and Human Rights*, New York: Columbia University Press.
Tibi, B. (1990) "The European Tradition of Human Rights and the Culture of Islam," in A.A. An-Na'im and F.M. Deng (eds.) *Human Rights in Africa*, Washington DC: The Brookings Institute.
Tolhurst, W. (1987) "The Argument from Moral Disagreement," *Ethics* 97: 610–21.
Turnbull, C. (1973) *The Mountain People*, London: Picador.
Turner, T. (1997) "Human Rights, Human Difference: Anthropology's Contribution to an Emancipatory Cultural Politics," *Journal of Anthropological Research* 53: 273–91.
Twiss, S.B. (1998) "Moral Grounds and Plural Cultures: Interpreting Human Rights in the International Community," *Journal of Religious Ethics* 26: 271–82.
United Nations (1995a) "Charter of the United Nations," in United Nations Department of Public Information (ed.) *The United Nations and Human Rights 1945–1995*, New York: United Nations Reproduction Section.
—— (1995b) "Universal Declaration of Human Rights," in United Nations Department of Public Information (ed.) *The United Nations and Human Rights 1945–1995*, New York: United Nations Reproduction Section.
Wainwright, W.J. (1986) "Does Disagreement Imply Relativism?," *International Philosophical Quarterly* 26: 47–60.
Waldron, J. (1994) "Disagreements about Justice," *Pacific Philosophical Quarterly* 75: 372–87.
—— (1999) *Law and Disagreement*, Oxford: Clarendon Press.
Walker, M.U. (1998) *Moral Understandings: A Feminist Study in Ethics*, New York: Routledge.
Walzer, M. (1987) *Interpretation and Social Criticism*, Cambridge MA: Harvard University Press.
—— (1994) *Thick and Thin: Moral Argument at Home and Abroad*, Notre Dame IN: University of Notre Dame Press.
Washburn, W.E. (1987) "Cultural Relativism, Human Rights, and the AAA," *American Anthropologist* 89: 939–43.
Wasserman, W. (1985) "What is a Fundamental Ethical Disagreement?," *Analysis* 45: 34–39.
Weinstock, D.M. (1994) "The Justification of Political Liberalism," *Pacific Philosophical Quarterly* 75: 165–85.
Weithman, P. (1994) "Liberalism and the Political Character of Political Philosophy," in C.F. Delaney (ed.) *The Liberalism-Communitarianism Debate*, Lanham MD: Rowman & Littlefield.
Welch, C.E., Jr. and Leary, V.A. (eds.) (1990) *Asian Perspectives on Human Rights*, Boulder CO: Westview Press.
Wellman, C. (1963) "The Ethical Implications of Cultural Relativity," *Journal of Philosophy* 60: 169–84.

—— (1975) "Ethical Disagreement and Objective Truth," *American Philosophical Quarterly* 12: 211–21.

Westermarck, E.A. (1932) *Ethical Relativity*, New York: Harcourt.

Wiggins, D. (1987) *Needs, Values, Truth: Essays in the Philosophy, of Value*, Oxford: Basil Blackwell.

Wiles, A.M. (1989) "Harman and Others on Moral Relativism," *Review of Metaphysics* 42: 783–95.

Williams, B. (1972) *Morality: An Introduction to Ethics*, New York: Harper & Row.

—— (1981) "The Truth in Relativism," in Williams, *Moral Luck: Philosophical Papers 1973–1980*, Cambridge: Cambridge University Press.

—— (1985) *Ethics and the Limits of Philosophy*, Cambridge MA: Harvard University Press.

—— (1995) *Making Sense of Humanity and Other Philosophical Papers*, Cambridge: Cambridge University Press.

Williams, E. (1947) "Anthropology for the Common Man," *American Anthropologist* 49: 84–90.

Wilson, B. (ed.) (1970) *Rationality*, New York: Harper & Row.

Wilson, J.Q. (1993) *The Moral Sense*, New York: Free Press.

Wilson, R.A. (ed.) (1997) *Human Rights, Culture and Context: Anthropological Perspectives*, London: Pluto Press.

Wines, W.A. and Napier, N.K. (1992) "Toward an Understanding of Cross-cultural Ethics: A Tentative Model," *Journal of Business Ethics* 11: 831–41.

Wiredu, K. (1996) *Cultural Universals and Particulars: An African Perspective*, Bloomington IN: Indiana University Press.

Wolf, S. (1992) "Two Levels of Pluralism," *Ethics* 102: 785–98.

Wong, D.B. (1984) *Moral Relativity*, Berkeley CA: University of California Press.

—— (1986a) "On Moral Realism without Foundations," *The Southern Journal of Philosophy* 24 (Supplement): 95–113.

—— (1986b) "Response to Kupperman's Review of *Moral Relativity*," *Philosophy East and West*: 36: 275–82.

—— (1989) "Three Kinds of Incommensurability," in M. Krausz (ed.) *Relativism: Interpretation and Confrontation*, Notre Dame IN: University of Notre Dame Press.

—— (1992) "Coping with Moral Conflict and Ambiguity," *Ethics* 102: 763–83.

—— (1995) "Pluralistic Relativism," *Midwest Studies in Philosophy* 20: 378–99.

Wright, C. (1992) *Truth and Objectivity*, Cambridge MA: Harvard University Press.

—— (1996) "Truth in Ethics," in B. Hooker (ed.) *Truth in Ethics*, Oxford: Blackwell.

Yearley, L.H. (1993) "Conflicts among Ideals of Human Flourishing," in G. Outka and J.P. Reeder, Jr. (eds.) *Prospects for a Common Morality*, Princeton NJ: Princeton University Press.

Zechenter, E.M. (1997) "In the Name of Culture: Cultural Relativism and the Abuse of the Individual," *Journal of Anthropological Research* 53: 319–47.

INDEX

261